Studies in Marxism and Social Theory

Capitalist Collective Action

Studies in Marxism and Social Theory

Edited by G. A. COHEN, JON ELSTER, AND JOHN ROEMER

The series is jointly published by the Cambridge University Press and the Editions de la Maison des Sciences de l'Homme, as part of the joint publishing agreement established in 1977 between the Fondation de la Maison des Sciences de l'Homme and the Syndics of the Cambridge University Press.

The books in the series are intended to exemplify a new paradigm in the study of Marxist social theory. They will not be dogmatic or purely exegetical in approach. Rather, they will examine and develop the theory pioneered by Marx, in the light of the intervening history, and with the tools of non-Marxist social science and philosophy. It is hoped that Marxist thought will thereby be freed from the increasingly discredited methods and presuppositions which are still widely regarded as essential to it, and that what is true and important in Marxism will be more firmly established.

Also in the series

Capitalist Collective Action

Competition, Cooperation, and Conflict in the Coal Industry

John R. Bowman

Queens College
City University of New York

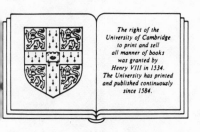

The right of the
University of Cambridge
to print and sell
all manner of books
was granted by
Henry VIII in 1534.
The University has printed
and published continuously
since 1584.

Cambridge University Press
Cambridge
New York   New Rochelle   Melbourne   Sydney

Editions de la Maison des Sciences de l'Homme
Paris

Published by the Press Syndicate of the University of Cambridge
The Pitt Building, Trumpington Street, Cambridge CB2 1RP
32 East 57th Street, New York, NY 10022, USA
10 Stamford Road, Oakleigh, Melbourne 3166, Australia
and Editions de la Maison des Sciences de l'Homme
54 Boulevard Raspail, 75270, Paris Cedex 06

© Maison des Sciences de l'Homme and Cambridge University Press 1989

First published 1989

Printed in the United States of America

Library of Congress Cataloging in Publication Data
Bowman, John R., 1952–
Capitalist collective action: competition, cooperation, and
conflict in the coal industry / John R. Bowman.

   p. cm. – (Studies in Marxism and social theory)
Bibliography: p.
ISBN 0–521–36265–2
   1. Bituminous coal industry – United States – History. 2. Cartels
– United States – History. I. Title. II. Series.
HD9545.B67   1988
338.2'724'0973 – dc19   88–16851
                                      CIP

British Library Cataloguing in Publication Data
Bowman, John R.
Capitalist collective action:
competition cooperation, and conflict
in the coal industry.
1. United States. Coal industries.
Competition & cooperation, 1880–1987
I. Title
338.6

ISBN 0 521 36265 2 hard covers
ISBN 2 7351 0284 X (France only)

To Esther C. Bowman
and in memory of John R. Bowman, Sr.

Contents

Preface

This book is about the problems of collective action and market organization that are generated by economic competition among capitalist firms. I first became interested in this subject several years ago when, in the course of doing some research on the response of American capitalists to the New Deal, I discovered that capitalists were using the language of collective action theory to describe their economic relations with one another and to justify their requests for government intervention. Capitalists clearly understood economic competition to be a collective action problem in which cooperation meant the maintenance of prices and the dominant defection strategy was embodied in price cutting. In several industries, the failure of voluntary efforts to maintain price stability led some firms to solicit state intervention in order to prevent "chiselers" from "selfishly" cutting prices. Two aspects of this sequence of events interested me particularly. First, I began to see that the organization of stable, predictable markets was a problem for capitalists. In an economic setting in which oligopolies predominate, it is easy to forget that markets are patterns of social interaction that must continually be produced and reproduced. Given the importance of markets in capitalist political economies, I was struck by how little scholarly attention the problem of market organization had received. The language used by capitalists during the economic crisis of the 1930s led me to conclude that the problem of market organization was a collective action problem for capitalists (perhaps *the* capitalist collective action problem) and that a collective action framework was the most appropriate way to address it. Second, it was clear that the efforts of capitalist firms to organize their markets generated serious political conflicts among capitalists and led some of them to seek support and intervention from outside actors, including other capitalists, workers, and the state. As a political scientist who had been accustomed to viewing capitalists as a relatively cohesive group, and as a Marxist who attached particular importance to the role of property relations in structuring political conflict, I found the virulence of the competitive conflicts among individual cap-

italists, along with their propensity to spill over into the arenas of political
conflict and industrial relations, intriguing, to say the least.

The basic argument of this book can be stated very simply in the
language of conventional Marxist analysis: Capitalist relations of production structure political conflict. What I mean by this, however, is
quite different from the standard argument that capitalist property relations define a basic conflict between workers and capitalists. Rather,
the relations of production on which I focus are the competitive relations among capitalists and the distinct collective action problems that
they produce. Competition places capitalists in various collective
action/gaming situations. By analyzing the ways rational firms behave
within these games and the ways they try to transform them we not
only can gain new insight into the question of how markets are reproduced, but we also can achieve a richer understanding of a political
reality that includes cleavages among capitalists, and alliances between
workers and capitalists, as well as conflict between workers and
capitalists.

The book is organized into three parts. In the first, which consists of
the first two chapters, I present the theory of capitalist collective action.
In Chapter 1, I argue that capitalist relations of production generate
conflict among capitalists as well as conflict between workers and capitalists. Capitalists must compete with one another, not only in order to
win high profits but also to secure their position in the market. Para-
doxically, this economic competition among capitalists takes the form
of a series of collective action problems. In most cases, the interests of
individual firms in high profits and economic survival can best be
achieved if they cooperate with their competitors and act in concert, but
each individual firm has an incentive to "free-ride" on the cooperation
of other firms. The question that occupies most of the chapter is: Under
what conditions will competing firms be able voluntarily to cooperate
with one another? I answer this question by depicting capitalist competition as a series of mixed-motive games among firms and by identifying a set of variables that affect the capacity of a group of firms to
achieve a cooperative outcome. The variable with the most far-reaching
consequences is the presence or absence of cost differentials. In industries where firms differ greatly in their production costs, common interests may not exist and the collective action problem faced by firms
may take on the form of a zero-sum conflict. I demonstrate in this chapter
that, under certain conditions, voluntary cooperation is likely, but that
there are a wide range of markets in which rational capitalist firms will

not choose to cooperate with one another, in spite of the fact that they can improve their profits by doing so.

What happens when a group of firms would be better off cooperating but is incapable of achieving the cooperative outcome through the independent rational action of its members? All things being equal, we would expect these firms to organize themselves so that cooperative behavior is forthcoming. This involves a transformation of their competitive game – usually through the addition of sanctions punishing noncooperative behavior – that makes cooperation the most attractive strategy. The problem is that all things are not equal. Such reorganizations of markets usually involve costs as well as benefits to individual firms. In Chapter 2, I analyze these costs and try to identify the factors that enter into a firm's decision to seek to reorganize its market to achieve a cooperative outcome or, alternatively, to maintain the competitive status quo. I then examine the various forms that capitalist collective action / market organization can take. I demonstrate that the solution of the capitalist collective action problems faced by a group of competing firms may involve intervention by firms in another industry, by workers, or by the state. The dilemma faced by capitalists is that the forms of collective action that are the most effective in delivering the benefits of cooperation – those that are enforced by the state – are also the most costly.

The theory presented in the first two chapters generates predictions about how individual firms will behave within a particular competitive situation and how firms will respond to particular competitive outcomes. These predictions are tested in the detailed empirical study of competition and collective action in the pre–World War II American bituminous coal industry contained in the five chapters of Part II. A second purpose of the case study is to extend the model presented in Part I by exposing it to the richness of historical reality. The theory of capitalist collective action elaborated in Chapters 1 and 2 is not determinate; it does not encompass every variable that could affect a firm's competitive behavior. Rather, it identifies a set of tendencies that "push" capitalist firms in one direction or another. These tendencies are powerful, but not omnipotent. The case study allows us both to test for the presence of these tendencies and to investigate the way they are reinforced, weakened, deflated, or, possibly, completely tamed by events and tendencies external to them. Besides testing the deductive aspects of the model, then, the case study is also intended to provide an empirical basis for extending and enriching it. As with other social phenomena, capitalist collective action will eventually be completely understood only through a combination of deductive reasoning and the inductive reasoning that proceeds from detailed empirical research.

Both economically and politically, the bituminous coal industry was one of the most important industries in the U.S. economy during the sixty-year period covered by this study. Coal was essential to the operation of railroads, manufacturing industries, and households. The coal industry provided employment to a very large number of workers whose unions played a central role in the American labor movement. Bituminous coal can claim the first modern labor union in the United States, the American Miners' Association, as well as the largest and most powerful single labor union during much of the first half of the century, the United Mine Workers of America.[1] The coal industry also contained the capitalists who were perhaps most averse to the unionization of their workers, or at least who were able to go to the greatest lengths to prevent it. As a result, the bituminous coal industry has a history of class conflict that is bloodier than that of any other American industry. Even during relatively normal periods, bituminous coal labor relations were marked by semiregular strikes that at times rocked the nation's economy. The bituminous coal industry also has a long history of involvement with the state. Coal operators not only solicited state intervention to correct their notoriously "disorganized" and "sick" condition, but also resisted a whole series of proposals, including the nationalization of the mines, designed to eliminate profiteering and other alleged abuses. Coal was distinguished by being the object of two pieces of special regulatory legislation in the 1930s, the latter of which, the Guffey–Vinson Act, made it one of the most regulated industries in American history. Certainly, if our main object is to understand the politics of market organization and to explain the complex and seemingly contradictory attitude of capitalist firms with respect to outside intervention in their markets, the coal industry provides at least as challenging a starting point as any other industry.

In Chapter 3, I employ the model of competition developed in Chapter 1 to identify the competitive games played by coal operators and to predict the competitive strategies that operators will select in these games. The principal game played by coal operators was a Prisoner's Dilemma in which the defection strategy was a combination of price and

---

[1] Edward Wieck writes that the American Miners' Association "may justly claim to have initiated the modern labor movement." (Edward A. Wieck, *The American Miners' Association* [New York: Russell Sage Foundation, 1940], p. 21.)

wage cutting. I demonstrate in Chapter 1 that, under some conditions, cooperation may be a rational strategy in the iterated pricing Prisoner's Dilemma. Much of Chapter 3 is devoted to showing that these conditions were not present in the pre–World War II bituminous coal industry. Sellers were numerous, buyers were powerful, the product was unstandardized, entry was easy, exit was difficult, and the presence of chronic excess capacity placed great pressure on firms to cut wages and prices. I then refine our picture of coal competition by examining cost differences among firms. In the coal industry, differences in freight costs, wage rates, and the quality of coal combined to produce conflicts of interest among operators as to whether and in what direction the universal defection outcome produced by unorganized coal competition should be transformed. Finally, I examine the effect of unionization on the structure of the competitive games played by operators. Because wage cutting was a principal element of the dominant defection strategy, unionized firms lacked the capacity to defect that their nonunion competitors enjoyed. This created another basis for conflict among operators over the degree and form of market organization.

In the next four chapters I turn my attention to the behavior of operators, arguing in general that both their behavior within their competitive games and their responses to the outcomes of these games can be predicted from the model of capitalist collective action developed in Chapters 1 and 2. Chapter 4 focuses on the pre–World War I period, in which several competitive games can be identified. Most of my attention is devoted to the new market organization problems caused by two major geographical shifts in the coal industry – the movement of eastern operators into traditional midwestern markets in the 1880s and the emergence in the early twentieth century of West Virginia and Kentucky as major centers of coal production. Both of these developments created new collective action problems for operators. The East–West competition of the 1880s led operators first to seek to organize themselves through internal means; then, when these efforts failed, to turn to the union of miners to organize competition among capitalists by helping them to prevent competitive wage cutting. Workers organized capitalists. When nonunion production in West Virginia threatened this arrangement, a worker–capitalist alliance sought to impose higher costs on southern operators, both through unionization and through other means. Thus our framework helps to make sense of a distinctive pattern of class struggle, one that appears to be driven by the competitive relations among capitalists and the "logic of collective action" that it generates.

I also briefly consider two other competitive games in this chapter. One involves operators competing in the Atlantic Coast market, who eventually turned to the coal-carrying railroads to organize their competition. The other involves midwestern operators who, in the years immediately prior to World War I, were led by the failure of alternative forms of market organization to solicit state intervention to enforce collective action in their markets.

By 1920, the attitude of coal operators toward state intervention in their markets had undergone a complete reversal, as operators became fierce opponents of even the mildest forms of state intervention. In Chapter 5 I argue that this change in operator attitudes was the product of a change in the structure of their competitive game. On the one hand, the sharp increase in the demand for coal, produced by World War I and the postwar industrial boom, placed operators in the novel position of being able to sell as much coal as they could produce, almost regardless of price. The pricing Prisoner's Dilemma was eliminated, along with the need for state intervention. On the other hand, the experience of operators with state regulation during the war increased the perceived costs of state intervention. During this period, the common interest of operators was not to prevent price cutting, but to maintain prices at a level *low* enough to forestall hostile maximum-price legislation.

In the late 1920s, the coal operators who had in previous decades defended collective bargaining as a necessary stabilizing influence in the coal market abrogated their agreements with the union. In Chapter 6, I examine the breakdown of collective bargaining, arguing that this process, like that which led to the institution of collective bargaining during the nineteenth century, can best be understood as a response by individual capitalist firms to their competitive games. In the earlier period, coal operators had sought to enforce cooperation among themselves through collective bargaining agreements that would prevent competitive wage cutting. Cooperation was a sensible strategy in this context only as long as a sizable majority of other firms cooperated. This condition ceased to hold in the years after World War I, when southern Appalachian, nonunion coal came to dominate the market. Unable to "beat" the nonunion firms by forcing them to cooperate, unionized firms had little alternative but to "join" them and defect. In order to do so, however, they had to free themselves from the constraints of their contracts with the union. They did so reluctantly, in the knowledge that the eventual result of their defection would be the disorganization of the market – a universal defection outcome that would benefit no one.

Just as the labor–capital alliance of the turn of the century was in part a product of the logic of competitive relations among capitalists, so was the capital–labor conflict of the 1920s largely structured by capital–capital competition.

In Chapter 7, I analyze the response of coal operators to the various competitive games that they faced during the period of the Great Depression. Having undermined the only mechanism that was exerting any constraints on their competitive behavior – interstate collective bargaining – bituminous coal operators entered the decade of the 1930s facing the same price- and wage-cutting game that they had first tried to escape forty years earlier. As in the nineteenth century, this game generated suboptimal outcomes that elicited efforts by operators to act collectively to organize their competition. By the time that the National Industrial Recovery Act (NIRA), which authorized industry "codes of fair competition," was passed in 1933, the failure of operators to organize themselves voluntarily had led many of them to espouse external intervention – either from workers or from the state. However, the code that operators finally agreed to did not institute centralized administration of prices but, instead, replaced the price and wage competition of thousands of individual operators with price competition among twenty-two regional code authorities. These code authorities felt the same pressure to reduce prices that formerly had been experienced by individual operators. To the extent that the industry was organized during the period of the code, and price-cutting pressure was suppressed, this was again the achievement of the United Mine Workers, who were able to prevent competitive wage cutting and, in some cases, competitive price cutting as well. When the NIRA was found to be unconstitutional, many coal operators responded to the prospect of a reimposition of self-destructive price competition by turning again to the state to organize them. As was the case during previous conflicts over market organization, the attitude of operators toward post-NIRA state regulation was largely determined by their competitive positions.

In Chapter 8, I return to the principal propositions of the first two chapters in an effort to reexamine them in the light of the empirical material presented in Chapters 3 through 7 and to explore briefly some of the theoretical implications of the study.

Acknowledgments

Although I am glad to bear the ultimate responsibility for the contents of this book, it could never have been completed without the advice and support that I received from a number of friends, teachers, and colleagues. I first addressed the problem of capitalist collective action in a seminar conducted by Adam Przeworski, and Adam's encouragement and advice have been an indispensable ingredient of my subsequent progress. Jon Elster and Ira Katznelson have also been extremely helpful with their careful and insightful readings of the book's various previous incarnations. I also owe a special debt to Philippe Schmitter for the encouragement that he gave me during the early stages of my work. As teachers, critics, friends, and role models, these four individuals have had an impact on my intellectual development that goes far beyond the present text.

I also wish to thank Russell Hardin, John Roemer, and Maurice Zeitlin for their comments on earlier versions of the book, and Christa Altenstetter, Irving Leonard Markowitz, Henry Morton, Burton Zweibach, and my other colleagues at Queens College for providing a hospitable working environment. Finally, I am grateful to John Echeverri-Gent, Argelina Cheibub Figueiredo, Marcus Faria Figueiredo, Rich Horowitz, Michael Wallerstein, and especially, Sandra Robishaw, both for their intellectual comradeship and for helping to remind me that there is more to life than the writing of books.

Earlier versions of portions of the text appeared in *Social Science Information* 21 (1982): 571–604 (published by Sage Publications); *Political Power and Social Theory* 5 (1985): 35–88 (published by JAI Press); and *Politics & Society* 14 (1985): 289–328 (published by Butterworths). I am grateful to each of the above publishers for granting me permission to include revised material from those articles in this book.

1. Economic competition and market organization: the logic of capitalist collective action

Introduction

In this chapter I argue that capitalist relations of production, besides producing conflicts of interest between workers and capitalists, also produce conflicts among capitalists; and that these latter conflicts, which take the form of economic competition, generate a distinct set of collective action problems for competing firms. By analyzing the structure of these problems and the behavior that they generate, we are led to an enhanced understanding of the manner in which capitalist relations of production structure the political behavior of capitalists.

I begin by recalling Marx's argument that capitalist relations of production have a dual character – that they generate antagonism among capitalists at the same time that they generate antagonism between workers and capitalists. I then suggest that the fact of competition among capitalists undermines some common assumptions about the interests of capitalists. Not only do the interests of individual firms often contradict one another, but it is also sometimes the case that the collective interest of the capitalist class contradicts the interests of individual firms.

Next, I argue that economic competition presents capitalist firms with a series of collective action problems. These are exemplified by price competition. Each firm shares a common interest in a relatively high industrywide price, but it is in each firm's interest to "free-ride" on the cooperation of its competitors and to reduce its own price. If each firm behaves rationally and lowers its prices, the outcome will be suboptimal – a lower level of profits than that which could have been achieved if all firms would have cooperated by keeping prices high.

The main body of the chapter is devoted to analyzing these capitalist collective action problems from a game-theoretical perspective, describing various competitive situations as games played among capitalist firms. This enables us to do two things. First, once we have identified the structure of the game, we can predict the strategy that a rational player will select. Second, we can predict the outcome that will be produced by the combination of these strategies. Of particular interest, of course, are those competitive situations that generate suboptimal outcomes because, in these cases, we can expect firms to attempt to transform the structure of their interaction and to try to organize their market, perhaps by appealing to outside actors, including the state, to intervene. An important subset of competitive games of this type includes those markets in which firms have different levels of production costs. In these cases, it is likely not only that the achievement of a collectively optimal outcome will elude the voluntary efforts of competing firms, but that an optimal outcome acceptable to all firms in the market does not exist. Here, the mixed-motive collective action problem becomes a zero-sum game of outright conflict.

Capitalist relations of production and the conflicting interests of capitalists

In the analysis of collective action, the principal problem is to determine under what conditions a group of actors will cooperate in pursuit of a common interest. Our first task in analyzing capitalist collective action, then, is to identify the common interests of capitalists. For most Marxists, and many non-Marxists as well, capitalists are a class whose common interests are rooted in capitalist relations of production. These production relations define a shared interest in high profits and in maintaining control of the production process that opposes capitalists to workers. The principal collective action problem faced by capitalists, in this view, is to organize themselves in defense of those interests that oppose them to workers. There can be no doubt that the conflict between capitalists and workers defined by capitalist relations of production is critically important to our understanding of political life, nor that this conflict generates collective action on the part of capitalists. We would be mistaken, however, if we concluded that the worker versus capitalist conflict was the only politically relevant conflict generated by capitalist relations of production, and that the capitalist collective action problem implied by this conflict was the only one, or even the most important one, faced by capitalists. As Marx wrote in *The Poverty of Philosophy*, capitalist relations of production have two aspects. On the one hand, they define the familiar antagonism between worker and capitalist; however, they also determine a fundamental conflict among capitalists. "If all the members of the modern bourgeoisie have the same interest inasmuch as they form a class as against another class, they have opposite, antagonistic interests inasmuch as they stand face to face with one another."'[1]

Few observers would go so far as to deny that capitalists compete, but this competition is rarely taken seriously by political analysts. When the fact of competition is recognized, it is usually treated as a sideshow, on the margins of the main event, the conflict between workers and capitalists. In this view, economic conflicts among short-sighted capitalists complicate the more important struggle, but they are clearly seen as of secondary importance to it. In fact, economic competition represents a very real high-stakes struggle among capitalists whose most fundamental individual interests are in conflict with those of their competitors, and, sometimes, with the collective interests of their class. It is essential to note that these competitive relations are a constituent element of capitalism – any capitalism. The form of competition, the strength of competitive pressures, the capacity of capitalists to control competition – all of these things have varied greatly both across time and across industries within the same time period, just as the worker–capitalist struggle has varied in form and intensity. But in neither case should the vicissitudes of the surface phenomena deceive us into thinking that the defining relationships of the mode of production have disappeared. Whether the object of our analysis is competitive capitalism, monopoly capitalism, late capitalism, or advanced capitalism, capitalist relations of production define a basic antagonism among competing capitalists.

This competitive antagonism has several important implications for political analysis. First, unlike membership in most other groups, the status of being a capitalist is achieved, not ascribed, and, moreover, it is achieved in struggle against other capitalists. The most fundamental interest of any firm is to continue to exist in the market, and, except during periods of the most extreme political crisis, the major threat to this basic interest of each capitalist in economic survival comes not from workers but from other capitalists.

Second, whatever the common interests are that capitalists share in opposition to other groups, their enjoyment by any firm is contingent upon its successful defense of its market position against competitors. The common interests of capitalists are only "common" to surviving capitalists. Thus, competitive struggles are not secondary to struggles between workers and capitalists, but rather they occupy a position of

'Karl Marx, *The Poverty of Philosophy* (New York: International Publishers, 1963), p. 123.

logical primacy with respect to them.[2] Each capitalist must secure his or her position as a capitalist in the market before he or she can act as a capitalist in any other arena.

A third implication of economic competition is that the interests of individual firms may be incompatible with the collective interest of capitalists in the continued survival of capitalism. In Marx's words, "the individual capitalist is in constant rebellion against the general interests of the capitalist class as a whole."[3] The continued existence of the capitalist system is certainly a necessary condition for the achievement of the firm's interest in economic survival; however, it is not sufficient to ensure the firm's survival. While the continuation of capitalist reproduction ensures that there will be some firms, it does not guarantee the survival of any particular firm.[4] Not only is it a fact of life in capitalist economies that firms sometimes go out of business, but it is in the interest of the preservation of the allocative efficiency of the capitalist economy that this occurs. The reproduction of capitalism – the accumulation of capital – requires capital to be shifted away from less efficient firms and sectors to more efficient ones. Insofar as capital accumulation requires such a redistribution of capital, the long-term reproduction of capitalism implies developments which contradict the interest of some individual firms. Marx writes in *The Poverty of Philosophy* that

From day to day it thus becomes clearer that the production relations in which the bourgeoisie moves have not a simple, uniform character, but a dual character; ... that these relations produce bourgeois wealth; i.e., the wealth of the bourgeois class, only by continually annihilating the wealth of the individual members of this class and producing an ever-growing proletariat.[5]

Perhaps the most important implication of competitive relations, and one whose consideration occupies most of the present study, is that in dividing capitalists, economic competition presents them with a set of collective action problems distinct from those they face in their opposition to workers, and which sometimes "overdetermine" these latter problems. Capitalist competition creates a paradoxical situation in which

[2]This expression is somewhat misleading in that the struggle between labor and capital within each firm is part of the competitive struggle between firms. However, it is competition among firms that is the motor behind the labor–capital struggle within the firm. In its absence, capitalists would not be forced to increase the rate of exploitation.
[3]Quoted in Jon Elster, *Making Sense of Marx* (Cambridge: Cambridge University Press, 1985), p. 189.
[4]Adam Przeworski, "Toward a Theory of Capitalist Democracy" (Unpublished Paper, University of Chicago, 1980), p. 24.
[5]Marx, *The Poverty of Philosophy*, p. 123.

the attainment of each firm's individual interest in profits and economic survival is dependent on the cooperation of its competitors.

Economic competition as a collective action problem

In everyday usage, the verb *to compete* implies rivalry and interdependence among the competing units. Capitalist firms compete when they pursue policies that affect each other's sales. Price cutting, advertising, investment, product differentiation, and so forth are all undertaken with the aim of increasing a firm's market share at the expense of other firms in the market. Curiously, this sense of rivalry and interdependence is absent from the economic theory of the competitive market, where firms respond passively to a set of impersonal constraints which they are unable to affect. "A persistent weakness of the concept of competition," writes Paul McNulty,

has been the tendency of economists to minimize, ignore, or deny its interdependent nature, that is, the extent to which the competition of one economic unit tends to affect the economic position of others, and, thus, the overall market structure. Despite the etymology of the verb (literally "to seek together"), to compete, in economic theory, has generally meant to act independently.[6]

The basic neoclassical economic model of competition is set in the perfectly competitive market, in which each firm's share of output is so small that an increase or decrease in the quantity that it produces will not affect the price of the commodity. In this type of market, each firm faces a horizontal demand curve (price is therefore a given) and the firm "competes" by setting output at the level at which price and marginal costs are equivalent. A reduction of output from this level would generate a loss of revenue greater than the cost savings of reduced production, and an increase in output would cost more than the revenue brought in by increased sales. Graphically (see Figure 1.1), this quantity $(q)_1$ is determined by the intersection of the marginal cost (MC) and demand (DD_1) curves. The average cost curve (AC) gives the cost of each unit as a function of output. When each competing firm's MC and DD_1 curves are aggregated, the industry supply (S) and demand (D) curves are the result (see Figure 1.2). The downward slope of the industry demand curve reflects the fact that while the price level is not

---

[6]Paul McNulty, "Economic Theory and the Meaning of Competition," *Quarterly Journal of Economics* 82 (November, 1968): 654. As Joe Bain points out, this interdependence encompasses not only firms within the market, but potential entrants as well (see his *Barriers to New Competition*, Cambridge: Harvard University Press, 1965, p. 4).

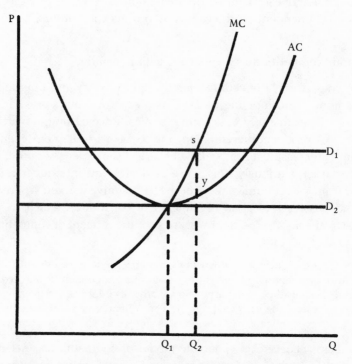

Figure 1.1. The individual firm in the perfectly competitive market. *Source:* Scherer, *Industrial Market Structure*, p. 12.

responsive to the output decisions of the individual firm, it will respond to the industry supply level, which is the aggregate of the output decisions of all of the firms in the industry. If the firm's demand curve cuts the marginal cost curve at a point to the right of the intersection of MC and AC (see D_2 in Figure 1.1), the firm's output will be at q_2. The gap between average costs and marginal costs means that the firm will earn supranormal "economic profits" equivalent to $s-y$ for every unit produced. These high profits will attract new entrants to the industry, causing the industry supply curve to shift to the right (from S_1 to S_2). This increased output will reduce price from p_1 to p_2, lowering the individual firm's demand curve until, at equilibrium, AC, MC, and D intersect (see D_1 in Figure 1.1).

In this model, the individual firm's output level is determined by its marginal cost curve and by the industry demand curve. It chooses an output level, then, independently of its perception of what the other firms in the industry are doing. However, this does not mean that the

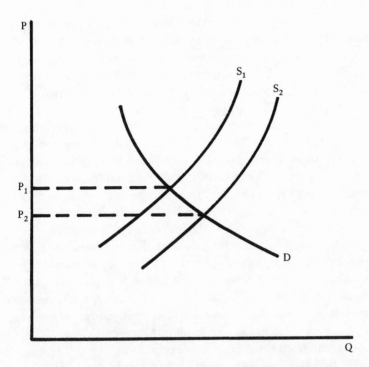

Figure 1.2. The industry in the perfectly competitive market. *Source:* Scherer, *Industrial Market Structure*, p. 12.

behavior of the other firms has no effect on the profit of each individual competitor. The industry price level – a given from the point of view of the individual firm – is in fact determined by the sum of the output decisions of each of the industry's firms. Thus each firm's subjective independence – its inattention to the activities of its competitor – is coupled with an objective interdependence which operates "behind its back." While independently pursuing their own economic survival by selecting the profit-maximizing output level, individual firms are jointly producing the conditions which largely determine both their own economic fate and the fate of their competitors. Capitalist competition, then, has two dimensions. On the one hand it involves the individual, independent pursuit of economic survival through the selection of a profit-maximizing strategy. It is this aspect of competition, which places capitalist firms in conflict with one another, that was the focus of the previous section. On the other hand, competition also involves the joint shaping or "seeking together" by competitors of an economic environment in which individual economic survival will be more or less likely. The industry price and output levels are collective goods.[7] Firms contribute to their provision through their price and output policies, and, once they are provided to one firm in an industry, they cannot be withheld from other firms. A firm's success in its struggle against other firms, then, is largely determined by the capacity of the firms as a *group* to "seek together" a benign price and output level.

The fact that the success or failure of each firm depends on the actions of all firms implies that if the firms in the market could communicate with each other and coordinate their activities, they could enhance their collective position. This can be demonstrated graphically with a simple monopolistic pricing model. Figure 1.3 presents the cost, demand, and marginal revenue curves for an industry with the capacity to act in concert as a single monopolistic decision maker. The demand curve (D) is downward sloping, reflecting the fact that the industry as a whole has the capacity to influence price with its output decisions. The negatively sloped demand curve implies a marginal revenue curve (MR) falling to the left of D. This is the critical difference between the industry/monopolist and the individual competitive firm. For the former, facing a horizontal demand curve, marginal revenue (the additional income accruing from the marginal sale) equals price. For the industry as a whole, however, an increase in output can be sold only at a lower price than was previously offered, and, of course, this lower price applies to total, not just marginal, output. Thus the increased revenue from the additional sales is offset in part by the decrease in revenue produced by the across-the-board price reduction that made the increased sales possible. Like the competitive firms, the industry/monopolist maximizes profits by setting marginal revenue equal to marginal cost. However, for the monopolist, this point will not be where the MC and D curves intersect, but where the MC and MR curves intersect. In Figure 1.3, this implies an output of q_1 and a price of W. If price and output were determined competitively, they would be given by the intersection of MC and D: Z and q_2, respectively. The area enclosed by WABZ is the quantity of the "excess" profit available to the firms in the industry if they could act in concert.

In real-world markets, of course, individual firms, however interde-

---

[7]Mancur Olson defines a collective good as "any good such that, if any person X_i in a group $X_1, \ldots, X_i, \ldots, X_n$ consumes it, it cannot feasibly be withheld from the others in that group "(*The Logic of Collective Action* [Cambridge, MA: Harvard University Press, 1971], p. 14).

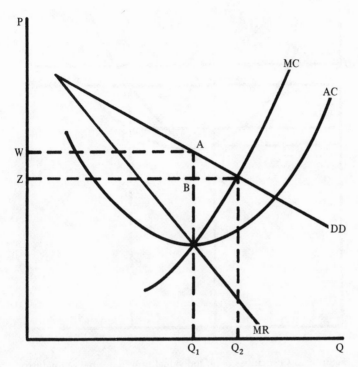

Figure 1.3. The cost and revenue curves of a monopolistic firm. *Source:* Scherer, *Industrial Market Structure*, p. 14.

pendent their competitive situations, retain an independent decision-making capacity. The industry, in other words, consists not of a single, joint decision maker, but of a number of individual decision makers. Dropping the assumption of the unified collective actor completely alters the situation. In this more realistic context, the individual firms face a collective action problem in which the rational pursuit of individual interests interferes with the attainment of a collectively optimal outcome. Return to the market described by Figure 1.3. Clearly, the firms in this situation have a common interest in maintaining the monopolistic price and output level. The relatively high price is a collective good to which each firm contributes with its pricing policy and from which each firm benefits by receiving abnormally high profits. However, as is the case in other collective-good situations, the "enjoyment" of the collective good cannot be denied to any member of the group, whether they contribute to its provision or not, and each member faces a strong in-

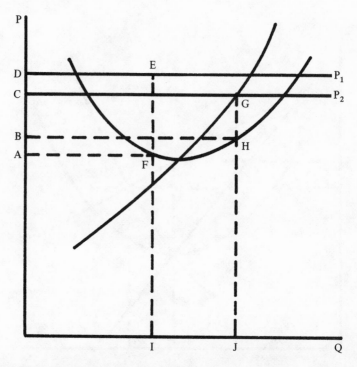

Figure 1.4. Cost curves of an individual firm in a cartelized industry. *Source: Dewey, Monopoly, p. 19.*

centive to refrain from contributing, and to free-ride on the contributions of others.[8] In the present case, the temptation is to exploit the high prices charged by competitors and to reduce one's own price and expand one's own output. The result, if all other firms continue their "cooperative" policies, will be higher profits for the price-cutting free-rider. Figure 1.4 shows how each firm can benefit from reducing its price below the cooperative level observed by its competitors. Let us set the cooperative price at D and stipulate that this price implies an output of I from the individual firm. At that price and output level, the firm's profits are equal to the area of DEFA. However, the firm that shades its price below the cooperative level (say, to C) and expands its output to J can increase its profit to the area enclosed by CGHB. The problem is that every firm faces this same temptation, and if each of them yields to it, industry price and output will end up at the competitive level (the intersection of D and MC in Figure 1.3) and each firm's excess profits will be erased.

[8]Ibid.

	B	
	Maintain prices (cooperate)	Reduce prices (defect)
A Maintain prices (cooperate)	3,3	1,4
Reduce prices (defect)	4,1	2,2

Figure 1.5. Two-person/firm Prisoner's Dilemma. (Numbers have ordinal values only: 4 is the most valued payoff.)

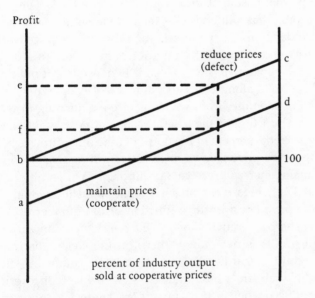

Figure 1.6. The profit of a firm as a function of its own pricing decision and those of its competitors.

Like many other collective action problems, the situation described above can be conceptualized in game-theoretic terms as a Prisoner's Dilemma.[9] The simple, two-person/firm version is depicted in Figure 1.5 above. Each firm faces a choice between two strategies – maintain prices (cooperate) and cut prices (defect). Rational firms will choose their dominant strategy – cut prices – and will generate the suboptimal outcome found in the bottom right quadrant.

Figure 1.6, which is based on a model developed originally by Thomas

[9] Russell Hardin, *Collective Action* (Baltimore: Johns Hopkins University Press, 1982).

Schelling, presents a graphic version of the n-firm pricing Prisoner's Dilemma.[10] Assume an industry containing n firms in which the following conditions are present: (1) the total demand for the industry's product is relatively unresponsive to changes in prices; (2) within the industry, the distribution of sales is responsive to price, demand shifting to the lowest-price firms; (3) each firm has a choice between two prices – the present price and a reduced price; (4) each firm's profits are a function of its own price decision and the price decision of the other $n-1$ firms; (5) all firms are the same size; (6) price discrimination is not possible. The x axis in Figure 1.6 measures the proportion of the output of the other firms that is sold at the cooperative price level. The y axis measures the profits that will accrue to the individual nth firm, based on its own price decision. Segment bc is the profit that a price-cutting firm will receive as a function of the proportion of the other firms' output that is sold at the cooperative price. Thus, if I choose to cut my price, my profit will increase along bc as the number of cooperating firms increases. Segment ad is the profit which a price-maintaining firm will receive, again as a function of the level of cooperation present among the other $n-1$ firms. If k percent of the output of the other firms is being sold at the cooperative price level, a price cutter will receive a profit of $\$e$ and a price maintainer will receive a profit of $\$f$. Two points should be emphasized. First, regardless of what strategy an individual firm chooses, its own payoff is a positive function of the number of other firms that select the cooperative strategy. Each firm's attainment of its interest in high profits is dependent, then, on the cooperation of its competitors. Second, regardless of what strategy competing firms choose, the individual firm's best strategy is always to reduce prices. The outcome produced when all firms pursue this strategy is suboptimal; it is worse for every firm than the outcome produced by universal cooperation. In short, the prosperity of each firm depends on the cooperation of its competitors, but no firm has an incentive to engage in such cooperation.

As we shall see later in more detail, what makes such situations interesting is the probability that rational actors whose independent behavior is generating suboptimal outcomes will seek to organize them-

[10]Thomas C. Schelling, "Hockey Helmets, Concealed Weapons, and Daylight Saving: A Study of Binary Choices with Externalities," *Journal of Conflict Resolution* 17 (September, 1973): 381–428.

selves.[11] It is these organizational efforts on the part of capitalist firms that are the principal focus of this study.

Raising the stakes: the case of the depressed market

So far, we have viewed the capitalist collective action problem generated by price competition as one of providing capitalist firms with a collective good – a supracompetitive price level. In doing so, we have followed the economic tradition of viewing the problem of capitalist collective action as a problem simply of cartel formation. What is missing from this traditional view is explicit recognition of the fact that the competitive price level that is optimal for the economy's overall efficiency may not be acceptable to many of the individual firms that constitute the economy. Again, we must face the possibility that what is good for the capitalist economy may not be good for individual capitalists. The exit of capital from the market and its movement from the less efficient to the more efficient firms and sectors – the process that is behind the market economy's allocative efficiency – takes place precisely because prices are too low in relation to costs for some individual firms. It is usually assumed that it is only the marginal firms that are victims of this process. However, depending upon demand and supply conditions, many, and perhaps all, firms in an industry may operate at a loss under competitive conditions.[12] When this situation persists, the equilibrium price generated by the independent behavior of competitors becomes a collective *bad* that they must eliminate in order to survive. In this case, which is depicted in Figure 1.7, the stakes involved in the competitive game have escalated. Cooperative or cartel prices and profits are no longer a luxury, but a necessity. The alternative, the universal defection outcome, yields negative profits for all firms.

Rational cooperation in the pricing Prisoner's Dilemma

The pricing Prisoner's Dilemma discussed above was a one-shot game that was divorced from all social context. Real-life Prisoner's Dilemmas, both in the market and in other areas of social life, are more likely to be ongoing interactions rather than single-play encounters, and they are

[11]Jon Elster, *Logic and Society* (London: Wiley, 1978), p. 137.
[12]See Lloyd Reynolds, "Cutthroat Competition," *American Economic Review* 30 (December, 1940): 736–47.

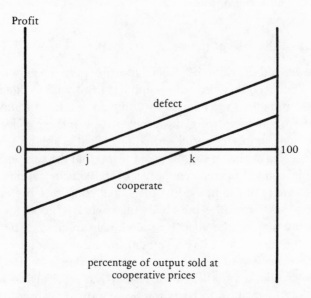

Figure 1.7. A firm's profit function in a depressed market.

likely to occur among a group of people who are enmeshed in other social connections. Under some conditions, both of these additional factors – the iteration of the Prisoner's Dilemma and its integration with other social relations – can increase the probability that rational players will select the cooperative strategy. Of course, if this occurs, further efforts at organization will not be forthcoming.

When we place the Prisoner's Dilemma in a context in which the individuals involved have continuous dealings of the sort that may lead them to know, like, and trust each other, it is possible that their individual motivational structures may become transformed, and while they still behave rationally, their actions may be in pursuit of a "self-interest" that has been tempered by guilt feelings, solidarity, or an altruistic concern for the well-being of others.[13] Jon Elster argues that such a transformation of the Prisoner's Dilemma into an Assurance Game – in which the joint-cooperation outcome is preferred over the outcome in which I defect and all other players cooperate (my preferred outcome in Prisoner's Dilemma) – may explain collective action among workers. "Through continued interaction the workers become both concerned and informed about each other."[14] On the surface, this dynamic does not seem to be applicable to capitalists. As Elster writes, "we would not expect . . . capitalists to be motivated for concern for each other's profit."[15] Michael Useem, though, has argued that there is a set of leading corporation officers – which he terms the "inner circle" – who, through their interaction in corporate board rooms, social clubs, and business associations develop an "inadvertent" sensitivity to the interdependencies of their decisions and become sensitive to classwide political concerns.[16] However, according to Useem, this "classwide rationality" is only operative with respect to decisions that "have no immediate bearing on company profits."[17] Thus, we should not expect this kind of capitalist class consciousness significantly to alter the motivation of firms facing pricing Prisoner's Dilemmas, whose very point is that they very much have a bearing on company profits.

For capitalist firms, the iteration of the Prisoner's Dilemma and the self-interested fear of retaliation is a more likely source for collective action than the evolution of an Assurance Game.[18] Real-world competition differs from the abstracted game discussed above in that it involves not just a single choice and a single outcome, but a sequence of choices and outcomes. In effect, a firm can alter its price strategy each time that it enters into a contract with a buyer. Over the course of a year, a quarter, or even a day, each firm faces several choices between maintaining and lowering prices, none of which is likely to make or break it. The iteration of the single-play price game can substantially alter its character by making the selection of the cooperative strategy during any given play of the game more attractive.

This can be seen more clearly if we view the pricing Prisoner's Dilemma faced by a set of n competing firms as a *supergame* composed of an indefinite series of discrete, single-play, *ordinary* games possessing the characteristics described above. In this ordinary game, there are only two strategies available to the nth player: Reduce prices (defect) or maintain prices (cooperate). In the supergame created by the indefinite

---

[14]Elster, "Marxism, Functionalism, and Game Theory," *Theory and Society* 11 (1982): 468.

[15]Elster, *Making Sense of Marx*, p. 362. The exception that proves the rule is a case described by Perrow in which a manufacturer's plant was destroyed by fire. While his plant was being rebuilt, his competitors volunteered to him the use of their own facilities during off-shift time periods (see Jeffrey Pfeffer and Gerald R. Salancik, *The External Control of Organizations: A Resource Dependence Approach* [New York: Harper and Row, 1978], p. 103).

[16]Useem, *The Hidden Circle* (New York: Oxford University Press, 1984), pp. 141–4.

[17]Ibid., p. 195.

[18]Elster, *Making Sense of Marx*, p. 363.

repetition of the basic, single-play pricing Prisoner's Dilemma, each strategy consists of a *series* of single moves. Instead of simply choosing between maintaining or reducing prices during a single production cycle, each player must select a pricing *policy* that will govern price choices in future production cycles as well. Such strategies could include "maintain prices until the majority of my competitors has lowered theirs" or "maintain prices for ten plays, then lower them indefinitely," and so on. Michael Taylor has reduced the multitude of supergame strategies to five general strategies.[19] These are easily adaptable to our pricing game.

1. Maintain prices in every ordinary game.
2. Reduce prices in every ordinary game.
3. Maintain prices in the first ordinary game and in every subsequent ordinary game as long as firms representing at least k percent of total output also maintain prices; if less than this number of firms cooperates, then choose the price-reduction strategy for a specified number of additional ordinary games before cooperating again.
4. Maintain prices in the first ordinary game; in subsequent games, if the number of firms who have chosen to cooperate in the previous ordinary game does not represent k percent of output, then cooperate; if not, defect.
5. Reduce prices in the first ordinary game. Thereafter, reduce prices only if the number of cooperators in the previous game represents less than k percent of output.

If each player discounts future payoffs at a relatively low rate, if the supergame is of indefinite length, if firms representing at least k percent of output choose to cooperate during the first ordinary game, and if every player has accurate information about the choices of the other players in each ordinary game, then the incentive to cut prices during any given ordinary game is virtually eliminated by the certainty that the long- or medium-term retaliatory price cutting of one's competitors will erase the gains of short-term price cutting.[20] Similarly, the risk of being the sole price maintainer in a market full of price cutters is minimized when one can reduce prices as soon as one finds that one is being victimized by one's competitors. Under these conditions, mutual cooperation will be the outcome in each ordinary game.

[19]Michael Taylor, *Anarchy and Cooperation* (London: Wiley, 1976), p. 90.
[20]Ibid. When the game is not of an indefinite length, the incentive to cooperate becomes eliminated as the end of the game approaches. See R. D. Luce and Howard Raiffa, *Games and Decisions* (New York: Wiley, 1957), p. 98.

Analogous reasoning has led many economists to predict a "tendency toward the maximization of collective profits" in oligopolistic industries containing a relatively small number of competitors.[21]

If each seeks his maximum profit rationally and intelligently, he will realize that when there are only two or a few sellers his own move has a considerable effect upon his competitors, and that this makes it idle to suppose that they will accept without retaliation the losses he forces upon them. Since the result of a cut by any one is inevitably to decrease his own profits, no one will cut, and, although the sellers are entirely independent, the equilibrium result is the same as though there were a monopolistic agreement between them.[22]

To the extent that the payoff structure of individual competitors is transformed by the threat of retaliation from other firms in the market, price competition is unlikely to generate demands for a further reorganization of the market. Since such demands, and the struggles they produce, are our primary focus, our first task is to identify the market conditions that will facilitate the emergence of such a cooperative outcome. They are listed and discussed below.

1. *Number of seller firms.* As the number of firms in the industry increases, the likelihood that they will successfully cooperate without outside intervention decreases. This is true for several reasons. First, it will be more difficult for them to arrive at an initial agreement on the content of the cooperative strategy.[23] As the number of firms increases, the number of interests that must be accommodated by the agreement also increases, as does the complexity of the bargaining process. Second, the success of any cooperative agreement depends largely upon the capacity of cooperating firms promptly to detect and retaliate against noncooperative behavior. Individual firm size held constant, the impact of each firm's choice of strategies on the industry outcome diminishes as the number of firms increases, tending to render the detection of noncooperative behavior more difficult.[24] Third, once the cooperative strategy has been satisfactorily defined, its longevity requires continued communication among the firms involved. They must be able to adjust the

[21]F. M. Scherer, *Industrial Market Structure and Economic Performance* (Chicago: Rand McNally, 1980), p. 168; William Fellner, *Competition among the Few* (New York: Alfred A. Knopf, 1949), p. 33.

[22]Edward Hastings Chamberlin, *The Theory of Monopolistic Competition* (Cambridge, MA: Harvard University Press, 1962), p. 48.

[23]Richard Posner, *Antitrust Law: An Economic Perspective* (Chicago: University of Chicago Press, 1976) pp. 52–3; Almarin Phillips, *Market Structure, Organization, and Performance* (Cambridge, MA: Harvard University Press, 1962), pp. 29–30.

[24]Scherer, *Industrial Market Structure*, pp. 199–200.

terms of the agreement to meet changing circumstances and they must be able to distinguish accidental and temporary departures from the agreement from a policy of conscious repudiation. Such continued communication among firms is more costly as the number of firms increases.[25] Fourth, as numbers increase, so does the likelihood that the industry will contain a maverick firm, determined to torpedo any effort to maintain price stability, for "irrational" ideological or psychological reasons. Finally, a necessary condition for cooperation among competing firms is that the firms recognize their interdependency and its logic in generating suboptimal outcomes. When the number of firms is very large, there is a greater probability that firms will attribute their payoffs to the operation of reified "market forces" and will lack the motivation to seek to cooperate with their competitors. Implicit in the above discussion is the assumption that all firms are of equal size. The effect of large numbers on the likelihood of cooperation is altered if the industry contains large, dominant firms. In this case, the number of firms that is responsible for producing k percent of the industry's output could be very low. Cooperation then would be correspondingly easier to achieve.

2. *The number of buyers.* Successful price cutting becomes more difficult as the number of buyers in the market increases. When a firm is selling to a large number of buyers, each of whom represents a relatively small proportion of its total sales, it cannot achieve significant gains from price cutting unless it reduces prices for many buyers. However, the larger the number of buyers who must know about the lower prices, the greater the difficulty in keeping this information from rival sellers as well.[26] Where buyers are few and each one represents a large proportion of a firm's sales, a price cut to benefit a single customer may be both worthwhile and easy to conceal. Moreover, in the latter case, the bargaining strength of the buyer may be such that it can force sellers into price reductions.[27] Also, as George Stigler argues, the observation of the movement of buyers in an industry can be an effective technique for monitoring a price-fixing agreement. All things being equal, a firm cannot attract more than its share of old and new buyers without tipping off its competitors that it is cutting prices. Stigler shows that this constraint

[25]Ibid., p. 176.
[26]George Stigler, "A Theory of Oligopoly," *Journal of Political Economy* 72 (February 1964): 44–61.
[27]Phillips, *Market Structure*, pp. 34–5.

operates so as to lead to a reduction in the incentive to cut prices as the number of buyers increases.[28]

3. *Newness of the market.* If, as Stigler argues, the disruption of old market patterns can provide a clue that price cutting is taking place, then it follows that price cutting is more difficult to detect in relatively unestablished, "new" markets. This is what Naomi Lamoreaux concluded from her study of competition in the turn-of-the-century iron and paper markets. "Established marketing habits and consumer loyalties had not had time to take root, and there seemed to be the possibility that a manufacturer could make a 'coup,' capture enough orders to run his plant full before his competitors found out and were able to retaliate."[29]

4. *Transaction characteristics.* The size and frequency of purchases affect both the incentive to cut prices and the likelihood of detection in much the same way as does the number of sellers. When transactions are "small, frequent, and regular," the incentive to cut prices on any given order is low. However, a large order that will suffice "to keep operations humming at capacity for several months" may be tempting enough to overcome a firm's fear of retaliation.[30] When purchases are frequent and regular, price cutters will be detected more easily by the disruption in the customary pattern of trade that they cause. This method of detection is denied competitors in industries in which repeat purchases never take place.[31] An exception to the above assertion is the case where sellers are selected on the basis of sealed bids, which facilitates the detection of price cutters.[32]

5. *Demand.* When demand is expanding, price cutting is less tempting because increased sales can be achieved without recourse to price reductions. The opposite, of course, is true during periods of declining demand.[33] However, while the incentive to cut prices increases during downturns in demand, the probability of price cutting being detected also increases. When total industry sales are increasing, an increase in the sales of a rival "can occur through the additional purchases of existing

[28]Stigler, "A Theory of Oligopoly."
[29]Naomi Lamoreaux, *The Great Merger Movement in American Business, 1895–1904* (Cambridge: Cambridge University Press, 1985), p. 62.
[30]Scherer, *Industrial Market Structure*, pp. 220–1.
[31]Stigler, "A Theory of Oligopoly," p. 46.
[32]Scherer, *Industrial Market Structure*, pp. 223–5; Posner, *Antitrust Law*, p. 61; Stigler, "A Theory of Oligopoly," p. 46.
[33]See, for instance, Karl Pibran, *Cartel Problems* (Washington, DC: Brookings Institution, 1935), p. 37.

customers, whereas where industry sales are stable or declining, an increase in sales must be at the expense of a rival."[34]

6. *Product durability.* In industries producing goods which can be easily stored or which won't be quickly rendered obsolete by changing consumer tastes or technological requirements, firms may be able to resist the pressure to dump excess goods on the market at bargain prices by using their inventory as a cushion aginst drops in demand. However, where obstacles to storage exist, the incentive to cut prices so as to unload inventories will be stronger.[35]

7. *Industry cost structure.* When a high proportion of a firm's costs are fixed costs, then small reductions in output are more likely to raise average costs above price, squeezing profits. The profits of high fixed-cost firms depend upon their maintaining output at a high level. Since these firms cannot safely maintain price stability in recessionary periods by reducing output, we can expect they will be particularly vulnerable to price-cutting incentives.[36] The tendency is likely to be aggravated if the fixed capital is of a highly specialized sort and is not readily susceptible either to liquidation or adaptation to other uses.[37] Under these conditions, exit from the industry is very expensive and firms will prefer to operate at a loss (as long as they can recover variable costs) rather than leave the market and realize their loss on their fixed capital. We conclude, then, that, in general, the incentive to defect is higher in high fixed-cost industries.

8. *Entry conditions.* The probability of successful cooperation increases with the difficulty of entry. This is a result, first of all, of the increase in numbers consequent upon new entry, which, as we have seen, increases communication costs. New entrants will add to total output, as well, however, and in doing so will generate price-cutting pressure on existing firms who wish to maintain their market shares. Barriers to entry include state-enforced patents, licenses, and entry restrictions; economies of scale, which increase the optimum size of the new entrant; differentials between new and old firms in the terms on which the necessary technology, labor, capital, raw materials, and marketing outlets can be secured; and cus-

---

[34]John E. Howard, "Collusive Behavior," *Journal of Business* 27 (July 1954): 202–3. Also see Stigler, "A Theory of Oligopoly."

[35]Scherer, *Industrial Market Structure*, p. 193.

[36]Ibid., p. 203. The impact of high fixed costs is likely to be greater when firms have to pay back outside creditors than when investment funds are internally generated (see Lamoreaux, *The Great Merger Movement*, pp. 55–9).

[37]Phillips, *Market Structure*, p. 122.

tomer loyalty.[38] Increasingly, economists are viewing barriers to entry not as structural features exogenous to competitive behavior but as the consequence of strategic behavior by incumbent firms.[39]

Consider a dominant firm facing the possibility of new entry in its market. It threatens the new entrant with a price war if entry occurs. However, because the entering firm knows that, once it enters the market, the incumbent's best strategy is to share the market rather than engage in a price war, the threat lacks credibility. One way in which the dominant firm can commit itself to the threat, and convince its rival that it is so committed, is through incurring a cost – such as an investment in extra capacity – that will be experienced as "wasted" if the threat is not carried out. Thus, once the extra capacity is in place, the incumbent firm may find that it is less costly to utilize this new capacity in a price war then to allow it to sit idle under a market-sharing agreement with new entrants. If this is the case, then the incumbent's threat to retaliate against new entrants with low prices and expanded output *is* credible. Besides investing in excess capacity, other "strategic investments" which confer an advantage on a firm by establishing the credibility of its threats include expenditures on advertising and product promotion, investment in product differentiation and style changes, and the establishment of an extensive geographical presence in the market. In each case, these investments are unproductive burdens as long as the dominant firm making them is not challenged by new competitors or if the incumbent firm and the new entrant peaceably share the market. They repay their investment only in the case of a meaningful competitive challenge. They thus represent an investment in a competitive war before the event, and a demonstration of the dominant firm's willingness to pay the costs of such a war. In general, as the cost of these strategic investments increases, so does the credibility of the retaliatory threats made by the investing firm and the "height" of the barriers faced by new entrants.

9. *Credible threats.* The foregoing analysis of strategic investments to deter entry raises the general issue of the credibility of threats.[40] If a threat of

[38] Andreas G. Papandreou and John T. Wheeler, *Competition and its Regulation* (New York: Prentice-Hall, 1954), p. 179; Posner, *Antitrust Law*, pp. 58–9.

[39] This observation, along with the analysis contained in the remainder of the paragraph, is based on Alexis Jacquemin, *The New Industrial Organization: Market Forces and Strategic Behavior* (Cambridge, MA: MIT Press, 1987), pp. 107–20; also see David Encaoua et al., "Strategic Competition and the Persistence of Dominant Firms: A Survey," in *New Developments in the Analysis of Market Structure*, ed. by Joseph E. Stiglitz and G. Frank Mathewson (Cambridge, MA: MIT Press, 1986), and, in the same volume, Richard J. Gilbert, "Preemptive Competition."

[40] The classic analysis of credibility and commitment is Thomas Schelling, *The Strategy of*

retaliatory price cutting by other firms is to constitute a deterrent to noncooperative behavior, then the firm facing this threat must believe that it will, in fact, be carried out. While this is true in all collective action contexts, it is particularly important in the case of cooperation among competing firms, since the carrying out of the threat by the enforcing firm(s) is likely to be costly – price wars are damaging to all participants in them. We have seen in our analysis of entry barriers that one way in which a firm can convince other firms of its determination to pay the costs of carrying out a retaliatory threat is to commit itself by incurring some of the costs beforehand. What is true of threats against potential entrants is equally true of threats against current rivals.[41] Cooperation is more likely, then, if the threat (implicit or explicit) of retaliation from other firms is credible. All of the strategic investments listed in the previous section can serve to enhance the credibility of threats made against incumbent rivals as well as against new entrants.

10. *Product heterogeneity.* The first dimension of product heterogeneity that concerns us is product differentiation, or the degree of cross-demand price elasticity existing between two or more products. If a reduction in the price of product *A* will not win over any of product *B*'s customers, either because of objective characteristics which make the two products imperfectly substitutable or because of subjective consumer preferences, then, assuming that there are no other firms in the market, the producer of product *A* will have little incentive to engage in price cutting. According to one chronicler of the "incredible electrical conspiracy," it was an increase in cross demand-price elasticity that generated price-cutting pressure among American electrical equipment manufacturers during the 1950s. "Smaller companies were becoming bigger and were broadening their product lines. Customers had a wide choice, . . . alike in quality and design. Price consequently became the decisive selling point."[42] The industry had to resort to explicit price fixing when it was unable "to shift buyers' attention from price to other selling points like high quality, better service, and improved design."[43] In general, as substitutability among a set of competing products increases,

---

Conflict (Oxford: Oxford University Press, 1960); also, see Martin Shubik, *Strategy and Market Structure* (New York: Wiley, 1959).

[41] Jacquemin, *The New Industrial Organization*, p. 120; R. Caves and M. Porter, "From Entry Barriers to Mobility Barriers: Conjectural Decisions and Contrived Deterrence to New Competition," *Quarterly Journal of Economics* 91 (1977): 241–61.

[42] R. A. Smith, "The Incredible Electrical Conspiracy (Part One)," *Fortune* (April, 1961), p. 135.

[43] R. A. Smith, "The Incredible Electrical Conspiracy (Part Two)," *Fortune* (May, 1961), p. 222.

the individual incentive to engage in price cutting will also increase. Cooperation, then, is less likely when cross-demand elasticity is high.

Another aspect of product heterogeneity that affects the likelihood of successful cooperation concerns not the differences between the products of two firms, but the range of possible differences within the products offered by each firm. As a product lends itself to such differences, both the number of agreements necessary to maintain price stability and the difficulty of reaching a general agreement will increase. Thus cooperation among tire manufacturers requires not a single agreement on the price of a tire, but an agreement that takes into account the 324 ways in which tires can be graded.[44]

Finally, products differ dynamically.[45] In industries characterized by a rapidly changing technology or by rapidly changing consumer tastes, agreements will have to be continually renegotiated, and cooperation will be correspondingly tenuous.

In summary, the pricing Prisoner's Dilemma supergame does not always produce the suboptimal mutual price-reduction outcome. In a market such as the one posited above, in which there are no significant interfirm differences and each firm faces roughly the same payoff structure, we can predict that the success of the firms in achieving a cooperative outcome to their pricing Prisoner's Dilemma will be more likely when sellers are few in number; when buyers are many in number; when orders are "small, frequent, and regular"; when the product is not new; when buyers select sellers on the basis of sealed bids; when demand for the industry's product is strong; when products can be easily stored; when the demand for the industry's product is relatively inelastic with respect to price; when the proportion of fixed costs to variable costs is relatively low; when fixed capital is not overly specialized; when entry is difficult; when threats are credible; when industry products are imperfectly substitutable; when products are not complex; and when product characteristics do not vary over time.

From cooperation to conflict: the impact of interfirm differences

So far, we have been assuming that all firms are identical, particularly with respect to their cost curves and output levels. This implies, first, that the optimum price is the same for all firms; and, second, and most

---

[44]Scherer, *Industrial Market Structure*, p. 203.
[45]Ibid., pp. 200–1; George Hay and Daniel Kelley, "An Empirical Survey of Price Fixing Conspiracies," *Journal of Law and Economics* 17 (April, 1974): 5.

important, that each firm has an equal capacity to reduce or increase its price and that the industry price level will affect each firm in the same way. This is obviously not the case in the real world of economic competition, where interfirm differences in efficiency and output level mean that "some competitors may be better able to compete than others."[46] Such differences in efficiency, as well as in other dimensions (such as financial resources), greatly complicate the collective action problem faced by competitors, even to the point of making it virtually intractable.

Consider the market depicted in Figure 1.8, in which there are three types of firms: low-cost firms (type A); medium-cost firms (type B); and high-cost firms (type C). In this market, the different types of firms have different incentives and capacities to cooperate. The low-cost firm receives positive profits even at the universal defection outcome. While it can increase its short-term profits under a cooperative outcome, its long-term interests may be better served by short-term universal defection, which may drive its high- and medium-cost competitors out of business. The high-cost firms, on the other hand, cannot sell enough goods to make a profit unless they defect *and* firms producing at least k percent of total output cooperate. Their survival depends upon their ability to cut the cooperative prices offered by their competitors. Regardless of the presence of the market-structure characteristics described above, type C firms are unable to cooperate. Since the success of the contingent cooperative strategy in the Prisoner's Dilemma supergame depends on at least k percent of output being sold at cooperative prices, the presence of at least this number of type C firms will make it impossible to achieve the cooperative solution voluntarily.

This game shares the basic characteristics of the mixed-motive Prisoner's Dilemma. Defection is the dominant strategy for all firms, yet the defection of each firm will generate a suboptimal outcome. As was the case in the previous game, some firms in this market (actually, all firms, with the exception of the type A firms) receive negative profits at the universal defection outcome: They need the cooperation of their competitors in order to survive. What makes this game different is that some firms (the type C firms) *cannot afford to cooperate*. In short, there is no outcome that will provide a positive profit to all firms.

In this game, as in the games described in the two previous sections, the fundamental dynamic is the conflict between the individual interest in profit maximization and the collective interest in achieving the con-

[46]McNulty, "Economic Theory," pp. 645–6.

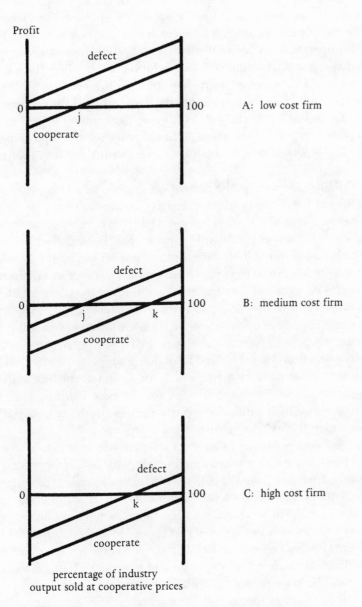

Figure 1.8. Profit functions of firms with different costs.

ditions required for profit maximization. In the earlier games, however, while these two interests did not parallel one another, they were not always completely incompatible; there was a solution – enforced universal cooperation – which satisfied the collective interest and approximated the best payoff that could be achieved by any firm through the unrestrained pursuit of its individual interest. If maximum profits and collectively optimal profits were not the same, at least the achievement of the latter still left each firm with very high profits. In the present game, however, the achievement of the collective interest is incompatible with high profits across the board, or even with the survival of every firm.

A further refinement of the market generates a similar conclusion. In all of the markets discussed so far we have assumed that profits increase with output. This implies that the reduced price covers operating costs. For each firm, however, there is a price level below which it cannot profitably sell commodities. When prices are set below this level, operating costs will not be recovered, and profits will decrease with output. In the market presented in Figure 1.9, the firms are differentiated by their capacity to reduce costs, and the price level is such that, unless each firm can reduce costs, it will be unable to recover operating costs at the reduced price. Firm A *is* able to reduce costs, possibly by lowering wages, while firm B is prohibited from doing so, perhaps by a collective bargaining agreement or a regional labor shortage. In this situation, cooperation is the dominant strategy for the type B firms, since they cannot increase their profits by reducing prices. In the language of collective action theory, they *cannot afford to free-ride*.

We began our analysis by likening capitalist competition to a collective action problem. As long as we limit ourselves to the homogeneous firm case, our departure from the collective action problematic lies primarily in the nature of the interests pursued, not in the structure of the game. However, when we introduce interfirm heterogeneity, we encounter an entirely new set of organizational problems. Not only do capitalist firms no longer have a common interest in universal cooperation, but when some firms can't afford to cooperate and others can't afford to defect, there may be no outcome in which all firms receive positive profits. Firms must organize themselves in order to receive optimal profits but, in order to do so, they must both overcome their own free-rider problems and force organization on those of their competitors whose survival depends on its absence. In these situations the attempt by firms to organize their markets is not a struggle to transcend particularistic in-

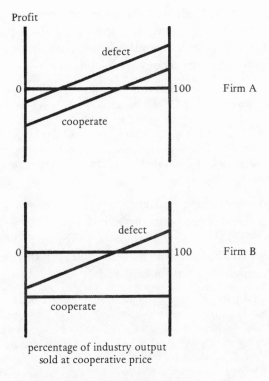

Figure 1.9. Profit functions of firms with different capacities to reduce prices.

terests in favor of a common interest, but a struggle between several particularistic interests. The question here is not whether individual interests can be subordinated to support a collective interest – they cannot – but which of two or more mutually exclusive versions of the "collective interest" will win out.

Other market-based collective action problems

The remainder of this study will focus on the pricing Prisoner's Dilemma and on the response to it of capitalist firms. Before proceeding, however, it should be noted that while the pricing game constitutes the most fundamental competitive collective action problem, it is not the only Prisoner's Dilemma faced by capitalists; nor is Prisoner's Dilemma the only game that generates capitalist collective action problems.

Consider, for instance, Marx's account in *Capital* of the decision to increase or maintain the length of the working day. By forcing their laborers to work long hours, individual capitalists can decrease variable costs and receive higher profits. Yet, according to Marx, if all capitalists did so, the health of the working class would be jeopardized, workers would perish, and, in the long run, labor costs would rise.

If, then, the unnatural extension of the working day, that capital necessarily strives after in its unmeasured passion for self expansion, shortens the life of the individual labourer, and therefore the duration of his labour-power, the forces used up have to be replaced at a more rapid rate and the sum of the expenses for the reproduction of labour-power will be greater, just as in the machine the part of its value to be reproduced every day is greater the more rapidly the machine is worn out.[47]

The choice between maintaining and lowering wages exhibits this same logic. It is in the interest of each capitalist to reduce costs by paying workers less money, yet, when all capitalists do so, the outcome will be a reduction in effective demand and a decrease in profits. In this game, a high wage level is a collective good for capitalists.

To each capitalist, the total mass of workers, with the exception of his own workers, appear not as workers, but as consumers. . . . Of course he would like the workers of other capitalists to be the greatest consumers of his own commodity. But the relation of every capitalist to his own workers is the relation as such of capital and labor. . . . Capital regards demand by the worker – i.e., the payment of the wages on which this demand rests – not as a gain but as a loss.[48]

Capitalists also play intertemporal Prisoner's Dilemmas. Consider a group of firms at time i. By cooperating in the pricing game they can achieve cartel profits. However, their high profits are likely to generate new entry and an eventual reduction in profits to the competitive level.[49] The firms maximize their long-term interest by restraining their desire to maximize short-term profits, and by moderating their prices so that profits are comfortably high, but not so high as to attract new entrants. In this game each player is the set of firms at time i ($i = 1, 2, 3, \ldots, n$). The "group" is constituted by the aggregation of these sets. The collective good is a future high price level to which every player contributes by keeping prices low enough to discourage new competition. Each player then benefits from the restraint shown by past players.

[47]Karl Marx, *Capital*, vol. 1 (New York: Modern Library, 1936), p. 292.
[48]Karl Marx, *Grundrisse: Foundations of the Critique of Political Economy* (New York: Vintage, 1973), pp. 419–20. Also, see John Maynard Keynes, *The General Theory of Employment, Interest, and Money* (New York: Harcourt, Brace and World, 1936), pp. 258–61.
[49]Jon Elster, *Logic and Society* (London: Wiley, 1978), pp. 129–30; and Mancur Olson, *The Rise and Decline of Nations* (New Haven: Yale University Press, 1982).

The key to the previous game lies in the fact that the outcome generated at time 1 leads to activity on the part of other capitalists – entry into the market – that alters future outcomes of the game. Aside from attracting new entry, the outcome of competitive games can also generate action on the part of political actors which may have adverse long-term consequences for capitalists. A public belief that corporations tend to do the "right" thing is a collective good which benefits all capitalists by moderating hostile demands for state regulation – or worse. Yet it is easy to imagine instances in which the collective, long-term interest in high standards of business conduct conflicts with the individual firm's short-term interest in high profits.

For instance, Useem suggests that while it may be individually rational for capitalist firms to exploit the low costs of doing business in South Africa, the capitalist class as a whole would benefit from a principled withdrawal from the racist South African economy.[50] This same logic would apply to any situation in which restraint from profit maximizing demonstrates business's "social responsibility."

Aside from Prisoner's Dilemma, capitalist competition also presents capitalists with coordination problems that may generate a demand for organization.[51] Thus, Jon Elster has pointed out that the decision whether to invest in labor-saving or capital-saving innovation can be understood as a game of Chicken, in which each firm does best by selecting a different strategy than that of its competitors.[52] If all other firms invest so as to save labor, the price of labor will decline, benefiting the firm that invested in capital-saving technology. As is the case in Prisoner's Dilemma, individual rationality alone is insufficient to produce a satisfactory outcome. Product-differentiation decisions may have a similar structure. Competing firms who wish to distinguish their products from each other and to position themselves in particular segments of the market may not care about what group of consumers they appeal to, as long as it is a different group than that sought after by their competitors.

Finally, when a set of competing firms could benefit from standard-

---

[50]Michael Useem, *The Inner Circle* (New York: Oxford University Press, 1984), pp. 144–5.
[51]For discussions of the coordination game as a collective action problem, see Duncan Snidal, "Coordination versus Prisoner's Dilemma: Implications for International Cooperation and Regimes," *American Political Science Review* 79 (1985): 923–42; and Andrew Schotter, *An Economic Theory of Social Institutions* (New York: Cambridge University Press, 1981).
[52]Jon Elster, "Marxism, Functionalism, and Game Theory," *Theory and Society* 11 (1982), pp. 470–1.

izing their products, they may find themselves in a coordination game in which each player prefers to adopt the same strategy as its opponent, but in which neither player knows which strategy its opponent will select. In the Battle of the Sexes variant of this game, the players still prefer to coordinate their choice of strategies, but they have different preferences as to what the common strategy should be. The game receives its name from a situation in which a man and a woman are faced with the decision of how to spend their evening. Their choice is between a prize fight and the ballet. "Following the usual cultural stereotype, the man prefers the fight and the woman the ballet; however, to both it is more important that they go out together than that each see the preferred entertainment."[53] An economic version of this game is created by the choice faced by competing manufacturers between two different product designs. Let us assume that each prefers coordination – a standardized product – but that each also prefers that its competitor bear the readjustment and retooling costs needed to bring the products into line. Like the man and the woman in Battle of the Sexes, the two firms prefer to coordinate their choice of strategies and standardize their products, but disagree as to the manner in which coordination will be accomplished.

Conclusion

The principal collective action problem faced by capitalist firms is not to organize themselves into a class actor vis-à-vis workers but to organize themselves into stable markets in which behavior is predictable and a live-and-let-live form of competition generates acceptably high profits and economic survival for all. Capitalist firms face this problem quite independently of the antagonistic relationship between workers and capitalists. Even if workers were quiescent and apolitical, capitalists would still face problems of market organization.

The analysis presented in this chapter gives us reason to believe that market organization will be an elusive goal. Under some conditions, to be sure, we can expect rational firms to select the cooperative strategy and for the optimal cooperative outcome to result. However, in the many situations in which these conditions are not present, particularly when there are important interfirm cost differences between firms in the industry, a spontaneous cooperative outcome will not be forthcoming.

[53]R. D. Luce and Howard Raiffa, *Games and Decisions* (New York: Wiley, 1957), p. 91.

This conclusion is the point of departure for the remainder of this study. In those markets in which cooperation fails to occur, we must expect firms to try either to escape from their competitive game or to organize themselves by transforming it. In the following chapter, I will analyze the various forms that capitalist collective action can take and the calculus behind the individual firm's decision to pursue particular forms of market organization.

2. Forms of capitalist collective action

Introduction

In the previous chapter I demonstrated that under some conditions, the rational behavior of individual firms will generate outcomes that are suboptimal, and perhaps intolerable as well. In this chapter I try to explain how firms will respond to these suboptimal competitive outcomes. Will they accept them or will they try to improve them by transforming the game and organizing themselves? As Anatol Rappoport has pointed out, the Prisoner's Dilemma model of a situation not only generates advice and predictions about rational behavior *within* the confines of the situation, but also leads immediately to a suggestion that the players should transform the game, that they should "seek ways of effecting enforceable agreements so as to turn the uncooperative game into a cooperative one."[1]

The problem is that the reorganization of markets imposes costs as well as benefits on individual firms, costs arising from a loss of autonomy that constrains the firm's pursuit of profit. I begin the chapter by identifying these costs and examining the way in which individual firms weigh the costs and benefits of various forms of market organization. In general, a firm's willingness to assume the costs of a particular form of market organization depends upon its "need" for a reorganization of the market and its capacity to achieve a less costly form of market organization than that which has been proposed. After discussing the calculus behind the decision to organize, I examine the costs and capacities of the various forms of capitalist collective action. I identify three general categories of capitalist organizational mechanisms: *internal* mechanisms, in which cooperation is enforced by the members of the industry; *external* mechanisms, in which cooperation is enforced by "private" actors outside of the industry – workers, suppliers, customers, and creditors; and *public* mechanisms, in which cooperation is enforced by the

---

[1]Anatol Rappoport, "Prisoner's Dilemma – Recollections and Observations," in Brian Barry and Russell Hardin, eds., *Rational Man and Irrational Society?* (Beverly Hills: Sage, 1982), p. 80.

state. I argue that the capacity of an organizational mechanism to enforce cooperation and to provide the benefits of collective action varies inversely with the costs that it imposes on the individual firms being organized. In some cases, these costs may be prohibitive. Firms may prefer *not* to act collectively.

A major implication of the analysis presented in this chapter is that the need for collective action – defined as the presence of suboptimal outcomes – does not automatically generate a solution. Not all firms experiencing suboptimal payoffs want to be forced to cooperate with their competitors; not all firms which do desire universal cooperation are willing to pay the costs to achieve it; and, finally, not all attempts at market organization, including those involving state enforcement, are successful.

Nonorganizational "solutions" to capitalist collective action problems

My principal concern in this study is with organizational solutions to capitalist collective action problems, solutions in which individual firms maintain their capacity for independent decision making and remain in a competitive relationship with each other, but organize themselves so that they act cooperatively. These solutions do not exhaust the ways in which competing firms can escape the suboptimal outcomes generated by rational, competitive behavior, however. Adapting Albert Hirschman's terminology, if transforming the game and reorganizing the market represent the "voice" option, firms still have several "exit" options at their disposal.[2] I will consider these various exit options briefly before returning to the discussion of market organization and collective action which constitutes my main theme.

First, a firm that finds its payoff to be unsatisfactory can exit from the market in the traditional economic sense and liquidate its capital. It will do so, however, only if the profit rate in other sectors of the economy, discounted by the transaction cost of liquidating its present capital, is higher than its present rate of profit. This condition is a more serious obstacle than the theory of the perfectly competitive economy implies. As we shall see in the case study of the bituminous coal industry, overcapacity, low profits, and "cutthroat competition" may persist for decades without generating significant exit from the market.

[2]Albert O. Hirschman, *Exit, Voice, and Loyalty* (New Haven: Yale University Press, 1970).

Another exit strategy open to individual firms acting unilaterally is product differentiation. Here a firm's object is to distinguish its product from those of its competitors to the extent that it monopolizes a segment of the market and is therefore insulated from competitive pressure. In her study of the turn-of-the-century paper and iron manufacturers, Lamoreaux found that those firms that pursued a product-differentiation strategy and sought profits in high margins rather than in high output, maintaining a high price level that was part of the product's quality image, were more successful in withstanding competitive pressures than those firms that pursued a mass-production strategy.[3] There are limits to the product-differentiation strategy, however, especially when consumers are industrial users whose purchases are guided by standardized specifications and who are not particularly susceptible to image-based marketing. Product differentiation is more likely to result in "monopolistic competition" (which is still competition) than in the absence of competition.

The third exit option involves the elimination of competition through a fusion of several interdependent competitors into a single decision maker. Because this involves joint action, as opposed to the two individual strategies described above, it is worth discussing in a little more detail.

Unlike human beings, organizations can effectively reconstitute themselves, either by fusing together in such a way that individual organizational identities and capacities for independent action are completely eliminated, or by combining pieces of themselves together so that their behavioral independence, but not their organizational identity, is sacrificed. These combinations can take a variety of forms, the most basic of which is the simple merger, in which the assets of two or more firms are joined together. The factors that cause mergers are varied and complex, and efforts to explain the pattern of merger activity (which, in the United States, has been characterized by "waves" of mergers) continue to occupy the energy of economists. In all probability, different sets of motivations and explanatory variables are dominant during different time periods. It is not necessary to enter this debate, however, in order to make the point that a merging of assets is a singularly effective way of eliminating competition; and to emphasize that whatever other benefits a merger might provide in terms of scale economies, improved financial resources, et cetera, we should not ignore the fact that mergers

[3]Lamoreaux, *The Great Merger Movement*.

are also a way to eliminate competitive interdependence. Certainly, capitalist firms have been conscious of this fact. In the words of one manufacturer, "it is proven that the most effective way to cure a bad situation is to buy up the offenders."[4] Mergers have also had the effect of eliminating competition, particularly in the pre–World War II period. Markham estimates that seventy-one competitive or near-oligopolistic industries were transformed into near monopolies as the result of merger between 1890 and 1904.[5] Similarly, in his study of ninety-two major mergers, most of which took place between 1890 and 1902, Moody found that seventy-eight ended up by controlling at least 50 percent of their markets; fifty-seven controlled at least 60 percent of their markets; and twenty-six controlled at least 80 percent of their markets.[6] Nelson's study of roughly the same period (1895–1904) yielded similar results, leading him to conclude that "a substantial share of . . . merger activity did result in securing a leading and often dominant share of the market" and that this finding demonstrates "the existence of a fairly strong desire to avoid rigorous competition."[7] As Scherer notes, "monopoly power was such a striking result of the numerous mergers around the turn of the century that one could hardly deny with a straight face that it was unintended."[8]

In the United States, the availability of the merger device as a monopolizing measure has declined considerably as the result of antitrust developments. In 1904, the Supreme Court found the Northern Securities Co., a holding company controlling the major rail lines operating between the Great Lakes and the Pacific Coast, in violation of Section 2 of the Sherman Act, which prohibits monopolizing, attempting to monopolize, and conspiring to monopolize trade. Although the Northern Securities Co. was not the product of a merging of assets, this decision signified that capitalists could no longer combine all of the firms in a market into "one big union." This interpretation of the antitrust laws did not eliminate the reduction of competition as a motive behind

---

[4]Quoted in Frederick M. Scherer, *Industrial Market Structure and Economic Performance* (Chicago: Rand-McNally, 1980), p. 129.
[5]Cited in Scherer, *Industrial Market Structure*, p. 121.
[6]John Moody, *The Truth about the Trusts* (Westport, CT: Greenwood Press, 1968), p. 487. Lamoreaux's analysis of these mergers yielded different numerical findings: Of 93 consolidations, 72 controlled at least 40 percent of their markets and 42 controlled at least 70 percent of their markets. These findings continue to support my major point, that mergers had the effect of eliminating competition. See Lamoreaux, *The Great Merger Movement*, pp. 1–4.
[7]Ralph C. Nelson, *Merger Movements in American Industry* (Princeton: Princeton University Press, 1959), pp. 95–107.
[8]Scherer, *Industrial Market Structure*, p. 128.

mergers, however; nor did it prevent "horizontal" mergers between competing firms if, in the courts' opinion, their results were not monopolizing. In both the 1926–1930 and 1940–1947 periods, over 60 percent of merger disappearances were horizontal, involving competing firms; and between 1948 and 1953, 36.8 percent of all assets acquired by merger fell into the horizontal category.[9] The decline in horizontal mergers was the result of the passage, in 1950, of the Celler–Kefauver Amendment, which prohibits mergers in industries in which they would result in a substantial reduction in competition and in which there is already a trend toward concentration. Horizontal mergers have declined significantly since 1950, but there is evidence that, on those occasions when they were undertaken, the reduction of competitive uncertainty was a motive.[10] Of course, mergers other than horizontal ones can still alter the parameters of the competitive game by changing relations between buyers, sellers, and suppliers. As Hannah notes,

The trend away from horizontal mergers is ... not so conclusive in showing the decline of this [market domination] motive as it might at first sight appear. Vertical integration ... may confer substantial market control, and a merger that outwardly appears to be a conglomerate may nonetheless frustrate potential entry....[11]

However, at best, the effect is "oligopoly by merger," not "monopoly by merger"; competitive relationships may be made more manageable, less uncertain, and more amenable to an organizational solution, but they still persist.[12]

The corporate form of ownership, by making it possible for the owner(s) of a minority of shares to gain control over the operation of a firm, provides the basis for a number of devices which effectively place two or more firms under control of the same decision maker while enabling them each to maintain their separate legal identities. In effect, the number of firms in the market remain the same, but the number of decision makers is reduced, conceivably to a single one. As is the case with mergers, however, the monopolizing possibilities promised by

[9]Carl Eis, "The 1919–1930 Merger Movement in American Industry," *Journal of Law and Economics* 12 (October 1969): 294; Scherer, *Industrial Market Structure*, p. 128.

[10]Jeffrey Pfeffer and Gerald R. Salancik, *The External Control of Organizations* (New York: Harper and Row, 1978), p. 125.

[11]Leslie Hannah, "Mergers," in Glenn Porter, ed., *Encyclopedia of American Economic History* (New York: Scribner's, 1980), p. 648.

[12]The expression "oligopoly by merger" is taken from George Stigler, "Monopoly and Oligopoly by Merger," in *The Organization of Industry* (Homewood, IL: Irwin, 1968).

these devices at the turn of the century have been virtually eliminated by various practical and legal constraints. To the extent that some form of intercorporate control is presently being exercised, it is unlikely that a sufficient proportion of industry output is involved to warrant the conclusion that competition has been eliminated.

During the early history of the corporate form in the United States, state law prohibited corporations from holding the stock of other corporations. The earliest intercorporate-control device, the trust, was developed in 1877 and perfected in 1882 by the Standard Oil Company in order to circumvent this restriction. During the next decade several other industries followed suit. The owners of the various firms involved would turn their shares over to a small group of "trustees," who then had the means to control the operation of each company. In return, the original stockholders received "trust certificates" entitling them to a share of the trust's profits. By 1892, as the result of a series of adverse court opinions against the Sugar Trust, the Whiskey Trust, and the Standard Oil Company, the trust device was effectively killed as a means of interfirm consolidation in the United States. Most of the trusts responded to this development simply by reorganizing themselves into corporations, the member firms surrendering their properties in return for stock in the new organization.[13] The practical effect was the same, of course; competition was eliminated through the replacement of a set of interdependent decision makers with a single decision maker. However, this is indistinguishable from a horizontal merger and faces the same constraints.

The same can be said for the *holding company*, a corporation owning stock in other corporations. Although this device became legally feasible in 1889, when the state of New Jersey amended its corporation law to permit corporate stock ownership, the first important exploitation of the new device didn't occur until a decade later, with the formation of the Standard Oil Co. of New Jersey, a holding company which controlled the former members of the Standard Oil trust. Several other holding company consolidations followed but, again, the 1904 Northern Securities decision, which banned monopolization through the acquisition of corporate stock, significantly checked their proliferation. The holding company device was further restricted by Section 7 of the Clayton

---

[13]Hans B. Thorelli, *The Federal Antitrust Policy* (Baltimore: Johns Hopkins University Press, 1955), pp. 76–83.

Act (1914), which prohibited the acquisition by one firm of another firm's stock if the result would be to lessen competition in interstate commerce.[14]

Another possibility is that a financial institution could gain effective control over a group of nominally competing firms through control of investment capital. In the late nineteenth century, when investment capital was in short supply, investment banks were able to translate their access to outside investors into positions of control over their corporate clients. In a sample of 40 corporations during the years 1900 and 1901, Herman found that 31.25 percent of them were controlled by financial institutions.[15] In the years since World War I, however, there has been a steady decline in such "finance control." In 1975, only 0.5 percent of the 200 largest publicly owned nonfinancial corporations (i.e., one firm) was controlled by financial institutions.[16] In the contemporary economy, according to Herman, investment banks are more likely to be the instruments than the masters of corporations.[17]

Several writers have argued that the holding-company function can be, and is, exercised not by a single industrial or financial corporation, as was the case during the "classic" holding-company period, but by groups of individuals using a "complex holding pattern" built around kinship relations and controlling interests in major corporations.[18] In a path-breaking study of the 100 largest nonfinancial corporations and the 50 largest financial corporations in the United States, Sweezy identified 8 major "interest groups" of corporations, the members of each group linked together by a network of financial connections, stockholdings, interlocking directorates, and family ties.[19] Presumably, such interest groups, to the extent that they exist, are assembled in order "to combine

[14]James C. Bonbright and Gardiner C. Means, *The Holding Company* (New York: Kelly, 1969), pp. 69–74.
[15]Edward S. Herman, *Corporate Control, Corporate Power* (Cambridge: Cambridge University Press, 1981), p. 62.
[16]Ibid., pp. 58–9.
[17]Ibid., pp. 120–1.
[18]Raymond W. Goldsmith and Rexford C. Parmelee, *The Distribution of Ownership in the 200 Largest Nonfinancial Corporations*, U.S. Temporary National Economic Committee Investigation of the Concentration of Economic Power, Monograph No. 29 (Washington, DC: U.S. Government Printing Office, 1941); Paul Sweezy, "Interest Groups in the American Economy," in U.S. National Resources Committee, *The Structure of the American Economy* (Washington, DC: U.S. Government Printing Office, 1939); Maurice Zeitlin, "Corporate Ownership and Control: The Large Corporation and the Capitalist Class," *American Journal of Sociology* 79 (March, 1974): 1,073–119.
[19]Sweezy, "Interest Groups." More recently, Herman found that only four of these groups were still visible. (Herman, *Corporate Control*, p. 230).

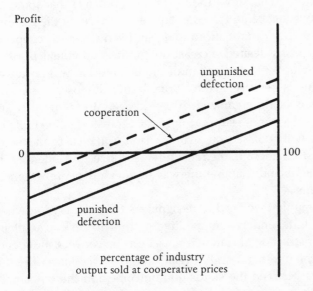

Figure 2.1. Profit function of a firm in a reorganized market.

the constituent companies into a system in such a way as to maximize the profits of the entire system irrespective of the profits of each separate unit."[20] However, for our purposes, the important question is whether the firms involved are competitors, and if so, whether combination effectively eliminates competition in entire markets. The available evidence does not suggest that this is the case.

The decision to organize

A group of competing capitalist firms whose independent rational behavior generates a suboptimal outcome can be said to be *organized* when their game has been transformed in such a way as to make cooperation the dominant strategy. This usually involves the introduction of sanctions that punish defection. Figure 2.1 depicts a payoff structure that has been transformed in this way. All things being equal, one would expect firms suffering from suboptimal payoffs to welcome such a transformation, since it would increase their profits. All things are not equal,

[20]Zeitlin, "Corporate Ownership," pp. 1,097–8; Bonbright and Means, *The Holding Company*, pp. 45–6.

however. We have already seen in Chapter 1 that when we introduce interfirm cost differences into the model, it is possible that some high-cost firms may resist being forced to cooperate, since, in the absence of side payments, they cannot afford to do so. Even when the cooperative payoff represents a desired increase in profits, individual firms may hesitate to pursue a reorganization of the market that will produce co-operation. This is because market organization imposes costs on the individual firms being organized. It would seem to follow that an individual firm's decision to support or resist a transformation of its competitive game will be based on a comparison of the costs and benefits of such a transformation. In the remainder of this section I identify these costs and benefits and examine the way in which they are weighed by individual firms.

The first thing that we need to recognize is that the decision whether to pursue an independent, competitive path or to seek to implement some form of market organization is not a decision between independent behavior on the one hand and "organization" *in general* on the other, but is a choice between the status quo outcome and the outcome that would be produced by a *specific* program of market organization. A firm's evaluation of the outcome that it expects will be produced by a particular organizational mechanism is determined by (a) the benefits that it will confer on the firm (i.e., the mechanism's effectiveness in enforcing co-operation); (b) its costs to the firm (i.e., the degree to which it constrains present and future profit maximization); (c) the firm's *organizational need*, which determines the degree to which it is willing to suffer costs in order to enjoy the benefits of organization; and (d) the *organizational capacity* of the industry in which the firm is competing – the degree to which market-structure features are present which facilitate the emergence of a cooperative outcome.

The principal cost imposed on capitalist firms by an organization of competition is a loss of autonomy. All forms of organized collective action involve some sacrifice of individual autonomy as decisions that were once left to the individual members of a group are taken over by a collective actor who either acts for the group as a whole or forces the individual group members to act as a whole. Capitalist firms value their autonomy not as an end in itself but because it allows them to make decisions that maximize profits – to continue to select the defection strategy. As their autonomy is limited, so is their capacity to organize production for profit and to take the profit for themselves.

This loss of autonomy has two dimensions. The first of these concerns the immediate impact of the new regime on the firm's payoff. Here, intraindustry heterogeneity plays a critical role. Even at the very general level of the model presented in Chapter 1, we have seen that high-cost firms may not be able to earn an acceptable level of profits by selecting the cooperative strategy, regardless of how many other firms in the market cooperate. These firms, of course, will resist any form of market organization that forces them to cooperate, unless some system of side payments is devised that compensates them for their losses. Several such devices are described below, in my discussion of internal organizational mechanisms. We will also run across an ingenious system of side payments when we turn to the bituminous coal industry. The industry's collective bargaining system was designed to enable high-cost operators to pay lower wages, thereby compensating them for their participation in the cooperative arrangement. Firms differ along more dimensions than simply the level of costs, however, and every organizational mechanism is likely to have a differential effect on competing firms.

Thus a concern rather poor in mechanical equipment but employing many hands may be in a position, by heavy payroll deduction, to prevent a reduction of volume from increasing its unit costs appreciably. It may therefore prefer a policy of restricted production and high prices. On the other hand, a competitive concern loaded with large capital costs may be less interested in curtailing its payroll than in exploiting fully the expensive mechanical equipment which becomes a dead burden if left idle. Reduced output even at high prices may be detrimental to it.[21]

The differential impact of organized collective action on firms with different costs and technologies means that support for market organization by one set of firms can be an effective strategy against a set of competitors who will be adversely affected by it. A fascinating example of this is provided by Marvel's analysis of English factory legislation that placed constraints on the number of hours that workers could be employed.[22] This legislation had a differential impact on firms according to whether they used water power or steam power to run their mills. Water-powered mills were vulnerable to interruptions in production caused by droughts. When this occurred, they needed to operate overtime to make up for lost output. The factory legislation put a stop to this pattern of production and thereby in-

[21]Karl Pibran, *Cartel Problems* (Washington, DC: Brookings Institution, 1935), p. 78.
[22]H. Marvel, "Factory Legislation: An Interpretation of the Early English Experience," *Journal of Law and Economics* 20 (1977): 379–402.

creased the market share of the steam-powered mills. Marvel claims that the legislation's support came principally from those districts in which steam power predominated.

The second dimension of costs concerns future, rather than immediate, losses of autonomy. In most cases, the actors that enforce cooperation have at least some capacity to redefine and perhaps to extend the content of cooperation, once the mechanism is in place. The individual firm must ask itself whether there is any chance that the actor with the capacity to enforce a relatively acceptable cooperative strategy in the present will decide to enforce an unacceptable cooperative strategy in the future. Thus the market-sharing agreement that gives to a firm a "fair" share of output may subsequently be altered so as to squeeze it out of the market. Similarly, firms that embrace collective bargaining in order to limit competitive wage and price cutting may regret their rashness if future wage demands are confiscatory. The probability that such future costs will result from present organization is determined by the degree to which the firm can influence the actors who control the mechanism and the degree to which the interests of these actors diverge from the firm's interest in its own profits. Thus a firm would prefer to be controlled by a "pool" of competitors which could only be moved into action by a vote of three-fourths of its member firms, rather than by a public commission in which consumers or workers may have the controlling voice. If the costs that a firm expects to suffer from a particular organizational mechanism are indeterminate, we can expect that it will value them as relatively high.

Another type of cost associated with the intervention of an organizational mechanism into a market is simply the material costs – in time and money – of establishing it and administering it. As these costs to capitalists increase, the particular mechanism in question becomes less attractive to them.

The sole benefit that an organizational mechanism can provide to an individual firm is the cooperation of the other firms in the market. Consider Figure 2.1, the payoff structure faced by a firm in a market in which some external actor is attaching negative sanctions to the defection strategy. In effect, we now have a game with three strategies: cooperation, punished defection, and unpunished defection. The coercive capacity, or effectiveness, of the intervening actor is indicated by the number of firms which have access to the unpunished-defection strategy. Regardless of its payoff structure and regardless of whether or not it has access to the unpunished-defection strategy, each firm benefits from the cooperation of its competitors, and the greater the number of other firms that cooperate, the more it benefits.

The major determinant of both the coercive capacity and the external costs of an organizational mechanism is the identity of the actors charged with defining and enforcing cooperation: competing firms, acting either individually or collectively; nonstate actors who are not among the firms being organized; and the state. Corresponding to these three categories of enforcement agents are three categories of organizational mechanisms: internal, external, and public. In deciding whether to seek to impose cooperation on other firms, then, a firm must weigh the benefits of their cooperation against the costs of its own cooperation – costs arising from its being forced to pursue a strategy other than its best, profit-maximizing one. The problem is that those mechanisms which are most effective in forcing other firms to cooperate also pose the greatest threat to an individual firm's autonomy (i.e., they are the most costly).

The manner in which a firm balances the cost and benefits of an organizational mechanism is a function of its *organizational need*. In order to understand this concept, we need to extend our time frame. Up until now we have been assuming that, except when the payoff structures have been transformed by an external actor, the competitive games played by capitalists are not significantly changed by their repetition, hence, that neither the number of players in the game nor the payoff structure faced by each player is altered as a result of the competitive process. While this assumption may be plausible in the short run, in the long run shifts in demand can raise or lower the profits of all players and the basic connections among a set of competing capitalists can be thoroughly transformed as some firms lose and others win their respective competitive struggles. Capitalists gauge their organizational need, then, not solely on the basis of their short-term payoffs but also on the basis of their prospects for surviving an alteration of the game that will leave them in an improved competitive position. These prospects, in turn, depend upon a firm's present payoff, its time frame, and its expected future payoff should "unorganized" competition continue. All other things being equal, the organizational need of a firm increases as its payoffs decrease, especially if they fall below zero. Thus, in Figure 1.8, the organizational needs of firms B and C are greater than that of firm A. A firm's time frame is determined primarily by its financial resources (or its access to financial resources). All other things being equal, financially strong firms have relatively low organizational needs.

They can afford to withstand short-term losses and are therefore able to place a relatively high valuation on future, rather than present, profits. Capitalists may have several reasons for believing that however low their present profits may be, their future profits in an "unorganized" market will be high enough to justify the continuation of their non-cooperative behavior. Thus, they may believe that low present profits are the result of a cyclical, temporary decline in demand. While their expected profit during the subsequent period of prosperity may still be suboptimal, it may not be unacceptably low, given the costs of organizing competition. In addition, some firms may possess competitive advantages that lead them to believe that they will be among the few survivors of an unorganized competitive struggle. These firms will prefer to behave independently rather than to seek to reorganize the market, a process that may perhaps erase their competitive edge and their prospects for future market domination.[23]

In general, capitalist firms attempt to minimize the costs of market organization. Because, as we shall see, the lower-cost mechanisms are also the least effective, the process of market organization assumes a sequential character: If a low-cost mechanism fails, firms face anew the choice to compete or to seek organization. As the process continues, the proposed organizational mechanisms become more effective (and more costly). Thus, a firm's willingness to accept a form of market organization will be dependent in part on whether or not a lower-cost mechanism could be effective in organizing the market. This, in turn, depends on the *organizational capacity* of the industry in question – the degree to which the various market-structure features contributory to cooperation (discussed in Chapter 1) are present.

In summary, individual capitalist firms in the competitive price game face two sets of decisions. The first is their decision within the game: whether to cooperate by maintaining prices or to defect by reducing prices. As we saw in Chapter 1, in many cases the outcome of this game, if rational strategies are selected, will be suboptimal. This presents firms with a second decision: whether or not to try to transform the game. On the one hand, individual firms wish to limit the intrusions of other actors into their own internal decision mak-

---

[23]Thus, Pearce found that a major cause of trade association collapse was the failure of the largest firms in the industry to cooperate (Charles A. Pearce, *Trade Association Survey*, U.S. Temporary National Economic Committee Investigation of The Concentration of Economic Power, Monograph No. 18 {Washington, DC: U.S. Government Printing Office, 1941}, p. 18).

ing; on the other hand, they wish to secure the cooperation of their competitors. The dilemma here, as we shall see in the following sections, is that these two goals are contradictory. The organizational mechanisms that impose the lowest external costs are frequently unable to induce cooperation, whereas the mechanisms with the greatest coercive capacity generate cooperation only by greatly reducing the autonomy of individual firms.

Internal organizational mechanisms

We saw in Chapter 1 that one way in which competing firms whose "unorganized" interaction generates suboptimal profits can enforce cooperation is through the economic retaliation of individual firms, who by responding quickly to noncooperative behavior prevent price cutters from reaping any long-term benefits from their defection. My earlier discussion of this phenomenon was limited to the case in which cooperation arose spontaneously, through a kind of "conscious parallelism." We can expect, however, that the chances of cooperation emerging are much greater when the firms involved can engage in explicit communication and coordination. Capitalists have devised a variety of internal organizational mechanisms which rely for enforcement on individual retaliation, but which enhance the communication and detection capacities of the firms. Such mechanisms are attractive to firms from the cost point of view; they impose limited constraints which are often easy to elude. However, these same factors also limit their effectiveness.

The most basic internal mechanism is a formal price-fixing agreement by which individual price and output levels are regularly negotiated and agreed upon. Similar results can also be achieved through informal gatherings of the "Gary dinner" sort, where no explicit agreements are struck, but which leave participants in no doubt as to which pricing and output policies are "best for the industry." Thus, in a letter cited by Wilcox, an official of the Borden Co. encouraged a local sales representative to cooperate with competitors by reminding him that "just a little sane and civil cooperation between manufacturers' representatives will go a long way toward keeping harmony in the market . . . ." The author of this letter urged his correspondent to stay on the right side of the fine line separating "civil cooperation" from illegal price fixing, but the implication of his advice was clear and casts doubt whether such a line exists: "Under no circumstances do we want you to discuss or agree to anything that may be termed illegal, but sit down and talk your problems over."[24] In his survey of trade associations, Pearce found that among their "most significant contributions" from the point of view of capitalists was their fostering of the kind of personal relations that make this type of communication possible.[25] Similarly, Herman argues that general purpose business associations such as the Chamber of Commerce, the Business Roundtable, and the National Association of Manufacturers "play a role as vehicles for communication and the development of community interest and collective behavior. The number of points of contact afforded by these organizations is large."[26]

Trade associations provide a more systematic and formalized means of interfirm communication. Thus, when direct communication among competitors is impossible, trade associations or similar institutions can perform a clearing-house function and collect and disseminate "average" past prices or current prices, which, with very little imagination, can be transformed into minimum prices.[27] The same end can be achieved through the circulation of studies which calculate "average" or "typical" costs.[28] A more subtle method of coordinating pricing among competing firms is through "cost education" – making sure that firms know all of their costs and circulating rules of thumb that tend to equalize costs (at a relatively high level) throughout an industry. Thus, the associations surveyed by Pearce recommended methods of calculating depreciation rates, assets, wages and salaries, raw material costs, overhead costs, loss and waste in raw material use, administrative expense, and distribution costs; and they circulated base-price lists, average markups, and various aids to differential pricing, such as quantity and trade discounts.[29]

Data on general industry conditions can also help those firms that wish to cooperate to adjust supply to demand and to bolster current prices. Many of the associations studied by Pearce kept each member informed of their current relative market share. In the words of one trade association administrator,

if the rate of growth of an individual producer's volume exceeds the rate of growth of his industry's total market; it represents business acquired from a

---

[24]Clair Wilcox, *The Structure of Industry*, U.S. Temporary National Economic Committee Investigation of the Concentration of Economic Power, Monograph No. 27 (Washington, DC: U.S. Government Printing Office, 1941), p. 143.

[25]Charles A. Pearce, *Trade Association Survey*, p. 40.

[26]Herman, *Corporate Control*, p. 214.

[27]Arthur R. Burns, *The Decline of Competition* (New York: McGraw-Hill, 1936), pp. 60–4.

[28]Pearce, *Trade Association Survey*, p. 290.

[29]Ibid., pp. 265–79; also Burns, *The Decline of Competition*, pp. 47–55.

competitor. Every businessman within my hearing knows the inevitable result of a continued loss of volume from one competitor to another.[30]

The pattern of trade association growth in the United States lends support to the view that they are perceived by competing firms as a possible means of organizing competition. An initial burst of trade association formation occurred in the years immediately following the Civil War, when regional markets broke down under the impact of improved communication and transportation. Other spates of trade association expansion occurred in the years during World War I (in part, a response to the passage of the Clayton Act) and during the 1920s and 1930s, when they constituted part of business's quest for "stability."[31]

Aside from informal agreements and trade associations, another type of internal organizational mechanism that can facilitate communication among competing firms (when the firms are corporations) is the interlocking directorate. These are of two types: direct interlocks, in which a member of one corporation's board of directors sits on the board of a competing corporation; and indirect interlocks, in which board members of competing corporations serve as members of a third corporate board.[32] According to Herman, direct interlocks are not of much importance in the contemporary American economy.[33] A 1969 study, however, found that nearly one in eight interlocks among the largest corporations in the United States fit into this category.[34] The communication possibilities of such direct interlocks are obvious. They

might . . . reinforce the propensity of oligopolies to establish norms of market behavior and to impose greater uniformity of action. . . . Interlocks could help establish norms about prices, costs, and innovations so that departures from the norm are easily decoded. . . . [They] contribute to the development of focal points and facilitate the monitoring of behavior that is subject to these norms.[35]

Indirect interlocks can serve a similar function, simply by providing a large number of contacts between competing firms.[36] Thus Michael Useem argues that a principal function of the interlocking directorate is to provide participating executives with what he calls "business scan, the continuous monitoring of new developments in government policies,

[30]Quoted in Pearce, *Trade Association Survey*, p. 182.
[31]Herman, *Corporate Control* 1981: 212–13.
[32]Ibid.
[33]Ibid., p. 202.
[34]Peter C. Dooley, "The Interlocking Directorate," *American Economic Review* 59 (1969, no. 3): 314–23.
[35]Johannes M. Pennings, *Interlocking Directorates* (San Francisco: Jossey-Bass, 1980), p. 27.
[36]Herman, *Corporate Control*, pp. 202–3.

labor relations, international tensions, markets of many kinds, technology, and business practices." In doing so, according to Useem, it emphasizes general business information rather than specific interfirm information.[37]

The presence on corporate boards of representatives from financial institutions such as banks and insurance companies, even when they are not directly linking competing firms, can also play an important communications function, which Pennings likens to the trade association survey.

Trade associations collect information from member firms...that...permits comparison between similar firms on a number of performance attributes. Banks are also repositories of market information.... For satisfying a firm's need of information about its industry, directional interlocks from financial institutions may be more attractive than horizontal interlocks, because they can provide a more panoramic view of the industry.[38]

The authors of the U.S. National Resources Committee's report on the structure of the American economy argued that the security underwriting, accounting, legal, advertising, engineering, and public relations firms which serve large corporations could perform a similar messenger function.[39]

A fourth internal mechanism which promotes interfirm contact is the joint venture, in which two or more firms pool their resources in order to pursue a particular project. The economic rationale for joint ventures is to permit firms to participate in projects that require levels of capital or technological expertise that are beyond their individual capacity to provide. If this was the reason why firms engaged in joint ventures, we would expect that most of these projects would involve smaller firms with limited resources. In fact, however, it is large firms that predominate.[40] The explanation for this fact would appear to be that joint ventures offer competing firms an opportunity to engage in the communication and coordination that facilitates market organization. The following passage from a European Economic Community report on a joint venture between General Electric and Weir Group, Ltd., applies equally well to any joint venture.

[37]Michael Useem, *The Inner Circle* (New York: Oxford University Press, 1978), pp. 45, 55.
[38]Pennings, *Interlocking Directorates*, p. 180. Also see Rudolph Hilferding, *Finance Capital: A Study of the Latest Phase of Capitalist Development* (London: Routledge & Kegan Paul, 1981), pp. 119–20.
[39]U.S. National Resources Committee, *The Structure of the American Economy* (Washington, DC: U.S. Government Printing Office, 1939), p. 155.
[40]Herman, *Corporate Control*, p. 211.

The very creation of the joint venture ... amounted to a restriction of competition, regardless ... of the specific restrictive provisions of the agreement. ...
The existence of the joint venture was seen by the Commission as providing
opportunities and inducements to the parties to enlarge their common activities
so as to impair free competition among themselves.[41]

In Japan, where an object of government economic policy is to restrain
foreign competitors, joint ventures between domestic and foreign firms
are encouraged *because* they have that effect.[42] These restrictive effects
are not accidental. Herman concludes that there is evidence that some
joint ventures "were designed specifically to avoid new competition and
to constrain and control supplies that threatened to destabilize
markets."[43]

A final means of interfirm contact, and one which has received very
little attention from researchers, is the government advisory body.

In literally scores of industries the government advisory body is a vehicle through
which major competitors meet regularly, under government imprimatur, with
a de facto exemption from antitrust, to advise the government on matters of
common interest. ... [They are] a vehicle through which business people of the
same trade can get together on a regular basis with the public excluded.[44]

The internal mechanisms discussed above all improve the ability of
competing firms to communicate with one another and to agree on
appropriate cooperative strategies. While knowledge of the content of
the cooperative strategy may be a necessary condition for cooperation
to emerge, it is the fear of retaliation from victimized competitors that
transforms the payoff structures of prospective price cutters. This fear
will be made more effective if the firms in the industry create an internal
organizational mechanism that improves their capacity to detect noncooperative behavior. If a firm knows that its own defection will be
quickly discovered and presumably acted upon, its incentive to defect
is practically eliminated; and if it knows that its competitors' defection
will be relatively visible, it has less reason to fear being victimized and
less incentive to engage in preemptory defensive defection.

There are a variety of internal organizational mechanisms which improve the detection capacity of individual capitalists and thereby facilitate cooperation. To the extent that cooperation is based on an explicit
agreement among competitors, the agreement can be supplemented by

[41]Ibid., p. 208.
[42]Ibid., p. 212.
[43]Ibid., p. 204.
[44]Ibid., p. 216.

a formal monitoring and reporting system. Thus, the members of one early American combination, the Gunpowder Association of the United States, elected a council which met weekly to monitor the agreement and to investigate complaints.[45] Also, of course, the price-reporting systems described above improve detection as well as communicate the cooperative price level.

In many cases, price competition can be hidden in various "trade practices," such as discounts, credit terms, and trade-in allowances, which render it less detectable. By standardizing these trade practices, the members of an industry can make defection more conspicuous and can force price cutters into the open. Such standardization of trade practices can include common credit terms, uniform customer classifications, standard discounts, prohibitions against free deals, limits on guarantees, restrictions on the return of merchandise, minimum trade-in allowances, fixed handling charges, and delivered pricing.[46] The impact of such rules on detection is illustrated by Wilcox's account of the steel industry's delivered price system, which required sellers to charge standard freight rates based on the cost of rail shipment from a few common "basing points":

If no common mode of transportation were agreed upon, a seller might cut his price on the ground that a cheaper method was available, whether it was or not. If competitive pricing were to be avoided, the industry would have to check all such quotations in great detail. With a uniform schedule of freight rates, based upon a common method of delivery, this door to competition in price is closed.[47]

Because it is more difficult to conceal a shipment of commodities than to conceal the price at which they are sold, a price agreement can be monitored more easily if the industry publishes market-share statistics or, better yet, arrives at a formal agreement whereby firms are assigned fixed shares of the market or even specific customers. The most extreme type of output-monitoring device is the joint selling agreement, in which all of the members of the industry agree to distribute their products through a single seller – either an association of manufacturers, a paper firm set up by the manufacturers, or an existing distributive firm – which

---

[45]Stevens, "A Classification of Pools," p. 552.
[46]Wilcox, *The Structure of Industry*, p. 230; Pearce, *Trade Association Survey*, p. 54.
[47]Wilcox, *The Structure of Industry*, p. 149.

then acts as the exclusive sales agent for their combined product, setting price and allocating orders among the member firms.[48]

In some industries, firms have attempted to retaliate against defection collectively, by fining defectors a fixed amount for each unit sold below the cooperative price level or beyond the agreed market share. These fines are then pooled and redistributed among the "sucker" firms. In an interesting variant of this arrangement, firms that behave noncooperatively are required to make direct payments to their competitors. Thus, if a member of the American Veneer Package Association wished to expand its output, it purchased market shares from the other members of the association.[49] Similarly, the 1886 explosives agreement divided the twelve U.S. seller firms into "the nine" and "the three." "The nine" were each given an annual sales allotment based on their past performance. If they sold more powder than they were allotted, they agreed to purchase from "the three" an amount of powder equal to the difference between their sales and their quota. "The three," on the other hand, could sell as much powder as they were able.[50] The 1887 steel rail agreement, which assigned each seller a fixed market share, embodied another kind of compensation for "suckers." About one-third of the estimated 1888 market was placed under a Board of Control, which could apportion it "as and to whom it may deem equitable, in the adjustment of any differences that might arise."[51]

Rather than fine violators after the fact, some industries have requested the participants in their agreements to make large deposits to be held against fines or to pool their profits, which are then redistributed on the basis of output. A good example of the latter type of arrangement is provided by the major manufacturers of cast-iron pipe in the 1890s. The U.S. market was divided into "reserve cities," in which only one firm could do business; "free" territory, in which competition was unrestricted; and "pay" territory, in which competition was governed by a profit-pooling scheme. A board representing the six member firms would set prices on all jobs within the pay territory; then each job would be auctioned off by the board to the firm offering to pay the highest

[48]William S. Stephens, "A Classification of Pools and Associations Based on the American Experience," *American Economic Review* 3 (September, 1913): 564–71.
[49]Wilcox, *The Structure of Industry*, p. 255.
[50]Stevens, "A Classification of Pools," pp. 559–60; Lewis H. Haney, *Business Organization and Combination* (New York: MacMillan, 1921), pp. 167–8.
[51]Quoted in Haney, *Business Organization*, pp. 168–9.

"bonus" into the pool's coffers. These bonuses were then redistributed on the basis of annual shipments within the pay territory.[52]

These internal organizational mechanisms are tempting to capitalist firms because of their low costs. They promise the cooperation of competitors in return for an utterly voluntary (and, if necessary, a temporary) sacrifice of autonomy. If at any time the short-term gain to be had from defection exceeds the discounted value of long-term cooperative profits, there is nothing to prevent a firm from defecting.

> Whatever may have been the period for which an association was originally formed, no member need belong to it or observe its rules a day longer than he likes. Nothing can keep him to his contract except a sense of honorable obligation, and that does not always resist the temptation of an advantageous order.[53]

Also, actors who are not competing members of the industry play absolutely no role in the definition and enforcement of the cooperative agreement. In the extreme case, "a dinner is arranged for and with their feet under the same table the competitors reach a general understanding ... [T]here is no certificate of incorporation to secure, and no taxes to pay."[54]

However, the relatively low costs characteristic of internal mechanisms are matched by their relatively low coercive capacity. By improving the communication capacity and detection capabilities of capitalists, internal mechanisms can produce cooperation only in those markets in which an absence of communication and poor detection are the only obstacles in its path, that is, only in markets in which other conditions are present which will lead to the cooperative outcome. In order for a firm to choose cooperation, the discounted value of the profits generated by universal cooperation must exceed the discounted value of the profits generated by solitary defection followed by universal defection. This, in turn, presupposes a market with special characteristics. Even if we grant some degree of formal communication among firms, the success of internally organized cooperation is unlikely except in markets in which firms are relatively few in number; where the product is sufficiently standardized to permit interfirm price comparisons; and where easy entry, buyers

[52]Eliot Jones, *The Trust Problem in the United States* (New York: MacMillan, 1922), pp. 12–13.
[53]Henry W. Macrosty, *The Trust Movement in British Industry* (New York: Agathon Press, 1968), pp. 22–3.
[54]Haney, *Business Organization*, p. 160.

with great market power, high fixed costs, and weak demand do not generate excessive downward pressure on prices and thereby magnify the short-term gains from defection. The success of these mechanisms also depends on the willingness and ability of firms representing a large proportion of an industry's output to retaliate in the face of defection by their competitors.

On the surface, it may appear that those internal mechanisms providing for collective enforcement, rather than retaliation by individual firms, would possess a greater coercive capacity. This is not true for two reasons. In the first place, the various fines and other enforcement procedures provided for in these agreements are useless in securing initial participation and are equally ineffective in securing the subsequent cooperation of those who do not enter the agreement. Second, in the absence of state enforcement of contracts, even those firms that do agree to pay penalties cannot be forced to live up to their promise by any other means than individual economic retaliation. These collectively enforced internal agreements, then, rest on the same coercive basis as do the individually enforced internal agreements.

The question of the enforceability of contracts points to another aspect of internal organizational mechanisms which greatly impedes their effectiveness, at least in the United States – the fact that they are often in violation of restraint-of-trade legislation. In the United States, explicit price-fixing agreements were on an extremely shaky legal foundation even before the turn of the century. In 1898, the U.S. Supreme Court found a price-fixing agreement in restraint of trade, even though the prices charged were not "unreasonable," because the participants had the *power* to set unreasonable prices. This decision was extended in 1927, when the Supreme Court found price fixing to be illegal per se. Output restriction was equated with price fixing in a 1940 Supreme Court decision.[55] The prosecution of these agreements depends largely on the zeal and resources of the U.S. Department of Justice, however, and while they have certainly been driven underground, it would be naive to believe that judicial decisions have eliminated them. Horizontal interlocking directorates are also illegal per se in the United States, under Section 8 of the Clayton Act. However, the enforcement of this provision has been "neither prompt nor vigorous," and while the Clayton Act

[55] Alan D. Neale and D. G. Goyder, *The Antitrust Laws of the United States of America* (New York: Cambridge University Press, 1980), pp. 36–8.

may have had some effect there is still a substantial amount of horizontal interlocking.[56] The other communication devices that are described above – the exchange of information, standardization, cost education, price leadership, etc. – are not illegal per se, but they are prohibited to the extent that they constitute a form of price fixing.[57] Again, however, given the limited resources of the Federal Trade Commission and the Department of Justice, and the improvement in the means of communication available to firms, a considerable amount of illegal behavior can be assumed to persist in the face of these legislative prohibitions.

Because of their low costs, we can expect that internal mechanisms will be the first type of market organization proposed by firms facing the suboptimal payoffs of the pricing Prisoner's Dilemma and that most firms will offer their nominal support. This does not mean that capitalist firms can always organize their competition on such a voluntary basis, however. Increased communication, which is really all that they have to offer, cannot in itself generate a cooperative outcome. In markets where other conditions are present that facilitate cooperation, conditions discussed already in Chapter 1, an internal organizational mechanism may provide what is required to make cooperation possible. Where these conditions are not present, internal mechanisms do not possess the capacity to organize capitalist markets. Even when conditions are ideal, market organization achieved through internal means is fragile and is likely to collapse during economic downturns. When the need for market organization persists, firms will have to seek stronger means to achieve it.

External organizational mechanisms

When conditions are such that competitors will be unable to detect noncooperative behavior promptly or will be unlikely to retaliate against it if they do, firms that need to reorganize their market may turn to nonstate actors outside of the market who possess a greater capacity to enforce cooperation. These include suppliers, buyers, creditors, and workers. Because these actors have greater sanctions at their disposal

---

[56]U.S. Congress, House of Representatives, Committee on the Judiciary, Antitrust Subcommittee, *Interlocks in Corporate Management* (Washington, DC: U.S. Government Printing Office, 1965), p. 237; Dooley, "The Interlocking Directorate"; David Bunting and Jeffrey Barbour, "Interlocking Directorates in Large American Corporations, 1886–1964," *Business History Review* 45 (Autumn, 1971): 317–36.

[57]Neale and Goyder, *The Antitrust Laws*, pp. 48–59.

than do individual firms, external mechanisms possess a greater coercive capacity than do internal mechanisms. Yet their costs are greater. Enforcement of cooperative "agreements" is more difficult to escape; and there is a greater likelihood that the actors enforcing cooperation will use this capacity to pursue interests that diverge from those of cooperating firms in the organized industry.

Suppliers can enforce cooperation by refusing to deal with noncooperative "receiver" firms. Such a denial of supplies can either force a defector to cease production altogether or to seek supplies from a more distant (and more expensive) source. In either case, the initial increase in profits that is generated by defection can be erased – either through a reduction in output or through an increase in costs. The Coal Dealers' Association of California furnishes an early example of such an agreement. The organization's bylaws included the following passage, which, in Steven's words, left "the enforcement of the . . . rules and rates of the retailers' association . . . practically . . . in the hands of the wholesalers":

Upon receiving proof from the Coal Dealers' Association of the violation by any retail coal dealer of any of the rules of business printed on the rate card issued by said association and being satisfied that the charge is established, said wholesale coal dealers agree, and each of them agrees to, and will, charge the dealer so violating said rules or rule consumers' rates thereafter for coal, until said retailer dealer, if a member of said association, shall have been reinstated to membership in the Coal Dealers' Association by the vote of the board of directors of said association, or, if not a member, until he shall have paid such reasonable penalty as may be imposed upon him by said association.[58]

Capitalist firms have been as imaginative in seeking assistance from suppliers to enforce cooperation as they have been in designing internal organizational mechanisms. In the 1870s a group of sugar refineries turned to their insurers to assist them in a price-fixing scheme. Arguing that night operation of refineries constituted a fire hazard, they tried to convince the firms carrying their fire insurance to enforce a ban on night work that would have the effect of restricting output and reinforcing a high price level.[59] A group of German cement manufacturers described by Karl Pibran was perhaps even more creative. They entered into an agreement with local farmers whereby the latter pledged not to sell any

[58]Stevens, "A Classification of Pools," pp. 566–7.
[59]Adolph Eichner, *The Emergence of Oligopoly* (Baltimore: Johns Hopkins University Press, 1969), p. 59.

land suitable for the erection of cement plants for a period of twenty years.[60]

The problem with having suppliers enforce cooperation among "receivers" is that generally suppliers are interested in the expansion of output in the receiver industry, not in its profitability. They thus lack an incentive to assist the receiver industry in restricting its output and maintaining a high price level. One way in which this obstacle can be overcome is through a system of mutual sanctions in which receivers force suppliers to force receivers to cooperate. Suppliers who continue to deal with defecting receivers are boycotted by the latter firms' competitors. A typical case is that of the National Association of Retail Druggists, which circulated a list of "aggressive cutters" to all drug manufacturers and wholesalers. If the latter firms persisted in dealing with retail price cutters, their own names were circulated on pink slips among the members of the retail trade, who then proceeded to boycott them.[61]

Another way in which the interests of suppliers and receivers can be cemented is through a profit-sharing plan. This is essentially the relationship that existed between bituminous coal operators and coal-carrying railroads in the nineteenth century. Coal sales were handled jointly by the railroads and the operators; then they negotiated with one another over the division of the delivered price.[62] However, while this type of mechanism does bond the receivers and suppliers, it does not provide an incentive for a supplier to punish defecting price cutting by a receiver since, if other receivers cooperate, both the supplier and the defecting receiver will receive a greater profit through price cutting.

The primary interest of the buyers of an industry's products is in low prices. We would expect, therefore, that they would be unwilling to enforce a cooperative agreement among that industry's firms if it would result in higher prices. Yet, there are cases in which the supplying industry forced buyers to boycott defecting suppliers in order to induce them to cooperate. Both millinery manufacturers and dress manufacturers have tried to prevent the pirating and subsequent discounted sale of designs by refusing to deal with retailers who bought and sold cheap

[60]Pibran, *Cartel Problems*, p. 69.
[61]Haney, *Business Organization*; also see Joseph Palamountain, *The Politics of Distribution* (Cambridge, MA: Harvard University Press, 1955), pp. 98–9.
[62]Joseph T. Lambie, *From Mine to Market: The History of Coal Transportation on the Norfolk and Western Railway* (New York: New York University Press, 1954), p. 161.

imitations of original designs.[63] Here, again, the immediate gains from the defection of the supplier firms are offset by the decline in sales that will result from the loss of their markets. A related example is supplied by the American Sugar Refining Co., which enlisted the assistance of wholesale grocers in its efforts to prevent new entry in its market. The grocers had originally approached American to implement a rebate system that would reward grocers who refrained from cutting sugar prices. A few years later the refinery came up with the idea of using the same system to protect its own position. "The wholesale grocers were to be protected against competition among themselves in return for the American's being protected against competition from new refineries."[64]

Creditors can enforce cooperation among a group of competing firms by refusing to provide capital to defectors or by limiting credit and thereby controlling output. In his tract, *Can Business Govern Itself?*, Edgar Heermance concluded that "the commercial bank, acting as it were in the position of trustee, has very definite control if it wishes to exercise it, over the way business is carried on." Therefore, in order "to reach the company which is disturbing the economic balance, it will be necessary to work through the banker."

If the banker receives information which leads him to believe that his client's production policy is out of line with that of the organized industry, and that [this policy] may lead to reduced profit or actual loss, he is likely to . . . advise a change of policy. The alternative, from a banking standpoint, would be the calling of the loan.[65]

Rudolf Hilferding was also led to the conclusion that banks have the incentive and capacity to organize competition.

In general [a bank] can only stand to lose from competition among enterprises which are its customers. Hence the bank has an overriding interest in eliminating competition among the firms in which it participates. Furthermore, every bank is interested in maximum profits, and, other things being equal, this will be achieved by the complete elimination of competition in a particular branch of industry.[66]

[63]Wilcox, *The Structure of Industry*, p. 258.
[64]Eichner, *Emergence of Oligopoly*, pp. 191–4.
[65]Edgar Heermance, *Can Business Govern Itself?* (New York: Harper and Row, 1933), pp. 236–7; also see Rudolf Hilferding, *Finance Capital: A Study of the Latest Phase of Capitalist Development* (London: Routledge, and Kegan Paul, 1981), pp. 120–1.
[66]Indeed, in the conclusion of the quoted passage, Hilferding goes on to argue that the banks have achieved the organization of competition. (Hilferding, *Finance Capital*, p. 225; also see Zeitlin, "On Class Theory," p. 1,102.)

One way in which such an outcome can be achieved is through a tight credit policy that constrains output. Thus, in an example cited by Wilcox, the Wisconsin Canners' Association was able to reduce the acreage planted by pea canners by securing the cooperation of the Wisconsin Bankers' Association, whose members provided an amount of credit sufficient to finance only the "cooperative" acreage level.[67] Another fascinating instance of bank intervention is provided by the following account in *Fortune* magazine of a price war initiated in the retail grocery market by A&P.

In the course of the war A&P picked up some new enemies it could ill afford. In a most extraordinary statement last month, the First National Bank of Chicago declared that A&P had aimed at a 'cutting of corporate throats.' J. L. Dody, a vice president of First National's loan division, told the meeting of 1,500 of its correspondent bankers that it was up to them to come to the rescue of well managed firms that suffered from the . . . offensive by offering them loans at unusually generous terms.[68]

It is also possible, especially when the borrower is in a weak position, for the lender to insert "restrictive covenants" into a loan agreement. These establish guideposts which constrain such major areas of decision as mergers and new-product development. They are unlikely to apply to day-to-day competitive policy, however.[69] Beth Mintz and Michael Schwartz, who argue that banks are the "primary mechanisms for collective decision making within the business sector," claim that this role is effected less through the kind of direct intervention in specific decisions described above, than through the enforcement of more general "rules of corporate conduct" within which considerable entrepreneurial discretion is possible.[70]

Workers can enforce cooperation among competing capitalists in any of three ways – by standardizing labor costs, by limiting output, and by restricting entry. In industries in which labor costs constitute a significant proportion of production costs, an industrywide collective bargaining agreement can standardize costs and can eliminate the conflicts of interest arising from cost heterogeneity and differential capacities to reduce costs which, as we saw earlier, greatly impede cooperation. If a collective bargaining agreement between workers and capitalists establishes in-

[67]Wilcox, *The Structure of Industry*, p. 246.
[68]Quoted in Beth Mintz and Michael Schwartz, *The Power Structure of American Business* (Chicago: University of Chicago Press, 1985), p. 111.
[69]Herman, *Corporate Control*, pp. 126–8.
[70]Mintz and Schwartz, *The Power Structure*, p. 117.

dustrywide wages and working conditions, thereby standardizing labor costs for all firms covered by the agreement, then a firm covered by the agreement cannot reduce wages without incurring a strike and a subsequent drop in production, sales, and profits. In subsequent chapters I will argue that when bituminous coal operators accepted collective bargaining in the bituminous coal industry at the end of the nineteenth century, it was with the end of controlling competition through the standardization of labor costs, which they hoped would stop the self-destructive price cutting which their internal efforts had been unable to check.

Organized workers can also stabilize competition by helping to limit output. Consider a market plagued by overproduction, in which the decision faced by each firm is whether to increase prices and decrease output or to maintain current output and prices. (Note that in this situation the maintenance strategy is not the cooperative strategy). Since this decision also produces a Prisoner's Dilemma structure, voluntary production cutbacks will not be forthcoming. Maloney et al. have argued that the output reduction desired by the industry can be achieved by conceding to unions the right to strike. Periods of universal defection are offset by strike-induced shutdowns, so that, in the medium run, production is reduced sufficiently to ensure cooperative profits, which are shared with workers through collective bargaining.[71] To anyone who has observed strikes, even from a distance, this model suffers from a certain surface implausibility, although before we discount it completely it is worthwhile to remember an incident recounted by Friedrich Engels, albeit one which, to his mind, was "unique in the history of modern industry." A group of speculators was attempting to corner the market in raw cotton and force a rise in the price paid for it by spinners. The spinners sought to retaliate by cutting back production, hoping to drive prices lower. Voluntary cutbacks, of course, were impossible. As an alternative,

the mill-owners, through their central committee, "semi-officially" approach the Central Committee of the Workers' Trade Unions with the request that the organized workers should, in the common interest, force the obstinate mill-owners to shut down by organizing strikes. Messrs. mill-owners, admitting their own inability to take concerted action, ask the formerly so much hated workers' trade unions, kindly to use coercion against them, the mill-owners, so that the mill-owners, induced by bitter necessity, should finally act in concert, as a class,

[71]Michael T. Maloney, Robert E. McCormick, and Ralph D. Tollison, "Achieving Cartel Profits through Unionization," *Southern Economic Journal* 46 (No. 2, 1979): 628–34.

in the interests of their own class. They have to be forced to do so by the workers, for they themselves are unable to bring this about.[72]

While the regulation of labor costs and output seems to be the major contribution that workers can make to the organization of capitalist competition, a strong union can also assist in the control of entry and the direct enforcement of price agreements. This was the case in the midwestern glazing industry in the 1930s. Glazing contractors used the glaziers union to limit entry and fix prices in both Indianapolis and St. Louis. In Indianapolis, union members refused to work for contractors who did not sign an agreement with the union and were not "recognized" by the other members of the industry. One writer concludes that the industry's recognition standards "effectively excluded many glazing contractors and glass distributors from seeking business within the Indianapolis trade areas."[73] A similar agreement in St. Louis prevented union members from setting glass except at the site of its final use, thus limiting the entry of sash and door manufacturers who installed glass on their products in factories.[74] According to Pibran, alliances of this type between workers and capitalists were common in Germany and England in the early part of the twentieth century. Organized workers who limited the supply of labor to the incumbent firms, thereby erecting a barrier to new entry, were rewarded with a wage level commensurate with the high, cooperative price level.[75]

If barriers to entry facilitate cooperation, barriers to exit from an industry have the opposite effect by generating overcapacity and pressure to cut prices. To the extent that wage cutting allows marginal firms to swell capacity in a crowded industry, unionization and other labor-market measures that limit wage reductions can help supply to adjust to demand and thereby ease competitive pressures.[76] In the end, this will increase the likelihood of successful cooperation among competing firms.

Aside from withholding labor, workers can also limit entry by enforcing a high wage rate. In industries in which some firms have a more labor-intensive technology than other firms, an increase in wage rates that is enforced across the industry will produce a disproportionate

[72]Friedrich Engels, "The Abdication of the Bourgeoisie," in Karl Marx and Friedrich Engels, *Articles on Britain* (Moscow: Progress Publishers, 1975), p. 397.
[73]J. P. Miller, *Unfair Competition* (Cambridge, MA: Harvard University Press, 1941), p. 221.
[74]Ibid.
[75]Pibran, *Cartel Problems*, pp. 67–8.
[76]See Lloyd Reynolds, "Cutthroat Competition," *American Economic Review* 30 (December, 1940), pp. 746–7.

increase in the cost burden of labor-intensive firms. At best, this places them at a competitive disadvantage; at worst, it raises their costs above the level that makes profitable entry possible. When market-structure conditions are such that large-scale (and presumably, capital-intensive) entry is impossible, high wage rates can constitute an effective barrier to entry and thereby facilitate cooperation among incumbent firms.[77] It is unlikely that this high wage rate can be secured without the assistance of workers, who of course have their own reasons for desiring it.

The costs associated with external organizational mechanisms are higher than those connected with the internal mechanisms discussed earlier because external actors are involved in both the definition and enforcement of the cooperative agreement. Each of these actors – suppliers, buyers, creditors, and workers – has an interest in the profitability of the industry being organized only as long as they can share in it. More often, their interest in their own profits or in a share of the organized industry's profits is likely to conflict with the interests of the individual firms in the organized industry. As Herman writes with respect to banks, they must be both very large and very astute to control competition among corporations. Bankers generally have a narrow profit orientation directed toward "capturing profitable business – not the imposition of order or reform."[78]

External mechanisms can possess a coercive capacity sufficient to induce cooperation, but only within a relatively narrow range of industries. In order for either suppliers or creditors to enforce an agreement, there must be a very high degree of mutual dependence between the firms at both stages of production. A threatened cutoff of supplies can transform the preferences of a firm in the Prisoner's Dilemma only if the particular raw material or commodity is indispensable and can be obtained only from a small group of firms whose own markets are so restricted that the threat of a boycott from one set of customers can outweigh the temptation to sell to another set. The same high degree of mutual dependence is also necessary if enforcement by buyers and creditors is to be effective. In order for workers to enforce agreements among competing firms, they must be highly organized and must possess the capacity to shut down any noncooperative plants. This, in turn, depends upon their possession of the material resources to undertake

[77]Oliver E. Williamson, "Wage Rates as a Barrier to Entry: The Pennington Case in Perspective," *Quarterly Journal of Economics* 82 (1968): 85–115.
[78]Herman, *Corporate Control*, pp. 128–9.

a strike and upon such institutional factors as the right to strike and the legality of collective bargaining agreements.

Public organizational mechanisms: the state

When competing firms "need" to organize their competition and when they are unable to do so by private means, either internal or external, state-enforced market organization is the only alternative to continued competition and suboptimal outcomes.[79] The state differs from private actors in three major respects: it has access to a wider range of devices with which to transform the payoff structures of individual firms; it can employ these devices more effectively; and a wider range of actors (and interests) is involved in all stages of the intervention process.

The state can organize competition in a variety of ways: by enforcing restrictive contracts and patent licenses among individual firms; by prohibiting or regulating various trade practices; by sanctioning a wide variety of cartel-type arrangements, involving price, output, and entry; and by using its fiscal policy to confer differential advantages on subsets of firms. The first of these categories is distinguished from the others in that the state adopts a passive role – ratifying and enforcing agreements whose contents are defined exclusively by the participants, who enter them voluntarily. Depending upon the legal environment, the state may enforce agreements to organize competition when they are put into the form of legally binding contracts. In the United States, before the Sherman Act placed statutory restraints on the degree to which capitalists could organize competition, legality in this field was determined by an amorphous legacy of common-law decisions and on their interpretation by contemporary jurists. Most nineteenth-century judges tended to adopt a procompetitive posture with regard to the common law, but this was by no means always the case, as the following judicial opinion demonstrates.

I apprehend it is not true that competition is the life of trade. On the contrary, that maxim is one of the least reliable of the host that may be picked up in any market place. It is in fact a Shibboleth of mere gambling speculation, and is hardly entitled to rank as an axiom in the jurisprudence of this country.[80]

---

[79]This is also a major thesis of the "economic theory of regulation." See George Stigler, *The Citizen and the State* (Chicago: University of Chicago Press, 1975) and Richard A. Posner, "Theories of Economic Regulation," *Bell Journal of Economics and Management Science* 5 (Autumn, 1974): 335–56.
[80]Quoted in Thorelli, *Antitrust Policy*, pp. 45–8.

Restrictive contracts that were validated in nineteenth-century U.S. courts covered both horizontal price fixing and vertical mutual sanctioning agreements.[81] In light of the relative uncertainty concerning the legality of these agreements, we can speculate that, in many cases, the belief that they were legally binding was as effective a sanction as an actual confirmation of their validity from the courts.

Since the passage of the Sherman Act, the only important case of state enforcement of voluntary restrictive contracts in the United States involves resale-price-maintenance contracts – agreements whereby the manufacturers of a trademarked, brand-named, or otherwise identifiable product prescribe the resale prices charged by wholesalers and retailers. Such agreements were almost universally upheld under the common law in nineteenth-century courts but, in 1911, they were found by the Supreme Court to be in violation of the Sherman Act.[82] Subsequently, retailer groups led by the National Association of Retail Druggists mounted a campaign to secure federal legislation authorizing resale price maintenance, introducing bills in virtually every session of Congress from 1914 to 1936. In the 1930s, in the face of continued congressional opposition, the campaign was taken to the state level, and between 1933 and 1938, fourteen states passed resale-price-maintenance laws.[83] In 1937, Congress passed the Miller–Tydings Amendment, which exempts from antitrust laws price-maintenance contracts covering goods moving in interstate commerce but resold in a state in which resale price maintenance is legalized. By 1940, 44 states had passed resale-price-maintenance laws, many of which included a nonsigner clause, stipulating that the observance of the resale prices set by a contract with any one distributor is mandatory for all other distributors, whether or not they actually sign the contract themselves.[84] After the nonsigner clause was invalidated by the Supreme Court in 1951, it was given explicit legislative legitimation in 1952 by the McGuire Act.[85] Although resale price maintenance can be used to enforce cooperation among manufacturers, its major purpose is clearly to provide a state sanction for the enforcement by manufacturers of cooperation among retailers and wholesalers.

[81] Ibid.
[82] Thorelli, *Antitrust Policy*, p. 48; S. G. Hollander, "The United States," in *Resale Price Maintenance*, B. S. Yamey (Chicago: Aldine, 1966), p. 68.
[83] Hollander, "The United States," p. 68.
[84] Joseph C. Palamountain, Jr., *The Politics of Distribution*, pp. 246–8.
[85] Hollander, "The United States," p. 70.

Patent law provides another basis for interfirm agreements that can be enforced by the state. The recipient of a patent enjoys a legal monopoly on the manufacture of a product or the use of a process. When he or she licenses other firms to share in this monopoly, he or she can include restrictive provisions in these licenses which will protect his or her own position. Often, however, the state-enforced power to restrict competition that is inherent in this licensing authority is extended beyond the strict requirements of the patent holder's legal monopoly. In effect, patent holders can organize competition through their control of technology, requiring individual firms to observe certain price and output practices before releasing technology to them, and punishing defection with patent-infringement suits. A further possibility is that several competing firms, each making the same product and each holding more or less complementary, overlapping, or mutually infringing patents, agree to pool their patents and to write market-sharing and price-fixing clauses into their licensing agreements. Perhaps the most notorious scheme to organize competition through patent licenses was mounted in the glass-container industry.

In summary, the situation brought about in the glass industry, and existing in 1938 was: Hartford, with the technical and financial assistance of others in the conspiracy, had acquired more than 600 patents. These, with over 100 Corning patents, sixty Owens patents, over seventy Hazel patents and some twelve Lynch patents, had been merged by cross-licensing agreements into a pool which effectively controlled the industry.... The result was that 94 percent of the glass containers manufactured in this country on feeders and formers were made on machinery licensed under the pooled patents.[86]

These licenses, which covered everything from prices and quantity to the size, weight, and color of glass that could be produced, were, in the words of an official with the Hartford Company, granted "only to manufacturers of the better type, refusing many licensees who we thought would be price cutters...."[87] By the late 1940s, court decisions had left very little scope for such practices in the United States, "but in the meantime," in many cases, "the profits of monopoly have been obtained."[88]

The public organizational mechanisms which contribute most toward the organization of competition are those which involve the enforcement of "agreements" which individual firms do not necessarily enter into

---

[86]Justice Roberts, quoted in Neale and Goyder, *Antitrust Laws*, p. 303.
[87]Clair Wilcox, *Public Policies toward Business* (Homewood, IL: Irwin, 1971).
[88]Neale and Goyder, *Antitrust Laws*, pp. 300–41, Wilcox, *Public Policies*, p. 171.

voluntarily. These fall into three general categories: trade practice restrictions; control over price, output, and entry; and fiscal policy.

I have already noted that one indirect method of enforcing an agreement not to cut prices is to adopt some method of standardizing costs that will place a common price floor under all sellers. In the United States, besides the private efforts discussed above, the state has also enforced prohibitions against various forms of cost cutting. Among the earliest examples of this type of legislation in the United States are the Meat Inspection Act and the Food and Drug Act, both passed in 1902 at the behest of manufacturers who were unable to protect their markets from the invasion of cheap competition by voluntary means.[89] Similarly, a desire to secure a state-imposed equalization of labor costs was at the heart of the support of coal operators for uniform mine-safety legislation and of cotton textile manufacturers for child-labor legislation during the first two decades of the twentieth century, and for minimum-wage legislation during the 1930s.[90] And by the mid-1920s, the Federal Trade Commission, created as an independent antitrust instrument, had become transformed into the promoter of "fair trade," attacking such cost-cutting practices as false advertising, trade-name appropriation, and misbranding, and encouraging industries to draw up "fair-practice codes." (These codes, however, were not enforced by the state.)[91] Perhaps the best-known example of state intervention to restrict cost-cutting trade practices occurred in distribution. In the 1930s, when many independent retailers and wholesalers saw their survival threatened by the growth of chain stores, which were able to secure lower prices from manufacturers, they successfully agitated for state intervention to prevent price discrimination by manufacturers. The result was the Robinson–Patman Act of 1936, which greatly reduced the scope of the quantity discounts obtainable by chain stores, while also limiting their access to the functional discounts enjoyed by independent wholesalers.[92]

---

[89]Gabriel Kolko, *The Triumph of Conservatism* (New York: The Free Press of Glencoe, 1963), pp. 98–109.
[90]William Graebner, *Coal Mining Safety in the Progressive Period: The Political Economy of Reform* (Lexington: University of Kentucky Press, 1976), pp. 101–3; Stanley Vittoz, *New Deal Labor Policy* (Chapel Hill, NC: University of North Carolina Press, 1987).
[91]G. Cullen David, "The Transformation of the Federal Trade Commission, 1914–1929," *Mississippi Valley Historical Review* 49 (No. 3, 1962): 437–55; Myron Watkins, *Public Regulation of Competitive Practices in Business Enterprise* (New York: National Industrial Conference Board, 1940).
[92]Palamountain, *Politics of Distribution*; Richard A. Posner, *The Robinson-Patman Act* (Washington, DC: American Enterprise Institute, 1976).

The capacity of the chain stores to engage in "noncooperative" price reductions is thus limited by law.

The state can also use its taxation policies to impose additional burdens on certain firms, thereby raising their costs and constraining their pricing behavior. Schattschneider's study of tariff politics provides several examples of subsets of competitors trying to use the tariff to build cost differentials onto other aspects of intraindustry heterogeneity with the aim of limiting the capacity of other firms to compete.[93] Similarly, in the 1930s, many states passed a "chain-store tax," a graduated license tax that rose with the number of stores that a chain operated in a state, in order to increase the operating costs of chain stores and to render their competition with independent distributors more "fair."[94]

The most effective way in which the state can organize competition is through a "regulatory agency" which controls entry, output, and prices. The prototype in the United States is the Interstate Commerce Commission (ICC), whose creation in 1887 was the culmination of fifteen years of private railroad cartelization that was only intermittently successful in curbing rail rate wars. The ICC organized competition by preventing price discrimination and secret prices, and by sanctioning collective rate making.[95] It was effectively emasculated by several court decisions in the 1890s, but its authority was gradually rebuilt, and, by 1920, it could set minimum rates and authorize pooling agreements. In 1935, ten years after a Supreme Court decision had foiled the efforts of the states to organize interstate truck competition, the president signed the Motor Carriers' Act, which gave the ICC the power to control entry and rates in the trucking industry. This measure restricted competition both among truckers and between rail and motor transport.[96] State-enforced organization of competition in the transportation industries was extended with the creation, in 1938, of the Civil Aeronautics Board, which, again, through control of entry, prices, and services, "protects producers by helping them form a cartel."[97]

Compulsory cartelization has also characterized U.S. agricultural pol-

---

[93]E. E. Schattschneider, *Politics, Pressure, and the Tariff* (New York: Prentice-Hall, 1935), pp. 153–6.

[94]Palamountain, *Politics of Distribution*.

[95]Paul W. MacAvoy, *The Economic Effects of Regulation* (Cambridge, MA: MIT Press, 1965); Gabriel Kolko, *Railroads and Regulation* (Princeton, NJ: Princeton University Press, 1965).

[96]James C. Nelson, "The Motor Carrier Act of 1935," *Journal of Political Economy* 44 (August, 1936): 464–504.

[97]William A. Jordan, *Airline Regulation in America: Effects and Imperfections* (Baltimore: Johns Hopkins University Press, 1970).

icy since the 1930s. The failure of voluntary production-control movements, led by farm journals and farm organizations in the 1920s, was followed by the passage of several major acreage-allotment and price-support measures, which have continued to define the basic features of U.S. farm policy.[98] As one commentator noted, this program "has many points of similarity with the cartel movement in industry."[99] Another important agricultural policy measure is the Agricultural Marketing Agreements Act of 1937, which authorizes the Secretary of Agriculture to create marketing cartels with the processors and distributors of agricultural commodities. This law is the basis for the U.S. system of milk-market controls.[100]

The most ambitious state-enforced cartelization plan attempted in the United States was the 1933–1935 National Industrial Recovery Act, which set up industry-dominated "code authorities" that developed "codes of fair competition" covering the whole gamut of production decisions. As is true of the other examples provided above, the origins of legislation lay largely in the failure of private methods of organizing competition.[101]

The state is the institution with the greatest capacity to organize capitalists by effecting transformations of their competitive games. However, state intervention can also be very costly to firms. The state is an institution capable of being mobilized by interests opposed to those of a particular individual firm or set of firms. Once the state has intervened in a market, these adversarial groups, which include everyone from consumers to competitors to revolutionary workers, can gain access to a firm's decisions. In George Stigler's words, "the political process automatically admits powerful outsiders to the industry's councils."[102] These outsiders can be expected to use their access to the state to pursue their own interests, interests which may contradict the interests of the firms being organized. In fact, the very process of organization by the state may *contribute* to the mobilization of groups affected by the competitive behavior of a set of firms. This is particularly likely when there

[98]Wayne D. Rasmussen, Gladys L. Baker, and James Ward, *A Short History of Agriculture Adjustment*, United States Department of Agriculture Information Bulletin No. 391 (Washington, DC: Government Printing Office, 1976).

[99]E. G. Nourse, quoted in Paul W. MacAvoy, *Federal Milk Marketing Orders and Price Supports* (Washington, DC: American Enterprise Institute, 1977), p. 21.

[100]Wilcox, *Public Policies*, pp. 776–7.

[101]Robert F. Himmelberg, *The Origins of the National Recovery Administration* (New York: Fordham University Press, 1976); Ellis W. Hawley, *The New Deal and the Problem of Monopoly* (Princeton: Princeton University Press, 1966).

[102]George Stigler, *The Citizen and the State* (Chicago: University of Chicago Press, 1975), p. 120.

is no tradition of state intervention in the market in question, and new legislation will be preceded by debate and political conflict. "The system invites opposition from groups or organizations who themselves have interests affected by the government.... The public forum of political debate makes opposition more likely, and the shifting positions of political figures, interested primarily in reelection, makes obtaining favorable political outcomes uncertain."[103]

It is well known that the state in a capitalist economy is greatly constrained by the private sector's control over the material resources that support the state's activities.[104] This does not mean, however, that a set of firms has nothing to fear from state intervention. As we have had occasion to emphasize repeatedly, the interests of the capitalist class as a whole, as well as the interest of the state in a flourishing private economy, do not necessarily coincide with the interests of individual firms or industries in their continued economic survival. Leaving aside the whole question of the capacity of outside actors to influence the state, the state as an institution may have its own interest in using its position as an organizer of a market to pursue goals which contradict those of the participants in the market. For all of these reasons, firms facing the suboptimal outcomes generated by competition may favor the uncertainties of the market over the risks of the political process.

Conclusion

As we saw in Chapter 1, capitalist competition is structured in such a way that the independent rational behavior of individual firms often generates a suboptimal outcome. They receive less profits than they would receive if they cooperated with each other and acted in concert. Faced with this knowledge, we would expect firms to attempt to organize themselves and to transform their competitive game so as to ensure a cooperative outcome. Since the state is the institution with the greatest capacity to effect such a transformation, it would seem to be the most likely choice as an organizational mechanism. Yet, even the most cursory examination of reality reveals that capitalist firms are far from unified

[103]Jeffrey Pfeffer and Gerald R. Salancik, *The External Control of Organizations: A Resource Dependence Perspective* (New York: Harper and Row, 1978), p. 216.
[104]See Claus Offe and Volker Ronge, "Theses on the Theory of the State," *New German Critique* 6 (Fall, 1975): 137–47; Charles Lindblom, *Politics and Markets* (New York: Basic Books, 1977).

in favor of state intervention in their markets. The analysis presented in the present chapter helps to explain why this is so.

In the first place, some firms simply prefer the suboptimal outcomes of the unorganized market. High-cost marginal firms may wish to see their competitors adopt a cooperative strategy, but will resist cooperating themselves as long as the payoff that cooperation yields is insufficient to ensure their economic survival. Financially strong firms possessing competitive advantages may willingly accept short-term suboptimal profits in the knowledge that competitors will be forced out of business and that, in the long run, their market positions will be strengthened.

Second, even when firms do wish to achieve a cooperative outcome, there are a variety of mechanisms besides state intervention that can help them to do so. A number of internal mechanisms can increase the communication and detection capabilities of individual firms and increase the likelihood that pricing Prisoner's Dilemmas will produce cooperation. Also, suppliers, workers, and creditors may be able to enforce agreements among competing firms by withholding raw material, labor, and capital from defectors.

Third, state intervention is costly. Not only do individual firms lose their autonomy, but possibly hostile actors may gain a measure of control over the firm's competitive behavior. For this reason, firms may prefer to take their chances with the market, even when state intervention is the only mechanism capable of organizing their competition and even when universal cooperation is their most preferred outcome.

A complete account of capitalist collective action, then, must focus on two sets of decisions. The first is the decision within the competitive game to cooperate or to defect. It is the outcome of this decision that may or may not generate a need for further organization. This need is not self-fulfilling, however. A firm's decision to pursue a particular form of market organization is the culmination of a second decision-making process, one in which the costs of market organization are weighed against its benefits. Of course, the final outcome will depend also on the interests of noncapitalist actors and on the relative power of the various coalitions participating in conflicts over market organization. In Part 2 we will have an opportunity to examine several such conflicts within the bituminous coal industry.

PART II

3. Price and wage games in the bituminous coal industry

Introduction

Market organization is a process that is constantly taking place in capitalist economies. In the previous two chapters I showed why capitalist firms wish and need to organize their markets and I identified some of the factors that determine the general shape of this process. In this and the following five chapters I examine the process of market organization in detail as it occurred in the pre–World War II American bituminous coal industry. We saw in Chapters 1 and 2 that a firm's response to a competitive game (i.e., whether or not it wishes to transform it) depends largely on the structure of the game, the outcome that it generates, and the firm's position within that outcome. Some competitive games "spontaneously" generate optimal, cooperative outcomes; others generate suboptimal outcomes of various degrees of severity; while others generate outcomes that are acceptable, and even preferable for some firms, and at the same time intolerable for others.

The nature of the game played by a set of firms is a function of (a) market-structure features which make communication and detection more or less difficult; (b) interfirm differences in the level of payoffs generated by various outcomes, which are largely the result of cost differences among firms; (c) differences in the strategies available to firms, or in their capacity to select the various strategies that are available to them; and (d) the absolute level of the payoffs, which can be expected to rise and fall with the general prosperity of the industry in question. In this chapter I discuss the bituminous coal industry in terms of each of these factors, concluding with a description of the competitive games played by coal operators and a set of hypotheses about their probable responses to these gaming situations.

Obstacles to cooperation

Coal operators, like other capitalist firms, faced a situation in which there were definite short-term gains to be had from reducing prices, but in which the profits of individual firms were actually lowered when each firm adopted such a strategy. We saw in Chapter 1, however, that under some conditions which facilitate communication among firms the incentive to reduce prices in the short term may be offset by a fear of subsequent retaliation by other firms. None of these conditions was present in the bituminous coal industry.

The bituminous coal industry was one of the least concentrated of American industries. If we assume that a stable price-fixing agreement requires the participation of about 70 percent of an industry's output, then, as Table 3.1 indicates, in both 1895 and 1905, a cooperative outcome in the coal industry would have required the cooperation of over 300 firms.[1] During the next thirty years this number increased. In 1920, 534 firms produced 66.5 percent of total U.S. bituminous coal output, and 1,080 firms produced 79 percent. In 1929, 553 firms contributed less than 80 percent of the coal produced in the United States. In each of these cases, the large number of firms would have made effective communication and detection practically impossible, at least in the national market. This last qualification is important, because, as we shall see shortly, not all coal operators were in active competition with each other. However, there was no major coal market in which the number of firms was so small as to reduce significantly the difficulty of communicating strategies and identifying defectors.[2]

The concentration and bargaining power of the buyers of bituminous coal also militated against cooperation. In a typical year during the mid-1920s, approximately 40 percent of the nation's coal output was consumed by such large users as railroads, electric utilities, and steel works. Other manufacturing operations accounted for another 19.5 percent.[3]

The bargaining power of coal users was reinforced by the transaction characteristics of the coal market. Of the nation's bituminous coal output, 75 percent was sold under contracts covering periods averaging one year

---

[1]Karl Pibran estimates that a successful cartel requires the participation of 70 percent of the industry (*Cartel Problems*, p. 65.).

[2]For a regional breakdown of the number of firms, see John R. Bowman, "Economic Competition and Collective Action: The Politics of Market Organization in the Bituminous Coal Industry, 1880–1940" (unpublished Ph.D. dissertation, The University of Chicago, 1984), p. 138. In 1929, only two coal fields – Virginia and Alabama – were so concentrated that over 60 percent (but still less than 70 percent) of total output was contributed by less than 10 firms, and neither field was important in the major national markets.

[3]U.S. Geological Survey, *Mineral Resources of the United States*, 1927, Part 2, p. 410. The Geological Survey described these data as representing a "typical year," although in fact they are an amalgam of data from several years, principally 1923, 1926, and 1927.

Table 3.1. *Number and size of bituminous coal companies, United States, 1895–1929*

Annual production (tons)	1895		1905		1920		1929[a]	
	Number of operators	% of U.S. output	Number of operators	% of U.S. output	Number of operators	% of U.S. output	Number of operators	% of U.S. output
Less than 10,000	1,055	2.1	1,492	1.6	2,349	1.6	2,277	1.3
10,000–50,000	590	11.6	961	7.8	2,121	9.4	1,043	4.8
50,000–100,000	285	15.4	403	8.9	727	9.1	408	5.5
100,000–200,000	268	41.7	331	14.6	543	13.4	331	8.7
200,000–500,00			199	18.8	348	18.7	335	19.9
500,000–1,000,000			49	10.8	109	13.3	131	17.0
1,000,000–3,000,000	32	29.2	39	19.8	64	19.5	70	22.9
More than 3,000,000			10	17.7	16	15.0	17	19.9

[a]The 1929 figures are not entirely comparable to the others.
Source: U.S. Geological Survey, *Mineral Resources of the United States, 1917,* Part 2, p. 644.

but sometimes extending to twenty years.[4] These selling arrangements added to the pressures on sellers to cut prices in order to win a long-term contract from consumers. One analyst testified before Congress that the "coal operator merely meets the price the purchasing agent of the railroad, utility, manufacturing plant, or retailer tells the producer he will pay."[5]

The ability of bituminous coal operators to maintain a cooperative price level was further hampered by the fact that, during most of our period, coal operators produced more coal than could be profitably sold, exerting a continual downward pressure on prices. This was due both to demand-side and supply-side factors. On the demand side, the aggregate demand for coal, which increased steadily through World War I, leveled off during the 1920s and 1930s. The price elasticity of the demand for coal was low. Because the principal use of coal was as an energy source in the production of other commodities, and because the existing technology did not permit manufacturers to change energy sources (e.g., from coal to natural gas) in the short run, the demand for coal was a derived demand that was dependent more on the level of industrial production than on the price of coal. Thus price competition among coal operators did little to generate additional demand for their product.[6]

However, even if we leave aside for the moment the impact of variations in the *magnitude* of the demand for coal, the fluctuating *pattern* of coal demand led coal operators continually to maintain high levels of output, even when their coal could not be sold at a price sufficiently high to cover costs and their operations had to be conducted at a loss. Because of its bulk, and because it deteriorates when it is handled and is liable to spontaneous combustion when it is stored, neither consumers nor operators maintained large stockpiles of coal above the ground. As a result, the pace of production was affected strongly by shifts in short-term demand, and coal shortages and high prices were likely to be produced by interruptions in production.

Even during the course of a normal year, seasonal weather patterns led to large fluctuations in the production of coal, which is in greater demand during periods of cold weather. During a typical year, production was lowest in April, the month when annual coal contracts were

[4]U.S. Geological Survey, *Mineral Resources of the United States*, 1918, Part 2, pp. 18–19.
[5]Quoted in James P. Johnson, *The Politics of Soft Coal* (Urbana, IL: University of Illinois Press, 1979), p. 22.
[6]U.S. Geological Survey, *Mineral Resources of the United States*, 1927, Part 2, p. 410.

traditionally signed. It continued at a low level through May, June, and July, then increased in August and September in anticipation of cold-weather needs. The months of peak production were from October through January. In the 1920–1934 period the average monthly production index for April was 80; for October it was 117.9.[7]

Another cause of uneven coal production was work stoppages. During the years when the interstate agreement between the United Mine Workers and the operators from Ohio, Pennsylvania, Illinois, and Indiana was to be renegotiated, consumers could expect a cessation of production for a period of a few weeks and were usually able to prepare for it by stockpiling. However, in the event of a major coal strike, such as occurred in 1919 and 1922, fears that consumer stocks were inadequate precipitated buyer panics and led to skyrocketing coal prices. The frequent inability of railroads to transport coal promptly to areas where it was most needed in the years before the mid-1920s also generated sharp short-term fluctuations in coal prices.

In short, bituminous coal was a boom/bust industry in which every operator had reason to hope that cold weather, labor troubles, or railroad-car shortages would "turn a depression in the coal trade into a comfortable prosperity."[8] "Perhaps you will say that the coal operator is an optimist," admitted one operator, but "if he were not an optimist, he would never be a coal man."[9] Thus, short-term fluctuations in coal demand and prices tended to reinforce the propensity of operators to keep unprofitable mines in operation. They wanted to be prepared for the next coal boom, which they often believed was just around the corner.

We are born gamblers, and there is not a man in the coal business today . . . but what hopes for a recurrence of that high tide of prosperity that occasionally comes to the industry will arrive before he is forced into bankruptcy. . . . We are satisfied in the summertime to trade a dollar for ninety cents in the hope that when . . . the winter months come we may trade the dollar for $1.75 or $2.00.[10]

Supply-side factors also contributed to overproduction in the bituminous coal industry. Principal among these was the high fixed cost of mining. The fixed costs of an idle coal mine that has not been completely

---

[7]F. E. Berquist et al., *Economic Survey of the Bituminous Coal Industry under Free Competition and Code Regulation* (Washington, DC: U.S. National Recovery Administration, Work Materials, No. 69, 1936), p. 54.
[8]Morton Baratz, *The Union and the Coal Industry* (Port Washington, NY: Kennikat, 1973), p. 4.
[9]*Coal Age* 19 (January 20, 1921): 133.
[10]Ibid., 1 (November 11, 1911): 143.

abandoned are virtually as high as those of a mine in full operation. Roofs and floors must be maintained, the pumping of water must continue, and the mine must be continually ventilated. Moreover, because mining operations are often carried out in remote areas offering no employment alternatives, the operator who shuts down a mine risks a permanent loss of the labor force that would be needed to resume mining. Idle miners also did not generate any company-store income, revenue that was of critical importance to the survival of many operations.[11] As one operator put it,

A mine is like a horse, which eats when working, or resting. When the mines are shut down, the headings are creeping, props are rotting, brattles falling, rails and pipes are rusting. Above ground the fixed force is idle, power is being used to pump water, the houses are empty, and the stock in the store long awaits tardy sales.[12]

Thus, rather than let a mine stand idle, and continue to pay out unrecoverable fixed costs, the mine operator had an incentive to mine and sell coal as long as variable costs and a portion of fixed costs could be recovered. Moreover, because total fixed costs were relatively constant, the mine operator had an incentive to produce in quantity, thereby minimizing average costs. In 1918–1921, for instance, coal produced in a mine that operated fifteen days per month (60 percent of capacity) cost from 13 percent to 14 percent more to produce than coal mined under conditions of full capacity. When working time was reduced by another five days, this percentage more than doubled to between 30 and 34 percent.[13] As one coal operator later lamented,

If you have a 50,000 ton a month mine, it will cost you $10,000 to $15,000 a month to let it stand idle. And that is the pressure that is in back of an operator, to try to operate his mine, to try to accumulate enough tonnage in order that he can reduce those losses, and he cannot do it by idle time.[14]

Other supply-side factors generating overproduction included easy entry, difficult exit, and transportation constraints. In the perfectly competitive economy, capital costlessly and rapidly pursues its most profitable form of employment. Capital invested in coal mining, however, is in practice stuck there. The shafts; ventilation and drainage systems; tipple; and customized cutting, loading, and transport equipment that

[11]W. P. Tams, *The Smokeless Coal Fields of West Virginia: A Brief History* (Morgantown, WV: West Virginia University Library, 1963).
[12]*Coal Age* 2 (August 8, 1912): 141.
[13]Isador Lubin, *Miners' Wages and the Cost of Coal* (New York: Macmillan, 1924), p. 286.
[14]Quoted in Baratz, *The Union*, p. 18.

make up a coal mine are truly "sunken capital" that cannot readily be liquidated and rechanneled elsewhere. Thus, even when an individual operator called it quits, the mine usually was kept in production by a new set of owners who tried to exploit its reduced capitalization.

> Universal experience shows that the coal property owners may, personally, be put out of business; COAL PROPERTIES, with their potential production, remain intact for reorganization by the creditors. . . . Coal companies . . . have frequently been driven to bankruptcy by intense, destructive competition. . . . Rarely, if at all, has the *producing capacity* of an average quality coal company been removed by bankruptcy.[15]

Just as the anticipation of high coal prices deterred exit, the actual high prices, when they periodically appeared, attracted the entry of new capacity, or the expansion of existing capacity. While it takes a large investment of capital and several years of time to open a large state-of-the-art coal mine, smaller mines can be put into operation cheaply and quickly. Of 2,846 coal companies canvassed by the United States Coal Commission in 1920, over 22 percent had less than $25,000 invested in their operation; 4 percent had investments of less than $5,000.[16] In the same year, which was one in which coal prices were extraordinarily high, the U.S. Geological Survey estimated that there were almost 6,000 noncommercial "wagon mines" or "snow-bird" operations in the country.[17] These were mines without railroad connections which were opened during periods of cold weather or high prices to serve the local trade. Although their output was not commercially significant, their rapid appearance signifies the ease with which more important commercial operations could be expanded, and the difficulty of restricting coal output.

A final influence on coal output was the railroads which transported the coal. Their primary interest in the coal business, of course, was in maximizing the quantity of coal that they moved, and they were willing to adjust their freight rates in order to do this. Thus, new, and usually more distant, competitors were granted a foothold in markets by their carriers, who accorded them preferential freight rates. Also, during periods of car shortage, the railroads typically allocated their cars among mines on the basis of the mine's output during the previous month. This tended to favor new entrants, whose coal was more accessible and

[15]S.A. Taylor, quoted in Glen L. Parker, *The Coal Industry: A Study in Social Control* (Washington, DC: American Council on Public Affairs, 1940), p. 25.
[16]Hubert E. Risser, *The Economics of the Coal Industry* (Lawrence, KS: Bureau of Business Research, School of Business, University of Kansas, 1958), p. 15.
[17]U.S. Geological Survey, *Mineral Resources*, 1921, Part 2, p. 524.

more easily mined, over established operations whose strength was in marketing rather than in production.[18] It also led operators to maintain high levels of output during periods of low demand so that they would be able to transport their coal when demand increased.[19]

We saw in Chapter 1 that product heterogeneity tends to make cooperation among competing capitalists more difficult by placing obstacles in the way of their agreement on the content of the cooperative price and by hindering the detection of price cutting. Although at first glance coal seems to epitomize the homogeneous commodity, in reality the name coal refers to a wide range of substances, which differ both in their physical composition and in their economic use. Coal is the outcome of a complex chain of chemical and geological processes that begins with the conversion of vegetal matter into peat.[20] All coals are composed of varying proportions of fixed carbon (which determines the ease of ignition and the amount of smoke produced during combustion); moisture (the burning off of which "wastes" part of the coal's energy); ash (extraneous nonignitable matter); and sulphur (which emits corrosive fumes when burned).[21] Coal is generally "ranked" according to the relative proportions of fixed carbon and volatile matter it contains. Anthracite has the highest percentage of fixed carbon. It is followed by semianthracite, a rare coal, of virtually no economic significance; semibituminous, also called low-volatile, smokeless, dry, or superbituminous coal; bituminous, also called high-volatile or fatbituminous coal; cannel coal, a relatively rare coal that is slightly higher in volatile content than ordinary-grade bituminous; sub-bituminous coal; and lignite, or brown coal, which ranks just above peat in terms of its carbon content.[22] For economic purposes these several ranks are generally collapsed into two, each embodying a distinct industry and market structure: (1) anthracite, or hard coal, including anthracite and semianthracite; and (2) bituminous, or soft coal, including semibituminous, bituminous, and cannel coal.[23] Within these general categories, the physical composition of soft

---

[18]Edward T. Devine, *Coal: Economic Problems of the Mining, Marketing, and Consumption of Anthracite and Soft Coal in the United States* (Bloomington: American Review Service Press, 1925), p. 292.

[19]Edward E. Hunt, F.G. Tryon, and Joseph Willits, *What the Coal Commission Found* (Baltimore: Williams and Wilkins, 1925), p. 67.

[20]Elwood S. Moore, *Coal* (New York: John Wiley and Sons, 1940), p. 1.

[21]A. T. Shurick, *The Coal Industry* (Boston: Little, Brown, and Co., 1924), pp. 160–2.

[22]Moore, *Coal*, pp. 92–106.

[23]Lignite is sometimes included in the bituminous coal industry, but I will not do so, since it was produced and consumed entirely in the western United States, and was not a factor in the major national markets during this period.

coal varied from district to district, and even from mine to mine. Customary marketing practices further impeded what would have been an extraordinarily difficult task of standardization.

Coal is not sold in terms of its heating properties..., but under trade names which either by accident or design conceal rather more than they tell of its real quality.... The outstanding fact about coal prices is their infinite variety. There are different prices for coals that differ in kind, or in name, or are taken from different mines.[24]

Aside from its physical properties, coal also differs in the amount of cleaning and sorting it undergoes at the mine, and in its size. Although coal is generally placed in 1 of 7 size classes (run of mine, lump or block, egg, nut, stoker, slack, and screenings), several coal-producing districts have distinguished over 100 different sizes of coal and there were several mines which sold coal in more than 40 size classes.[25] The near impossibility of standardizing coal for purposes of facilitating cooperation is indicated by the fact that during the most recent attempt at governmental price fixing of coal, the final price list took two years to prepare and contained over 450,000 entries.[26]

Interfirm differences

I emphasized in Chapter 1 that, in most industries, the capitalist collective action problems generated by economic competition are complicated by interfirm differences in production costs and in the capacity of firms to select various competitive strategies. The coal industry is no exception. Variations in geological conditions, in distance from the market, and in wage rates produced variations in the cost of production; and variations in labor-market conditions (the presence or absence of collective bargaining) affected the capacity of firms to compete by cutting wages.

The most important geological determinants of production costs were the size of the coal seam and (indirectly) the quality of the coal. All other things being equal, coal was more difficult and costly to mine when it lay in thin seams, where miners were forced to work in uncomfortable and inefficient postures, and where the most efficient mining equipment

---

[24]Walton H. Hamilton and Helen R. Wright, *The Case of Bituminous Coal* (New York: MacMillan, 1926), pp. 67–8.
[25]James B. Hendry, "The Bituminous Coal Industry," in Walter Adams, ed., *The Structure of American Industry* (New York: MacMillan, 1961), p. 100.
[26]Baratz, *The Union*, p. 19.

could not be employed.[27] Generally, labor productivity tended to increase with seam thickness, until the optimum height of 8 feet was reached. After this level, the relationship between seam thickness and productivity was less clear.[28] Other characteristics of the seam which could affect the costs of mining, at least in underground mines, included the presence of water, which necessitated a drainage system, the presence of faults and irregularities, which imposed an added sorting and cleaning burden upon the miners, and the character of the roof and floor, which determined the amount of "dead" or "unproductive" time that had to be occupied in timbering and in maintaining the tracks of the underground rail system.[29]

Coal quality is not, strictly speaking, a determinant of cost, but because inferior coal can compete with higher quality coal only by being sold at lower prices, coal quality can have an effect on profit margins that is analogous to that produced by variations in costs. By reducing the difference between costs and price, coal of inferior quality functions as an additional cost of doing business. High-quality coal, on the other hand, because it can command a higher price, can offset other cost disadvantages. Thus, a high-cost mine producing good coal may survive under conditions that will drive an equally efficient operation, mining low-quality coal, out of business.

Although the quality of coal deposits can vary greatly within a mining region, cross-regional differences were much more important. Spatially, the U.S. Geological Survey has classified the coal deposits of the United States according to province, region, field, and district.[30] While, in recent years, bituminous coal production in the western United States has become very important, during the period that concerns us the vast majority of the nation's coal output came from the Appalachian region of the Eastern province (Pennsylvania, Ohio, West Virginia, Maryland, eastern Kentucky, Tennessee, and Alabama) and the Eastern region of the Interior province, encompassing western Kentucky, Illinois, and Indiana. It was in these two areas that the "drama of coal [was] played."[31] Within these areas, Maryland's and Virginia's output was marginal, and most of Alabama's was consumed within the state and did not compete

---

[27]Baratz, *The Union*, pp. 9–11; James B. Hendry, "The Bituminous Coal Industry," p. 94.
[28]U.S. Geological Survey, *Mineral Resources of the United States, 1917*, Part 2, pp. 944–5.
[29]Waldo Fisher and Anne Bezanson, *Wage Rates and Working Time in the Bituminous Coal Industry* (Philadelphia: University of Pennsylvania Press, 1932), pp. 7–11.
[30]In the text, I use field and district interchangeably, as did most coal operators and coal-trade writers.
[31]*Coal Age* 26 (November 20, 1924): 729.

Table 3.2. *Eastern and midwestern coal fields grouped by the quality of their coal*

High quality Low volatile	Low volatile	High quality High volatile	High volatile
New River (WV)	Clearfield (PA)	Pittsburgh (PA)	No. 8 (OH)
Winding Gulf (WV)	Somerset (PA)	Connellsville (PA)	Cambridge (OH)
Pocahontas (WV)	Western Kentucky	Panhandle (WV)	Hocking (OH)
		Fairmont (WV)	Jackson (OH)
		Kanawha (WV)	Masillon (OH)
		Thacker (WV)	Illinois
		Kenova (WV)	Indiana
		Big Sandy (E.KY)	
		Hazard (E.KY)	
		Harlan (E.KY)	

Sources: Coal Age 33 (March, 1928): 162–3; *Coal Age* 35 (May, 1928): 286–7; *Coal Age* 23 (January 1, 1923): 111–15; Shurick, *The Coal Industry*, pp. 362–5; U.S. Interstate Commerce Commission, Investigation and Suspension Docket No. 744, *Bituminous Coal to Central Freight Association Territory*, 46 ICC 119–26, 1917; U.S. Interstate Commerce Commission, *Lake Cargo Rates*, 101 ICC 516, 1975.

in the major eastern and midwestern markets. For most purposes, then, including our own, the bituminous coal industry was contained in the states of Pennsylvania, West Virginia, Ohio, Illinois, Kentucky, Indiana, and Tennessee. Together, these states accounted for over 80 percent of U.S. production in the 1920s and 1930s.

Table 3.2 provides a summary listing of the major Appalachian and Eastern Interior coal fields, along with a description of the principal type of coal mined in each. In general, coal quality declines as one moves west. The country's best high-volatile coal was mined in western Pennsylvania, southern West Virginia, and eastern Kentucky. Ohio's coal was generally inferior to the Pennsylvania, West Virginia, and eastern Kentucky product, but superior to coal from Indiana, Illinois, and western Kentucky.

Aside from the characteristics of the seam and the quality of coal, geological conditions also determine whether the coal can be taken from surface pits or whether it must be mined underground. The type of mining process employed has an important impact on productivity. In strip, or surface, mining, the top of the seam lies fairly close to the surface and can be exposed through the physical removal of the covering strata or "overburden." The coal can then be removed with power shovels. In deep mining, on the other hand, the coal lies far below the surface and can only be mined by tunneling through the seams. Strip mines are much less expensive than deep mines – both to open and to operate. They require less specialized equipment; they can reach a state of full operation in shorter periods of time; they don't require timbering or ventilation; their haulage units are not limited by the size of underground passages; and they require less labor.[32]

Another factor connected to geological conditions which affected the cost of production was the age of the mine. Usually, the most accessible and easily mined portions of the seam were tackled first, so that, as time passed, the miners were working in less and less satisfactory conditions, and probably with older equipment.

Aside from the technological advance represented by strip mining, labor-saving mechanization also took place underground, consisting primarily in the replacement of hand picks with mechanical cutting tools, and of hand shovels with mechanical loading devices.

Labor costs accounted for most of the cost of producing bituminous coal. A Federal Trade Commission study of coal-industry costs found that, in 1916, average labor costs in the Appalachian and Eastern Interior regions ranged from 63 percent to 84 percent of the cost of mining a ton of coal.[33] The U.S. Coal Commission came up with similar findings for the years 1918 and 1922, when labor costs contributed 73 percent and 69.4 percent of total free on board (f.o.b.) – at the entrance of the mine, not including delivery – costs nationwide.[34] Wages were not only the largest component of mining costs, but were one of the only determinants of cost that was at all subject to the control of the operator, who could not improve the quality of his coal, the conditions under which it was mined, or its distance from consumers. As we shall see below, then, wage reductions were the principal competitive weapon in the operator's arsenal.

An early writer once noted that the story of coal was one of large numbers of workers and great distances. Coal, which was consumed primarily in regions where population and industrial production were concentrated, was mined in remote areas where local markets were nonexistent. Because of its bulk and the distances which it had to be shipped, shipping costs were the most important element in the price of a delivered ton of coal. Coal was actually more expensive to transport to consumers than it was to mine. Between 1928 and 1935, average freight

[32]Baratz, *The Union*, pp. 11–14.
[33]U.S. Federal Trade Commission, *Cost Reports of the Federal Trade Commission: Coal*, Volumes 1–6, 1920.
[34]Hunt, et al., *Coal Commission*, p. 106.

Table 3.3. *Index numbers of wages paid to mine workers 1912–1922*

Year (June 30)	Tonnage men		Day men	
	Union	Nonunion	Union	Nonunion
1912	53.8	45.5	35.5	28.3
1913	53.4	44.9	35.4	29.7
1914	53.2	44.6	35.4	29.6
1915	52.7	44.3	35.3	29.5
1916	55.4	48.4	36.9	32.0
1917	65.9	60.6	45.8	41.3
1918	75.8	72.7	65.3	63.5
1919	75.5	73.8	65.3	63.8
1920	99.4	95.6	79.3	82.1
1921	99.9	90.5	100.0	91.3
1922	100.0	71.3	100.0	62.0

Source: Fisher and Bezanson, *Wage Rates*, pp. 42–3, 74–5.

charges ranged from 54 percent to 63 percent of the total delivered cost of a ton of bituminous coal.[35] Freight rates, then, were a major factor in determining cost differences between coal mined in different regions. And, like wages, freight rates, which were in part the result of conflict among operators and carriers in the various mining regions, were not as inflexible as the costs associated with geological conditions.

Not only did coal operators vary in their costs of production and transportation; they also varied in their capacity to adopt the principal cost-reduction strategy – wage cutting. Here, different capacities were related to the presence or absence of collective bargaining. As Table 3.3 indicates, unionized miners, who were paid on a tonnage basis, and unionized day men, who were paid by the hour, consistently received higher rates of pay than their nonunion counterparts during the 1912–1922 period, the only one for which precise data are available.[36] More important, nonunion wage rates were much more flexible. Between January, 1912, and January, 1923, there were six union wage adjustments, all in an upward direction. In the nonunion mines, it was not unusual

[35]U.S. Bureau of Mines, *Minerals Yearbook*, 1936 (Washington, DC: Government Printing Office), p. 552.

[36]There were about 30 different occupations involved in the mining of coal. Generally, those workers who cut and loaded the coal were paid on a piece basis. Other workers, called "company men" or "day men," who performed auxiliary or service roles, were paid straight time rates. "Inside" day men worked underground; "outside" day men worked above ground.

to find as many as twelve to fifteen wage changes during the same period.[37] The most prominent of these was a 22-percent wage cut in 1921 which left nonunion wages almost 30 percent below the union rate.

Depression and prosperity

One final determinant of the structure of coal competition is the level of demand. When demand is high, operators may be able to sell their output without having to resort to price reductions. They may even be able to exploit coal shortages and *increase* their price as demand rises. Conversely, low demand increases the competitive pressure on operators to reduce prices in order to maintain sales. Aside from exerting pressure on the *direction* of coal prices, demand also affects the level of prices and payoffs, and, therefore, the need for individual operators to escape the payoffs generated by a particular competitive situation. During periods in which demand is relatively high, the payoffs to individual firms will be higher and their need to transform their competitive games will not be as great. In the following chapters, we will have occasion to examine the level of prosperity of the coal industry in more detail. For the present, it suffices to note that the industry passed through three broad phases between 1880 and 1940. The breakdown of insulated regional markets and the emergence of a national market for coal in the 1880s inaugurated a period characterized by overcapacity and low prices that lasted until the beginning of World War I. From 1916 through 1922, demand generated by the war, by the postwar industrial boom, and by distribution problems produced an unprecedented boom in the coal industry, leading to high prices and increased entry. This boom was short lived, however, and for the rest of the period, until World War II, the industry suffered through a prolonged depression.

Games played by coal operators

Coal competition existed on two levels. One involved the intradistrict competition among operators whose mining conditions, wage rates, and freight rates were very similar. Much more important, however, was the interdistrict competition that pitted sets of dissimilar mining operations against one another. It is this latter level that will be our principal focus. At stake in this interregional competiton were the major industrial

[37]Hunt et al., *Coal Commission*, pp. 178–9.

markets of the Northeast and Midwest, which furnished most of the demand for bituminous coal. There were five of these interdistrict markets: the tidewater market, the New England rail market, the lake-cargo market, the central rail market, and the midwestern market. The tidewater market involved coal shipped eastward to the Atlantic ports of New York, Philadelphia, Baltimore, and Hampton Roads, Virginia. Most of this coal was shipped on to New England or consumed near the ports.[38] The principal districts involved in this market were those located in central Pennsylvania and West Virginia.[39] Although the Pennsylvania and northern West Virginia districts were closer to the coast, this distance advantage over the southern West Virginia districts was offset by freight rates which favored the latter districts, by the superior quality of their coal, and by the fact that the Clearfield and Pittsburgh districts in Pennsylvania were unionized and paid higher and less flexible wage rates than their southern competitors, which were predominantly nonunion. As a result, the share of the southern West Virginia and eastern Kentucky districts in the tidewater market increased from 40 percent to 63 percent between 1919 and 1934.[40]

Coal also reached New England by all-rail routes. Pennsylvania generally dominated this market, largely because the absence of through freight rates from West Virginia forced operators there to pay a series of relatively high short-haul rates that were prohibitively expensive. This obstacle was removed by the ICC in 1927 but, as late as 1929, less than 10 percent of New England's rail shipments of coal originated in West Virginia.[41]

A third major locus of interdistrict coal competition was the lake-cargo market – coal shipped by rail to the Ohio ports of Ashtabula, Cleveland, Sandusky, Fairport, Toledo, and Lorain for water shipment to the Northwest. In terms of sheer quantity, the lake trade was not particularly large, but, in the words of *Coal Age*, "the tonnage [was] large enough to appeal to any producing district. Moving during the months of the year when production is generally caught in the valley of the seasonal rhythm, the lake trade is doubly attractive."[42] Most lake-cargo coal came

[38]U.S. Bureau of Mines, *Minerals Yearbook*, 1940, p. 783.
[39]Wilbert G. Fritz and Theodore A. Veenstra, *Regional Shifts in the Bituminous Coal Industry with Special Reference to Pennsylvania* (Pittsburgh: Bureau of Business Research, University of Pittsburgh, 1935), pp. 49–64, 73, 78.
[40]Ibid., p. 91.
[41]Ibid., pp. 49–64, 73, 78.
[42]*Coal Age* 29 (March 18, 1926): 389.

from Ohio, Pennsylvania, West Virginia, and Kentucky.[43] Even more than was the case in the tidewater market, distance conferred an advantage on certain fields, particularly those in western Pennsylvania and Ohio. Three of Ohio's most important coal fields, along with the Pittsburgh field, were less than 200 miles from Lake Erie. As was the case in the eastern markets, however, low freight rates, high-quality coal, and low labor costs combined to allow competition from coal fields in southern West Virginia and eastern Kentucky.

A fourth bituminous coal market was the central all-rail market, encompassing rail shipments to Ohio, Michigan, and northeastern Indiana, and including the cities of Toledo, Detroit, Grand Rapids, Fort Wayne, South Bend, and Columbus. The producing districts involved were basically the same Ohio, West Virginia, and Kentucky districts that shipped to the lakes; and this market resembled the lake trade in other respects as well. High quality, low freight rates, and low wages enabled the more distant southern districts to compete successfully with the closer Ohio districts.[44]

The final market worth noting is the midwestern market: western Indiana, Illinois, Missouri, and Minnesota. Although eastern coal was not absent from this market, it was generally the case that high transportation costs kept Ohio and Pennsylvania operators from becoming a major competitive force here. West Virginia coal was more successful (13 percent of Illinois's coal came from West Virginia in 1915),[45] but Illinois and Indiana coals, in spite of their relatively low quality and high production costs, were more protected by distance from southern competition in their home market than was the Ohio coal to the east.

Modeling coal competition along the lines of the competitive games presented in Chapter 1 allows us to make predictions concerning (*a*) the competitive behavior of each firm within the game; (*b*) the response of each firm to the outcome of the game (i.e., Is it acceptable or not? Will the firm seek to transform the game?); and (*c*) the response of the firm to various proposed transformations of the game.

At the interdistrict level of competition, we can distinguish three games played by operators during the relevant time period: (*a*) a price–wage game played by heterogeneous firms, none of which are union-

---

[43]Ibid.; National Industrial Conference Board, *The Competitive Position of Coal in the United States* (New York: National Industrial Conference Board, 1931), p. 283.
[44]U.S. Interstate Commerce Commission, *Investigation*, 46 ICC 66, 1917.
[45]U.S. Geological Survey, *Mineral Resources of the United States*, 1915, Part 2, pp. 487–92; Fritz and Veenstra, *Regional Shifts*, pp. 49–64, 73, 78.

ized, under recessionary conditions; (b) a price–wage game played by heterogeneous firms, some of which are unionized, under recessionary conditions; and (c) a price game played under conditions of prosperity.

Figure 1.8 depicts the price–wage game played by firms differing in their costs, under the recessionary conditions that were typical for the bituminous coal industry, except during the World War I boom. I refer to it as a price–wage game because as long as collective bargaining contracts were absent, price and wage reductions often went hand in hand. Wage reductions, then, were the major competitive weapon available to operators.

[T]he only formula that the operators know in managing their mines is to reduce wages to meet any lack of competition. If there is an inequitable freight rate, they meet that situation by reducing wages. If the mine is uneconomical, they order reduced wages so that the uneconomical mine can remain in the market. If the mine is a wet mine, or has a bad top or a soft bottom, or a high ash content, or too much sulphur, or a low carbon, to compete in the market, they order reduced wages and make the mine worker responsible for every deficiency of nature, for every act of bad judgment, and every maladjustment of the freight rate structure, and for every act of Providence.[46]

The position of the payoff curves with respect to one another and their upward direction are both a product of the basic structure of the competitive game discussed in Chapter 1. The y-intercepts of the curves are a function of the firm's costs of production and general market conditions. Given the price of coal and the level of demand for coal, the y-intercepts of the payoff curves of higher cost firms will be lower than those of low-cost firms. But holding costs constant, the y-intercepts will decline along with the level of demand and the price level. In other words, at any given point in time, the three firms depicted in Figure 1.8 differ on the basis of their costs. Lower-cost firms mine superior coal, pay lower wages, and/or pay lower freight rates than their higher-cost competitors. However, over time, a decline in the level of prosperity of the coal industry will have the effect of shifting payoff curves so that a low-cost firm might see its payoff structure shift, say, from A to B.

What do these payoff structures tell us? First, regardless of the cost level of the firm or the state of demand and prices in the coal industry, each firm's dominant strategy is to reduce wages and prices, and we can predict that it will do so. Second, it is evident that the outcome

[46]Testimony of John L. Lewis, U.S. Congress, House of Representatives, Committee on Ways and Means, *Stabilization of the Bituminous Coal Industry*, Hearings on H.R. 8479, 74th Congress, 1st Session, 1935, p. 645.

generated by universal wage and price cutting is suboptimal. All things being equal, then, each firm prefers a transformation of the game that will generate cooperative behavior on the part of its competitors. If Chapter 2's discussion of costs is valid, the effort to reorganize the market will begin with a low-cost internal mechanism, such as an informal price-fixing agreement. Such an effort will be doomed, however; first, by the market-structure characteristics discussed earlier in this chapter – the large number of firms, the difficulty of standardizing the product, and so forth; but also by the payoff structures faced by the individual firms. Not only does *every* firm prefer to defect from a price-fixing agreement, but firms facing the type C payoff structure cannot afford to cooperate. The three payoff structures, then, correspond to three attitudes toward market reorganization. Firms facing the type A payoff structure would like to see their competitors cooperate, but are probably unwilling to pay the costs associated with an organizational mechanism that would be capable of forcing them to do so. Type B firms not only would prefer that their competitors cooperate, but they *need* the cooperation of operators representing at least k percent of the industry's total output, and would be more willing than the type-A firms to agree to a more costly form of market organization. Type C firms, on the other hand, can be expected to resist being forced to cooperate.

Let us introduce unionization into the competitive situation. Firms that are unionized can in principle still adjust their prices, but they are deprived of the principal cost-cutting tool – wage reductions – that makes lower prices stick. Unionized firms are, in effect, then, forced to cooperate. Clearly, a unionized firm's acceptance of this outcome is a function both of its cost level and the level of unionization. As the level of unionization (and cooperation) declines past j and k, the medium-cost firm and the low-cost firm, respectively, will require a transformation of the game in order to recover positive profits. (The high-cost firm in this model cannot survive under conditions of forced cooperation.)

Two types of transformation are possible in this situation. A firm can transform its own payoff structure by "winning" the right to defect without being punished – the union-busting transformation – or the payoff structures of other, nonunion, firms can be altered so as to force defecting firms to cooperate. What type of transformation will be preferred by a firm that is forced to pursue a unilateral cooperative strategy? The answer to this question depends on two factors – the effect that its own renunciation of the cooperative strategy will have on the subsequent strategy choices of other cooperating firms, and the costs to itself of violating the cooperative agreement. If the firm believes that it will not be punished when it defects from the agreement and if it believes that its defection will not lead immediately to the unraveling of the cooperative agreement and to the suboptimal universal defection outcome, then it will prefer to defect rather than to seek the cooperation of more competitors. Low-cost firms, who are better able to survive at the universal defection outcome, will be more likely than medium-cost firms to choose this road away from the unilateral-cooperation payoff. However, if the immediate costs of defection are high – a strike-induced cessation of production, for instance – or if the firm's defection is likely to produce a bandwagon effect and the immediate unraveling of the cooperative agreement and the defection of all, then it will prefer to seek the universal cooperation outcome. On the other hand, if I am not the first defector from the agreement and the unraveling process has already begun, it is unlikely that universal cooperation is a realistic goal and I will probably join the defection bandwagon. As for the nonunion firms, those in the high-cost category will always resist unionization, which will ruin them. At fairly high levels of unionization, the other nonunion firms will also resist being forced to select the cooperative strategy. However, once the level of cooperation falls below k, the medium-cost firm will need more cooperation in the market in order to survive and can be expected to be receptive to some form of market reorganization. The low-cost firm can survive at the universal defection outcome and must weigh the benefits of increased cooperation against not only the costs of cooperating, but also against the hardship which the universal defection outcome imposes on its higher-cost competitors. It will therefore probably oppose a further organization of the market.

What all of this means is that however the organization of workers and collective bargaining fits into the *interclass* struggle between workers and operators in the bituminous coal industry, it also occupies a central place in the *intraclass* struggle over market organization. Collective bargaining and the enforced cooperation in the wage–price game which it implies provides both a means for operators to transform competitive games that are generating suboptimal outcomes and a competitive disadvantage to be wished on rival firms. Conversely, and again irrespective of the struggle with workers, collective bargaining and forced cooperation threaten the survival of the least-advantaged, high-cost firms.

The final competitive situation faced by operators during this period was one characterized by booming demand. Here, high demand transformed the competitive game and temporarily removed operators from their Prisoner's Dilemma. When a firm's output can be sold without price reductions, there is, of course, no incentive to cut prices. As we shall see, however, this situation did possess some Prisoner's Dilemma elements, since profiteering could be expected to result in some form of unpleasant state control. It was in the interests of each operator to raise prices as high as possible, but it was in the interests of the operators as a collectivity to maintain a socially responsible price level in the face of shortages, thereby defusing any demand for government-enforced price controls.

Conclusion

Before we proceed to investigate the response of coal operators to their competitive games, we might ask what means were available to them to organize their competition.

We saw in Chapter 2 that it is sometimes possible to eliminate competition through consolidation. Was this feasible in the coal industry? Our answer must be negative. In the first place, the large number and geographical dispersion of operators which made it so difficult to agree on prices and to monitor their mutual behavior also placed huge obstacles in the way of any agreement to consolidate their properties. Easy entry conditions had the same effect.

A second major problem, one which *Coal Age* called the "usual" stumbling block preventing mergers, was the difficulty of agreeing on the valuation of coal properties.[47] A consolidation of coal mines not only meant a combination of the capital invested in the operations, but also the merging of the coal deposits. Given the history of price fluctuation in the industry, and the importance of such possibly varying factors as freight rates and wage rates in determining the marketability of coal, it was extremely difficult to place a monetary value on coal reserves that probably would not be exploited for decades.

Third, unlike such industries as steel and railroads, centralizing administrative control over the mining, marketing, and distribution of coal produced few economies.[48] There was no technological imperative pushing operators toward combination and centralization.

Another factor that hindered consolidation was the fact that, in many

[47]*Coal Age* 35 (March, 1930): 178.
[48]Simon Whitney, *Antitrust Policies: American Experience in Twenty Industries*, 2 vols. (New York: Twentieth Century Fund), 1: 416.

coal operations, the management and the stockholders were one and the same.[49] Consolidation would have deprived many of them of employment. One speaker before the American Mining Congress told his audience that human nature bars the success of coal operators in consolidating their properties "because you would find many men who would thus lose their jobs when economies were put in."[50] A year later, a New York City management consultant made the same point in the pages of *Coal Age*. "The inevitable fact that some owners must retire from managerial positions and some managers must lose their positions if the necessary reduction in the number of management units is effected, militates against prompt action toward the reconstruction of the industry."[51]

Finally, the coal industry was not an industry that was very attractive to the investors who supplied the capital needed for large-scale consolidations. A steady stream of bankers addressing meetings of coal operators continually reminded them of "the sales resistance of the investing public" with respect to their industry.

Your labor difficulties have, as you know, received great publicity, and the public is not altogether uninformed as to the irregularity and spasmodic character of your production, as to the unfortunate interruptions of your car supply, and as to the important fact that the developed production of your industry has far outstripped the normal demand of the country for your product.[52]

As a citizen, and, as a business man, the individual of substance may be most interested in these problems; as an investor, however, he is most likely to turn his funds to other channels till greater progress is made toward their solution.[53]

Chapter 2 also described a variety of internal organizational mechanisms whose main contribution to a cooperative outcome lies in improving the communication and detection capacities of capitalists. As we have seen above, the obstacles to communication and detection in the coal industry were so enormous that it is very unlikely that an internal mechanism could have resolved them. Aside from these difficulties, the nature of demand in the coal market, the power of buyers, and the large and infrequent purchases characteristic of the coal trade greatly increased the incentive to cut prices.

[49]Ibid., p. 417.
[50]*Coal Age* 30 (December 16, 1926): 845.
[51]Ibid., 32 (July, 1927): 24.
[52]Ibid., 28 (June 11, 1925): 864.
[53]Ibid., 32 (July, 1927): 7.

In some industries, we have seen, seller firms can force buyer firms to force seller firms to cooperate with one another. From what we know about the relationship between the buyers and sellers of bituminous coal, we must conclude that the coal industry is not one of these industries. Coal was a buyers' market, both in terms of the relationship between supply and demand, and in terms of the relationship between the bargaining power of buyers and that of sellers. Operators lacked the capacity to prevent large buyers from adding to price-cutting pressures. The finance-capital solution, where capitalist firms are organized by creditors, was equally unfeasible in the bituminous coal industry. While creditors, unlike buyers, had an interest in the profitability of operations and a real incentive to boost coal prices, they did not possess the capacity to do so. Like the mining industry, coal financing was extremely decentralized, coming mostly from local institutions and individuals. Creditors, therefore, faced the same communication and detection obstacles as did operators.

The coal industry had two sets of suppliers: mining-equipment manufacturers and railroads. Since most equipment purchases were of a once-and-done character, operators didn't have the continuing relationship with equipment manufacturers that would give the latter firms the capacity to punish defection, even if they could be induced to do so, which was extremely unlikely. The relationship between operators and railroads was different, however. The mining railroads did possess some capacity to influence the behavior of operators. A single railroad monopolized coal transportation in each district and operators were totally dependent on the railroad to transport their coal to consumers. Certainly, the carriers could punish individual operators by allocating them less cars than they wanted, effectively limiting their output. As long as the carrier could fill its cars with coal from other mines, it would lose nothing by regulating production *within* its district. The problem, however, is that the railroads' principal interest lay in high levels of output, and at the level of *interdistrict* competition, the railroads benefited even more than the operators from low coal prices, because their own profits were a function of freight rates and coal output, not coal profits. Thus, they had no incentive to limit the output that they transported. If anything, they wished to increase it. Moreover, we should not forget that the railroads were major consumers of coal and shared the buyers' interest in low prices.

The only remaining private actors to consider are workers. Given the relationship between price cutting and wage cutting, they did have an incentive to enforce cooperation among operators. And because mining communities were so isolated and were unusually close-knit, and because mining was so labor intensive, one might infer that miners would have possessed a considerable capacity to punish operators by shutting down their mines. However, in order for miners to enforce cooperation among operators, they must be organized throughout the industry and possess the capacity to shut down every defecting operator. This was no easy achievement, given the repressive legal climate of the period and the same isolation of the mining communities mentioned above, which, besides leaving the operator dependent on the miners for labor, left the miners dependent on and vulnerable to the operator in virtually every dimension of their existence.

To the extent that price cutting and wage cutting went hand in hand, we would expect the organization of workers to constrain competitive behavior by removing the wage-cutting strategy. However, this would not prevent operators from engaging in other cost-cutting practices, nor would it keep them from taking further price cuts out of their profit margins.

In short, the capacity of coal operators to transform their competitive games through consolidation, internal organizational mechanisms, or external organizational mechanisms was low. This did not prevent them from trying, but it did limit their success. In the following chapters, we will unfold the logic of their competitive games and their efforts to transform them, showing how economic competition led operators simultaneously to cooperate and to struggle against competitors, to oppress and to ally with their workers, and to resist and to solicit state intervention.

4. Workers organize capitalists: collective bargaining and market organization, 1880–1914

Introduction

In this chapter I demonstrate that the economic and political behavior of bituminous coal operators during the pre–World War I period can be explained by the structure of their competitive games. Bituminous coal operators faced several different competitive situations during this period, each of which presented operators with a distinct collective action problem and each of which generated a distinct pattern of responses among them. These responses encompassed not only their pricing behavior, but also their relations with workers and with the state.

The first collective action/market organization problem was generated by the disruption of traditional regional markets by new entry. This occurred both in the Midwest and on the East Coast during the 1880s. In the Midwest, improvements in transportation and increased competition from natural gas drove coal from western Pennsylvania and Ohio westward into the "natural" market territory of Illinois and Indiana firms. The result was increased competition that took the form of both wage cutting and price cutting. As prices and profits declined, operators sought to escape the resultant suboptimal outcome by employing internal, voluntary means to discourage price cutting and raise profits. Predictably, these efforts failed. In the face of continued low profits, coal operators next turned to external intervention – in the shape of the union of miners. Capitalist firms in the bituminous coal industry sought to organize their competition by entering into a collective bargaining agreement with their workers. Operators viewed collective bargaining as a way to stabilize prices by closing off the main avenue of cost reduction – wage cutting. A strong union capable of enforcing wage agreements could simultaneously place an indirect check on price cutting.

New entry also intensified competition in the Atlantic Coast tidewater market. At about the same time that eastern coals were expanding into the Midwest, low-volatile coal from southern West Virginia was intruding into the tidewater market for the first time. The result was the considerable downward pressure on prices characteristic of the pricing

Prisoner's Dilemma. As did their midwestern counterparts, eastern operators first sought to escape the suboptimal outcome through internal means. When these failed, they also sought outside intervention – this time from the coal-carrying railroads.

An entirely different collective action problem was produced by the emergence of southern Appalachian coal as a major force in the inland markets of the East and Midwest in the early 1900s. Because the newer fields in southern West Virginia and eastern Kentucky were not unionized, operators there enjoyed a cost-cutting strategy that was not available to their northern and western competitors. In this new game, "cooperating" union firms were placed in a disadvantageous position by nonunion price and wage cutting. They responded by allying with the union against nonunion capitalists in an effort to raise the costs of the latter firms and to force them to cooperate. The nonunion firms, in turn, resisted such efforts to deprive them of their privileged competitive position.

The final competitive situation was the basic price-cutting Prisoner's Dilemma played by firms with similar capacities to reduce costs. While some unionized operators directed their attention toward raising the costs of their nonunion competitors, other unionized firms that were less vulnerable to nonunion competition continued to tackle the old problem of price cutting, which had not been completely eliminated by collective bargaining. On the eve of World War I, the failure of both internal and private external efforts to solve this problem led some operators to solicit state intervention to organize the coal market.

The rise of East–West coal competition: a new competitive game

Beginning in about 1839, improvements in transportation and an increased demand for energy in the American economy led coal production to take off at a rapid pace, climbing from 552,000 tons (1839) to over 6 million tons in 1860. By 1890, when production topped 111 million tons, bituminous coal was the nation's leading energy source.[1]

The improvement in transportation, along with increased demand and production in the decades following the Civil War, caused an important transformation in the way in which coal was marketed.

---

[1] See Table 4.1 for bituminous coal output data. For data on other energy sources, see Schurr and Netschert, *Energy*, p. 496; U.S. Geological Survey, *Mineral Resources*, 1915, Part 2, p. 358.

Although interdistrict competition before 1860 did exist on a small scale in some markets, more generally an abundant supply of an alternative fuel (timber), an underdeveloped transportation system, and the remote location of most important coal deposits combined to limit the consumption of coal to points adjacent to its production, where it was sold under near-monopoly conditions.[2] This all changed during the years that followed the Civil War. "Markets which had previously been supplied by adjacent mining districts were now . . . cut into by producers from distant coal fields; and this meant competition even more severe than that in the past and an inevitable increase in overproduction."[3]

The rise of interregional coal competition was given a further boost by the emergence in the 1880s of natural gas as a competitor to bituminous coal in the energy markets of western Pennsylvania and Ohio. The new fuel, which in the words of one coal-trade writer, "is cheaper, makes better iron, better glass, in fact, makes everything better," dislodged Pittsburgh and Ohio operators from their local markets and forced them to seek sales to the west, in territory traditionally dominated by operators from Indiana and Illinois.[4] These developments were reflected in a virtual halt in the growth of coal output between 1882 and 1886 (see Table 4.1). The coal industry revived from this recession between 1889 and 1892, thanks to a period of unusual industrial activity, but its difficulties were renewed by the 1893 depression and its aftermath. National output dropped 9.7 million tons, from 128.4 million to 118.8 million tons (see Table 4.1). Although total output reached 135 million tons in 1895, coal miners in Pennsylvania, the most prosperous of the major producing states, were working an average of only 206 days in 1895, 26 less than in 1890 (see Table 4.2). To the west, the depression lingered longer. Ohio and Indiana miners worked an average of

[2]Wieck, *Miners' Association*, pp. 57–8; Arthur E. Suffern, *Conciliation and Arbitration in the Coal Industry of America* (Boston: Houghton-Mifflin and Son, 1915), p. 4.
[3]Lubin, *Miners' Wages*, p. 51.
[4]*Black Diamond* 2 (January, 1886): 10; U.S. Geological Survey, *Mineral Resources*, 1886, pp. 232–3, 260; ibid., 1888, pp. 296, 335. Throughout the remainder of Part 2, I rely heavily on two primary sources, *Black Diamond* and *Coal Age*, for evidence of operator attitudes and behavior. These were both commercial publications that, while not affiliated with any organization of operators, were directed primarily at operators and reflected an operator perspective. They provided detailed reporting of commercial and marketing conditions in the industry, of the activities of operator organizations, of political and labor developments relevant to the coal industry, and, increasingly, of technological developments.

Table 4.1. *Bituminous coal output by state, 1880–1940 (millions of tons)*

Year	PA	OH	WV	IL	IN	E.KY	W.KY	KY Total	Total US
1880	18.4	6.0	1.8	6.1	1.4	—	—	0.9	42.8
1881	22.4	9.2	1.7	6.7	2.0	—	—	1.2	54.0
1882	24.6	9.4	2.2	9.1	2.8	—	—	1.3	68.4
1883	26.9	8.2	2.3	12.1	2.6	—	—	1.6	77.2
1884	28.0	7.6	3.4	12.2	2.3	—	—	1.6	83.0
1885	26.0	7.8	3.4	11.8	2.4	—	—	1.6	72.8
1886	27.1	8.4	4.0	11.1	3.0	—	—	1.6	74.6
1887	31.5	10.3	4.9	12.4	3.2	—	—	1.9	88.6
1888	33.8	10.9	5.5	14.3	3.1	—	—	2.6	102.0
1889	36.2	9.8	6.2	12.1	2.8	—	—	2.4	95.7
1890	42.3	11.5	7.4	15.3	3.3	—	—	2.7	111.3
1891	42.8	12.9	9.2	15.7	3.0	—	—	2.9	117.9
1892	46.7	13.6	9.7	17.9	3.3	—	—	3.0	126.9
1893	44.1	13.2	10.7	19.9	3.8	—	—	3.0	128.4
1894	39.9	11.9	11.6	17.1	3.4	—	—	3.1	118.8
1895	50.2	13.4	11.4	17.7	4.0	—	—	3.4	135.1
1896	49.6	12.9	12.9	19.8	3.9	—	—	3.3	137.6
1897	54.4	12.2	14.2	20.1	4.1	—	—	3.6	147.6
1898	65.2	14.5	16.7	18.6	4.9	—	—	3.9	166.6
1899	74.1	16.5	19.2	24.4	6.0	—	—	4.6	193.3
1900	79.8	19.0	22.6	25.8	6.5	—	—	5.3	212.3
1901	82.3	20.9	24.1	27.3	6.9	2.3	3.2	5.5	225.8
1902	98.6	23.5	24.6	32.9	9.5	3.0	3.8	6.8	260.2
1903	103.1	24.8	29.3	37.0	10.8	3.2	4.4	7.5	282.7
1904	97.9	24.4	32.4	36.5	10.8	3.2	4.4	7.6	278.7
1905	118.4	25.5	37.8	38.4	11.9	3.5	4.9	8.4	315.1
1906	129.3	27.7	43.3	41.5	12.1	3.8	5.9	9.6	342.9
1907	150.1	32.1	48.1	51.3	14.0	4.6	6.3	10.7	394.8
1908	117.2	26.3	41.9	47.7	12.3	4.5	5.8	10.2	332.6
1909	138.0	27.9	51.8	50.9	14.8	4.8	5.9	10.7	379.7
1910	150.5	34.2	61.7	45.9	18.4	6.3	8.3	14.6	417.1
1911	144.6	30.8	59.8	53.7	14.2	6.6	7.1	14.0	405.9
1912	161.9	34.5	66.8	59.9	15.3	8.6	7.8	16.5	450.1
1913	173.8	36.2	71.3	61.6	17.2	11.0	8.5	19.6	478.4
1914	148.0	18.8	71.7	57.6	16.6	12.4	7.8	20.4	422.7
1915	158.0	22.4	77.2	58.8	17.0	13.7	7.5	21.4	442.6

161 and 163 days, respectively, in 1896, while the figure for Illinois was 186.

These post–Civil War developments, particularly the westward movement of Pennsylvania and Ohio coal, constitute nothing less than the transformation of the earlier structure of coal competition and the imposition of a new competitive game involving different and more numerous players. In structure, the new game resembled the price–wage Prisoner's Dilemma played among firms differing in

Table 4.1. (*continued*)

Year	PA	OH	WV	IL	IN	E.KY	W.KY	KY Total	Total US
1916	170.3	34.7	86.5	66.2	20.1	17.5	7.8	25.4	502.5
1917	172.5	40.7	86.4	86.2	26.5	17.5	10.2	27.8	551.8
1918	178.6	45.8	89.9	89.3	30.7	20.7	10.8	31.6	579.4
1919	150.8	35.9	79.0	60.9	20.9	21.3	8.6	30.0	465.9
1920	170.6	45.9	89.8	88.7	29.4	24.5	11.0	35.7	568.6
1921	116.0	31.9	72.8	69.6	20.3	23.0	8.6	31.6	415.9
1922	113.0	26.9	80.5	58.5	19.1	27.9	13.7	42.1	422.3
1923	171.9	40.5	107.9	79.3	26.2	33.8	10.9	44.8	564.6
1924	130.6	30.5	101.7	68.3	21.5	36.1	9.0	45.1	483.7
1925	136.9	28.0	122.4	69.9	21.2	42.9	12.2	55.1	520.0
1926	153.0	27.9	143.6	69.4	23.2	47.5	15.5	62.9	573.4
1927	133.0	15.8	145.2	46.8	17.9	47.9	21.2	69.1	517.8
1928	131.2	15.6	132.9	55.9	16.4	45.6	16.3	61.9	500.8
1929	143.5	23.7	138.5	60.7	18.3	46.0	14.4	60.5	535.0
1930	124.5	22.6	121.5	53.7	16.5	39.6	10.4	51.2	467.5
1931	97.7	20.4	101.5	44.3	14.3	31.4	8.6	40.0	382.1
1932	74.8	13.9	85.6	33.5	13.3	25.8	9.5	35.3	309.7
1933	79.3	19.6	94.3	37.4	13.8	28.3	6.9	36.1	333.6
1934	89.8	20.7	98.1	41.3	14.8	30.3	8.2	38.5	359.4
1935	91.4	21.1	99.2	44.5	15.7	32.6	8.1	40.8	372.4
1936	109.9	24.1	117.9	50.9	17.8	39.1	8.4	47.5	439.1
1937	111.0	22.7	118.6	51.6	17.8	38.5	8.6	47.1	445.5
1938	77.7	18.6	93.3	41.9	14.8	31.2	7.4	38.5	348.5
1939	92.2	19.6	107.9	46.4	16.6	34.2	8.3	42.6	394.9
1940	112.9	22.1	126.3	49.5	18.6	40.3	8.9	49.1	460.8

Source: U.S. Geological Survey, *Mineral Resources of the United States*; U.S. Bureau of Mines, *Minerals Yearbook*.

costs that was described in the previous chapter. The cooperative strategy is to maintain the status quo price level; the defection strategy is to reduce prices. In this game, price reductions can be supported by cost (in particular, wage) reductions. The price-cutting strategy is dominant. Therefore, we can predict general price and wage cutting, leading to a suboptimal outcome.

How will operators respond to this outcome? We know from Chapter 2 that the willingness of individual firms to accept suboptimal outcomes varies according to their organizational need, which is largely a function of their costs. Without firm-level data on costs, it is impossible to identify precisely which firms fall into each cost category, but the aggregate data do provide the basis for some further refinement of the picture. The fragmentary price data suggest that Pennsylvania coal was considerably

Table 4.2. *Average number of days worked by bituminous coal mines by state, 1890–1940*

Year	PA	WV	OH	IL	IN	E.KY	W.KY	Total KY	Total U.S.
1890	232	227	201	204	220	—	—	219	226
1891	223	237	206	216	190	—	—	225	223
1892	223	228	212	220	225	—	—	217	219
1893	190	219	188	229	201	—	—	202	204
1894	165	186	136	183	149	—	—	145	171
1895	206	195	176	182	189	—	—	153	194
1896	206	201	161	186	163	—	—	165	192
1897	205	205	148	185	176	—	—	178	196
1898	229	218	169	175	199	—	—	187	211
1899	245	242	200	228	218	—	—	224	234
1900	242	231	215	226	199	—	—	227	234
1901	230	219	198	220	194	—	—	213	225
1902	248	205	200	226	205	—	—	209	230
1903	235	210	194	228	197	—	—	207	225
1904	196	197	174	213	177	—	—	197	202
1905	231	209	176	201	151	—	—	200	211
1906	231	220	167	192	175	—	—	212	213
1907	255	230	199	218	197	—	—	210	234
1908	201	185	161	185	174	—	—	186	193
1909	—	—	—	—	—	—	—	—	209
1910	238	228	203	160	229	—	—	221	217
1911	233	221	179	188	182	—	—	191	211
1912	252	266	201	194	182	—	—	201	223
1913	267	234	206	189	190	—	—	212	232
1914	214	201	108	173	168	203	159	187	195
1915	226	208	142	179	179	205	154	186	203

cheaper to produce than Illinois and Indiana coal in the mid-1880s (Table 4.3). The differential is less pronounced in the following decade, but it continues to exist, supporting the conclusion that, leaving aside transportation costs, Pennsylvania coal enjoyed a cost advantage over Illinois and Indiana coal during this period. This conclusion is also affirmed by the average working day data, which show that Pennsylvania operators were able to operate at a higher capacity than the midwestern operators during the 1890s (see Table 4.2). The same data also show that operators from Illinois were able consistently to fare better than operators from Indiana. As for Ohio, the 1880s data are even more fragmentary, but the data for the following decade indicate that Ohio operators suffered more (probably at the hands of competitors from western Pennsylvania) during the hard times of the early 1890s than operators from any other state. Squeezed out of their traditional markets by cheaper

Table 4.2. (*continued*)

Year	PA	WV	OH	IL	IN	E.KY	W.KY	Total KY	Total U.S.
1916	259	237	197	198	187	231	162	208	230
1917	261	225	210	243	221	209	225	214	243
1918	269	238	223	238	227	231	228	230	249
1919	218	200	164	160	148	196	170	189	195
1920	244	198	188	213	192	182	182	182	220
1921	151	149	134	152	128	160	131	152	149
1922	154	143	100	120	110	133	158	140	142
1923	213	169	150	158	136	161	127	152	179
1924	180	182	143	148	136	195	115	174	171
1925	200	225	151	161	159	226	152	206	195
1926	224	247	159	172	173	243	192	230	215
1927	203	235	98	114	120	238	235	237	191
1928	218	223	171	156	150	228	172	212	203
1929	230	247	201	177	172	239	177	222	219
1930	198	204	189	156	157	200	148	187	187
1931	169	176	174	136	146	168	130	159	160
1932	154	168	127	112	145	156	149	155	146
1933	162	196	169	141	163	179	137	170	167
1934	179	196	167	160	171	190	145	180	178
1935	180	192	162	171	176	193	157	182	179
1936	205	216	183	175	178	214	143	202	199
1937	199	209	185	168	174	204	145	192	193
1938	156	175	145	149	149	166	132	160	162
1939	176	202	175	163	177	185	153	180	178
1940	212	215	193	169	188	210	154	200	202

Source: U.S. Geological Survey, *Mineral Resources of the United States*; U.S. Bureau of Mines, *Minerals Yearbook*.

and higher-quality Pennsylvania coal, they were unable to offset their local losses with their westward incursions. The West Virginia coal industry was relatively underdeveloped during the 1880s, but the data from the 1890s indicate that West Virginia was producing the nation's cheapest coal and that it weathered the decade better than did every state but Pennsylvania.

In summary, the following state of affairs existed during the 1880s and 1890s. In Pennsylvania and Ohio markets, where freight costs did not significantly differentiate operators, Pennsylvania and West Virginia coals were generally cheaper to produce and of superior quality than Ohio coal. Pushed to the west, Ohio operators were able to take some business away from operators from Illinois and Indiana, but not enough to offset their eastern losses. Operators from the midwestern states of

Table 4.3. *Average value per ton of bituminous coal (F.O.B. mine) by state,*
1880–1940

Year	PA	OH	WV	IL	IN	E.KY	W.KY	Total KY	Total U.S.	Coal age spot price
1880	—	—	—	—	—	—	—	—	1.25	—
1881	—	—	—	—	—	—	—	—	1.12	—
1882	—	—	—	1.51	—	—	—	—	1.12	—
1883	—	—	—	1.48	—	—	—	—	1.07	—
1884	—	—	—	1.26	—	—	—	—	.94	—
1885	—	—	—	1.17	—	—	—	—	1.13	—
1886	.80	—	—	1.10	—	—	—	—	1.05	—
1887	.80	—	—	1.08	—	—	—		1.11	
1888	.95	.93	1.10	1.12	1.40	—	—	—	1.00	—
1889	.77	.94	.82	.97	1.02	—	—	.98	.99	—
1890	.84	.94	.84	.93	.91	—	—	.92	.99	—
1891	.87	.94	.80	.91	1.03	—	—	.93	.99	—
1892	.84	.94	.80	.91	1.08	—	—	.92	.99	—
1893	.80	.92	.77	.89	1.07	—	—	.86	.96	—
1894	.74	.83	.75	.89	.96	—	—	.88	.91	—
1895	.72	.79	.68	.80	.91	—	—	.86	.86	—
1896	.71	.79	.65	.80	.84	—	—	.78	.83	—
1897	.69	.78	.63	.72	.84	—	—	.79	.81	—
1898	.67	.83	.61	.78	.81	—	—	.79	.80	—
1899	.76	.87	.63	.85	.88	—	—	.79	.87	—
1900	.97	1.02	.81	1.04	1.03	—	—	.92	1.04	—
1901	.99	1.00	.87	1.03	1.01	—	—	.95	1.05	—
1902	1.08	1.14	1.01	1.03	1.10	—	—	.99	1.12	—
1903	1.18	1.29	1.17	1.17	1.23	—	—	1.06	1.24	—
1904	.94	1.09	.88	1.10	1.11	—	—	1.04	1.10	—
1905	.96	1.04	.86	1.06	1.05	—	—	.99	1.06	—
1906	1.00	1.09	.95	1.08	1.08	—	—	1.02	1.11	1.21
1907	1.04	1.10	.99	1.07	1.08	—	—	1.06	1.14	1.18
1908	1.01	1.06	.95	1.05	1.06	—	—	1.01	1.12	1.05
1909	.94	.99	.86	1.05	1.02	—	—	.94	1.07	1.04
1910	1.02	1.05	.92	1.14	1.13	—	—	.99	1.12	1.23

Illinois and Indiana, squeezed by coal from the east, also fared poorly.
Thus, while no doubt there existed low-cost, medium-cost, and high-
cost operators in every state, it appears that, in general, the need for a
reorganization of coal competition was less in Pennsylvania and West
Virginia than in Ohio, Indiana, and Illinois. We would expect operators
from these latter states, then, to be more willing to bear the costs of
outside intervention to organize the market, and to be the instigators of
efforts to transform the competitive game.

Finally, it should be recalled that these attempts to organize compe-

Table 4.3. (*continued*)

Year	PA	OH	WV	IL	IN	E.KY	W.KY	Total KY	Total U.S.	Coal age spot price
1911	1.01	1.03	.90	1.11	1.08	—	—	.99	1.11	1.07
1912	1.05	1.07	.94	1.17	1.14	—	—	1.02	1.15	1.21
1913	1.11	1.10	1.01	1.14	1.11	—	—	1.05	1.18	1.23
1914	1.07	1.13	.99	1.12	1.10	1.13	.85	1.02	1.17	1.14
1915	1.06	1.08	.97	1.10	1.10	1.01	.84	1.01	1.13	1.12
1916	1.30	1.33	1.18	1.25	1.27	1.27	1.00	1.19	1.32	1.85
1917	2.44	2.48	2.32	1.88	1.99	2.48	1.64	2.17	2.26	3.25
1918	2.59	2.58	2.56	2.32	2.29	2.71	2.25	2.55	2.58	2.58
1919	2.42	2.22	2.49	2.30	2.22	2.58	2.17	2.46	2.49	2.59
1920	3.77	3.82	4.34	3.08	3.16	4.44	3.37	4.11	3.75	5.64
1921	2.78	2.65	2.84	2.74	2.57	2.77	2.48	2.69	2.89	2.55
1922	2.84	3.23	2.93	2.89	2.85	2.97	3.06	3.02	3.02	3.64
1923	2.75	2.43	2.65	2.50	2.48	2.66	2.11	2.54	2.68	2.77
1924	2.26	2.03	1.82	2.27	2.16	1.90	1.78	1.88	2.20	2.08
1925	2.10	1.93	1.71	2.19	2.02	1.80	1.44	1.72	2.04	2.06
1926	2.13	1.96	1.84	2.14	1.98	1.36	1.87	1.74	2.06	2.21
1927	2.05	1.92	1.72	2.16	2.03	1.54	1.81	1.73	1.99	1.99
1928	1.90	1.69	1.59	2.00	1.78	1.23	1.68	1.56	1.86	1.80
1929	1.80	1.51	1.55	1.87	1.63	1.54	1.67	1.54	1.78	1.79
1930	1.72	1.40	1.50	1.74	1.59	1.49	1.58	1.49	1.70	1.75
1931	1.59	1.24	1.31	1.70	1.45	1.01	1.34	1.27	1.54	—
1932	1.34	1.11	1.06	1.53	1.30	.84	1.05	.99	1.31	—
1933	1.37	1.20	1.14	1.46	1.28	.88	1.20	1.13	1.34	—
1934	1.84	1.71	1.70	1.56	1.48	1.18	1.68	1.57	1.75	—
1935	1.88	1.66	1.71	1.56	1.51	1.18	1.73	1.62	1.77	—
1936	—	—	—	—	—	—	—	—	1.76	—
1937	—	—	—	—	—	—	—	—	1.94	—
1938	—	—	—	—	—	—	—	—	1.95	—
1939	2.03	1.63	1.76	1.64	1.48	1.30	1.85	1.74	1.84	—
1940	2.04	1.71	1.83	1.69	1.53	—	—	1.85	1.91	—

Source: U.S. Geological Survey, *Mineral Resources of the United States*; U.S. Bureau of Mines, *Minerals Yearbook*.

tition will probably begin with low-cost internal mechanisms before progressing to more costly mechanisms.

Price cutting and collective action: internal mechanisms

The history of the coal industry in the last two decades of the nineteenth century confirms the expectations derived from our model. Chronic price and wage cutting led first to internal, then to external, efforts to organize competition. The external organizational mechanism accepted by operators – interdistrict collective bargaining – was enforced by workers. By preventing competitive wage reductions, the organization of workers and the ensuing collective bargaining framework contributed to the organization of capitalists.

All of the available evidence indicates that considerable price and wage cutting did occur in the bituminous coal industry in the 1880s and 1890s. The average value of Illinois coal fell from $1.52 in 1882 to $1.08 in 1887 (Table 4.3). In most of the major producing states, this decline in price was halted during the early 1890s, but it resumed with vigor with the onset of the 1893 depression. In each of the states included in Table 4.3, prices declined from 1893 to an unprecedented low in 1897 or 1898. Nationwide, the decline was from $0.96 in 1893 to $0.80 in 1898. That this decline was not due to increased productivity is demonstrated by the alarm with which it was viewed in government and trade publications. At the end of 1885, a *Black Diamond* correspondent lamented that "in no trade, perhaps, have values suffered such a decline during the past year or two as in bituminous coal."[5] In the following year, the same publication reiterated that

there can be no question that the coal trade . . . is passing through a period of depression of rather unusual severity. . . . Cutting of rates and incessantly varying discriminations act as a constant stimulus to competition, and the laws governing supply and demand are often ignored. Corporations or individual operators, in their efforts to create demand by the means of extraordinary concessions, are simply dropping the coal trade into a quagmire from whence recovery to terra firma is impossible.[6]

Complaints of "excessively low," "unprofitable," and "ruinously low" prices persisted during the 1890s.[7]

Early on, as we have already seen, price was linked to cost cutting through wage reductions.

An operator finds the demand so dull, but competition so lively, that he is absolutely compelled to reduce the price of his product or retire from the market. . . . He cannot make the reduction unless he reduces the cost of production or spends his own money. Operators have been known to do the latter. . . . This may do for a few days, but could not last. Consequently, the diplomatic producer

[5] *Black Diamond* 2 (September, 1885): 8.
[6] Ibid., 2 (March, 1886).
[7] U.S. Geological Survey, *Mineral Resources*, 1888, pp. 175–6; *Mineral Industry, Its Statistics, Technology, Trade* 3 (1895); 132–3; *Black Diamond* 18 (January 2, 1897): 11; ibid., 18 (February 26, 1897): 207; ibid., 18 (March 5, 1897): 235.

calls his men around him; he will state to them in a frank, pleasant manner, the condition of the trade and the position of the market.[8]

In 1894 and 1897, the severity of such wage reductions led workers to strike.

The rational response to such a suboptimal situation, we have seen, is to promote collective action to overcome it. By the 1880s, the coal industry, at least at the level of the individual district, already had a long history of attempting to organize competition through internal means.[9] In fact, one of the earliest restraint-of-trade cases in U.S. history was brought in 1871 against a group of coal operators and dealers who had agreed to restrict output.[10] However, with the exception of a coal syndicate formed in Pittsburgh in 1887 "to stop the ruinous policy ... of driving competition beyond the limits of sound judgment," I have found no evidence of formal internal mechanisms in the 1880s.[11] Yet there was more than a small dose of prescription in the trade-journal reports of low prices.

Coal is not a luxury; it should and can command fair remunerative prices to the operator, shipper, and dealer, but for the selfish and shortsighted policy of a few, who, in a desire to increase their tonnage, bear the market heedless of the fact that with the sluices once opened, it will be impossible to close them again. ... As long as we are almost exclusively restricted to home consumption injudicious efforts at competition can and must result in disaster.[12]

Black Diamond's exhortations to "study the market," "to conform to the laws of supply and demand," and to "devise some plan whereby the production could in a measure be brought within the limits of demand" indicate that there were at least some efforts to induce operators to act to further their common interest in higher prices.[13]

The *Black Diamond* has repeatedly called attention to the constant and rapid decline in the values of coal; it has persistently held that overproduction is the sole cause, and restriction is the only practical remedy. To obtain the full benefits of this remedy, however, it is necessary, as a matter of self protection, for producers to organize, to merge individual interest into the common good.[14]

---

[8]Ibid., 2 (October, 1885): 6.
[9]Wieck, *Miners' Association*, p. 97.
[10]Harvey C. Mansfield, *The Lake Cargo Coal Rate Controversy* (New York: Columbia University Press, 1932), p. 24.
[11]*Black Diamond* 3 (January, 1887): 17.
[12]Ibid., 1 (April, 1885): 8.
[13]Ibid., 2 (June, 1886): 5; ibid., 3 (March, 1887): 13; ibid., 2 (September, 1885): 9.
[14]Ibid., 2 (June, 1886): 5.

Price cutting and collective action: the organization of capitalists by workers

The continued decline of coal prices, along with the lamentations over price cutting presented above, indicate that such appeals to the "common good" had no effect. This failure of coal operators to secure the cooperation of their competitors through internal means forms the background of their attempts to reorganize their markets through external intervention in the late 1880s. In the midwestern market that we have been considering, this meant accepting a jointly agreed upon wage floor enforced by organized workers. If workers could stop wage cutting, it was believed, they could also stop price cutting. At the very least, each operator would know the wages paid by competitors.

On the labor side, coal-mine workers understood early on that as long as wages were the main element in production costs, their own livelihoods were jeopardized by the disorganized state of the coal industry. One of the earliest recorded U.S. coal strikes, the anthracite strike led by John Bates, had as a major goal the restriction of production and the elevation of the *price* of coal.[15] A few years later, in 1871, anthracite operators supported a strike by miners, hoping that it would raise coal prices. According to Aurand, the small operators in the Schuylkill and Lehigh Valley regions of the anthracite field "acknowledged their inability to cope with the vicissitudes of the market, and urged labor to save them." The strike was seen as a "cooperative effort . . . to raise coal prices. As such, both sides agreed to maintain the strike in a friendly manner."[16] And in 1861 in Illinois, Daniel Weaver, the President of the American Miners' Association, published a "letter to the miners" in which he discussed the impact on prices of a uniform wage scale:

There is no such thing as uniformity among the bosses. True, the Missouri bosses appear anxious that a minimum . . . price of coal in the city should be established, and many of the miners . . . think we ought to cooperate with the bosses to effect this purpose. I am of a different opinion. The regulation of the selling prices of coal is beyond our prerogative. If our employers pay us for digging the price we demand . . . we can claim no more. This, of itself, will accomplish the purpose, provided the price of digging amongst ourselves be uniform.[17]

[15]Harold W. Aurand, *From the Molly Maguires to the United Mine Workers: The Social Ecology of an Industrial Union, 1867–1897* (Philadelphia: Temple University Press, 1971), p. 66.
[16]Ibid., pp. 71–8.
[17]Wieck, *Miners' Association*, p. 225.

Although there were miners' unions in the anthracite region in 1849 and in the 1870s, and a national miners' union, the American Miners' Association, existed during the 1860s, the history of modern collective bargaining in the coal industry begins with the formation in 1883 of the Amalgamated Association of Miners of the United States – a federation of worker organizations in Illinois, Ohio, Pennsylvania, and Maryland. In 1885, expanding their representation to Indiana, Iowa, West Virginia, and Kansas, the AAMUS became the National Federation of Miners and Mine Laborers. That same year, this organization, along with a handful of operators, issued a joint invitation to other operators to attend a joint conference to end the price wars that had been so injurious to both workers and capitalists.

The widespread depression of business, the overproduction of coal and the consequent severe competition have caused the capital in the mines to yield little or no profitable returns. The constant reductions in wages that have lately taken place have afforded no relief to capital, and, indeed, have but tended to increase its embarrassments. Any reduction in wages in any coal field usually necessitates and generates a corresponding reduction in every other competitive coal field. If the price of labor in the United States was uniformly raised to the standard of three years ago the employers of labor would occupy toward each other the same relative position in point of competition as at present.[18]

Operators were also aware of the importance of wage cutting as an essential element of the cycle of destructive competition through which they were suffering. They recognized the union of mine workers as a possible enforcement agent to organize their own competiton. In October, 1885, *Black Diamond* called for the formation of a national operator association to meet with the miners.

How easy it would be for an executive committee of the national producers' organization to join hands with the chief executive committee of the National Federation of Miners and Mine Laborers on all matters calculated to advance the interests of the coal industry and whenever refractory members of either organization are to be disciplined.[19]

As the 1886 joint conference approached, *Black Diamond* warmed to the idea of organizing workers.

Complete organization among miners as well as operators should . . . be vigorously pushed. Difficulties may present themselves in the adjustment of prices to be paid for mining in the several states. . . . Different grades of coal come into

---

[18]Quoted in Arthur E. Suffern, *The Coal Miners' Struggle for Industrial Status* (New York: Macmillan, 1926), pp. 37–8.
[19]*Black Diamond* 2 (October, 1885): 6.

the same market. . . . This, and the rates of freight, should be fully established when a certain price . . . should be agreed upon. . . . A persistent infraction of this rule on the part of an operator, by selling his coal at less than the circular price, should be followed by a cessation of work at his mines; the miners so called out to be supported by both organizations jointly.[20]

This initial joint-conference framework disintegrated over the next four years, however, as one group of operators after another failed to participate. They dropped out not because they opposed collective bargaining, but because they feared that collective bargaining would establish disadvantageous cost differentials that would benefit competitors.[21] The miners lacked the capacity to force operators to overcome this fear.[22]

The immediate result of the breakdown of this mechanism in the early 1890s was a return to the self-destructive wage and price cutting that had characterized the pre-1886 period (as well as the period in which the agreement was in effect, for that matter). As they did before, operators again turned to internal organizational mechanisms – this time the district sales agency and the price-fixing association – to transform the structure of their competition. Such organizations appeared in many fields during the 1890s, particularly in the wake of the 1893 depression.[23] Like their predecessors, these mechanisms were also unsuccessful in stopping the downward slide of coal prices.

The deterioration of the coal trade in the wake of the depression in the latter half of 1893 precipitated further price and wage cuts, and in April, 1894, the miners struck, shutting down production in the fields supplying the Midwest markets for a period of two months.[24] As a result, operators from Illinois, Indiana, western Pennsylvania, and Ohio agreed to maintain a union wage scale, but only under the condition that the union enforce it among their competitors.[25] Economic conditions continued to deteriorate, however, and by 1896, there was "a general disregard of contractual relationships on the part of both the operators and the mine workers. . . . The general weakness of the union was, of course, chiefly responsible for this condition."[26] In early 1897, there was a further

[20]Ibid., 2 (January, 1886): 6.
[21]Suffern, The Coal Miners, pp. 47–64.
[22]See Black Diamond 2 (July, 1886).
[23]William Graebner, "Great Expectations: The Search for Order in Bituminous Coal, 1890–1917," Business History Review 48 (Spring, 1974): 56–9.
[24]Mineral Industry 3 (1893): 132–3.
[25]Suffern, Conciliation, p. 40.
[26]David J. McDonald and Edward A. Lynch, Coal and Unionism: A History of the American Coal Miners' Unions (Silver Springs, MD: Lynald Books, 1939), p. 142.

round of wage reductions in Illinois and Indiana, and *Black Diamond* reported in June that

many operators would welcome a strike, as it would clean up stocks and might have the effect of establishing a sensible and practical differential in the four principal mining states of the middle west, thus enabling all miners to make fair living wages.[27]

When the strike came in July, it had the "practical endorsement" and, "with few exceptions, the sympathy and moral support of the operators," especially in Indiana and Illinois, where "the miners have the entire sympathy of the operators, who wish them success."[28] This strike resulted in the joint conference of 1898 between the mine workers and operators from the "Central Competitive Field" states – Ohio, Pennsylvania, Illinois, and Indiana – that established the union-enforced organization of the coal industry which endured with greater or less success for the next twenty-five years. This time the operators recognized that they would be better served by a union with a greater capacity to enforce cooperation, and granted the miners' union, now named the United Mine Workers of America (UMWA), a wage–dues check-off in order to increase their coercive capacity.[29] "Strong hostility among operators led them locally to foster the very unions they fought in order to weaken their opponents."[30]

It would be going too far to say that the joint-conference movement was solely the outcome of efforts by operators to organize competition. Their efforts would never have taken the turn that they did had not the workers struggled to organize themselves. Yet, the operators certainly were receptive to collective bargaining. According to *Black Diamond*, the operators pledged their "hearty support" to the miners' organizational campaign and "the miners concede that they were most materially assisted in securing their demands by the earnest support and cooperation afforded them by the operators of Illinois."[31]

Operators clearly saw collective bargaining as a means to eliminate the price wars that had disabled the industry. As one later testified,

Both the operators and the miners felt that if a cooperative arrangement could be worked out in the particular district so closely competitive, that if collective

---

[27]*Black Diamond* 19 (June 3, 1897): 11.
[28]Ibid., 19 (July 10, 1897): 43.
[29]F.G. Tryon, "The Effect of Competitive Conditions on Labor Relations," *Annals of the American Academy* 111 (June, 1924): 83–95; Mansfield, *Lake Cargo*, p. 19.
[30]Mansfield, *Lake Cargo*, p. 19.
[31]*Black Diamond* 20 (January 29, 1898): 126.

bargaining for the entire country could be had, and an organization among the miners built up that would be responsible and would respect a contract, it would be most desirable for the industry.[32]

"Strange as it may seem," an operator commented, *"the United Mine Workers of America, as a body, have forced the operators of the various competitive fields into one large combination."*[33]

Support of collective bargaining by those operators who could not afford to pay a cooperative wage and still sell their coal at a profit was won by a system of side payments under which they were granted the right to pay slightly lower wages than their better-situated competitors. This system was governed by a vague principle labeled "competitive equality." For the operators, competitive equality meant that miners working in areas which, because of freight rates or geological conditions, suffered from a competitive disadvantage with respect to other districts, should accept lower wages, thereby allowing all operators to enjoy roughly equivalent profit margins.

We have banded together here so that operators in every district might exist, notwithstanding the different conditions that prevail; and so long as we work on those lines some miners will have to accept less wages than others.[34]

For the miners, competitive equality meant

a uniform wage scale for all classes of . . . labor. . . . The basis of that is that the same prices shall prevail in one district that prevail in another; that you shall, as far as the interstate movement can provide, all be placed upon a basis of competitive equality, and that is the basic principle upon which this movement is founded.[35]

As it evolved through the struggles between operators and miners, the principle of competitive equality, in practice, meant that operators with competitive advantages retained them, but that disadvantaged operators received sufficient compensation to enable them to stay in business.[36] This system operated through a series of wage differentials. At the joint conference of 1898, four basing points were selected, one from each of the Central Competitive Field states, each representing typical (and similar) mining conditions. The operators and miners agreed on a basic eight-hour day, basic pick- and machine-mining rates for each

[32]Quoted in Lubin, *Miners' Wages*, p. 53.
[33]*Black Diamond* 35 (September 30, 1913): 27, emphasis added. Also see Graebner, "Great Expectations," p. 54.
[34]An operator quoted in Lubin, *Miners' Wages*, p. 74.
[35]Quoted in ibid., p. 79.
[36]Suffern, *The Coal Miners*, p. 319.

basing point, and basic wages for some classes of "inside" day labor. Then district and subdistrict conferences of miners and operators came to agreements that reflected the base-point wage rate with allowances for differences in geological conditions and freight rates. Altogether, there were four sets of differentials, some determined at the interstate conference and some at the district conferences. The first compensated operators whose coal was brittle and more likely to crumble into fine "screenings" or "slack," which, in the early part of the century, was less marketable than larger sizes of coal. According to this system, it was the practice until 1916 (except in Illinois) for miners to be paid only for the coal that was large enough to pass over a screen. Wages could be adjusted, then, to compensate operators whose coal was brittle and less marketable. Operators were enabled to pay their workers not for the tonnage brought from the mine (mine-run coal), but for the *marketable* coal brought from the mine (mine-run coal minus the screenings). At the joint conference, wages were set so that, in each mine, the miner's screen rate (the wage rate for coal that passed over the screen) was calculated on the basis of the proportion of mine-run coal that was likely to fall through the screen. If 50 percent of the coal was screenings, the screen rate was double the mine-run rate. Operators with inferior, brittle coal ended up paying their miners less per ton of mine-run coal than did their competitors who owned less brittle coal. Thus, if the hypothetical mine-run rate at two mines was $0.60 per ton but, in one of the mines, 50 percent of the coal passed through the screen, and in the other, 25 percent of the coal passed through the screen, then the miner who mined a ton of coal in the first mine would receive $0.30, while the miner who mined a ton of coal in the second mine would receive $0.45.

The machine differential compensated operators who ran less mechanized and less efficient mining operations, but without removing completely the incentive to mechanize. If mechanized operators would have paid their workers the same daily wage that pick miners received, their labor costs *per ton* would have been very much less than that of competing pick-mining operations. This would have seriously disadvantaged the latter group of operators. However, if miners in mechanized mines were paid the same *tonnage* rate as pick miners, most of the advantages of mechanization would have been captured by the miners rather than the operators, who would still face the same labor costs per ton of coal mined. This outcome, which would have protected the pick-mining operations from lower-cost competition as well as greatly increasing the earnings of machine-operating miners, was naturally favored by the union. As the President of the United Mine Workers re-marked in 1901, "we contend . . . that there should be no advantage to the operator who owns a machine mine over the operator who owns a pick mine."[37] In practice, the machine differential gave miners who operated machines a lower rate of pay (per ton) than pick miners, but not so low as to equalize the daily earnings of pick and machine miners. Machine-mine operators, then, were forced to share with the miners the benefits (in the form of higher earnings) of the competitive advantage that mechanization represented.

The freight and thin-seam differentials had similar effects. Workers who labored in distant mine fields or under unfavorable, unproductive conditions accepted a lower rate of pay in order to allow their operators to remain in the market, while these operators had to accept a lower profit margin.[38] The overall effect of the differential system, then, was to make it possible for mines that were in one way or another unfavorably situated to remain in operation.[39]

The joint-conference arrangement provided the background for the most important struggles over market organization in the coal industry over the next twenty-five years. Before looking at the operation of this mechanism in more detail, and analyzing the impact on it of other major shifts in the coal trade, it is necessary to consider another late nineteenth-century development, the rise of southern competition in the tidewater market and the organization of coal competition by the coal-carrying railroads.

North–South competition and the organization of coal competition by railroads

We have seen that the principal competitive development in the late nineteenth-century bituminous coal industry was the breakdown of re-gional markets and the emergence of direct competition between eastern and midwestern operators, leading them to accept collective bargaining as a means to control competitive wage cutting. A second stage in the development of interdistrict coal competition was the rise of coal pro-duction in the southern Appalachian states of West Virginia and eastern Kentucky. In later sections of this chapter we will have occasion to consider the impact of this development on the structure of coal com-

---

[37]Quoted in Lubin, *Miners' Wages*, p. 103.
[38]Suffern, *Conciliation*, pp. 323–30.
[39]Lubin, *Miners' Wages*, pp. 260–6.

petition between operators in the Central Competitive Field and the southern Appalachian operators, which were principally nonunion. In this section, I wish to focus on a narrower topic – the impact of new southern West Virginia competition on the Atlantic Coast tidewater market. As was the case in the Midwest, new entrants disrupted traditional market patterns and precipitated efforts to organize competition through internal means. And, as in the Midwest, the failure of these internal organizational mechanisms led operators to turn to more effective external devices. In the case of the tidewater market, however, it was the coal-carrying railroads, not an organization of workers, that were supposed to enforce cooperation among operators.

The tidewater market, which had been dominated by the mines along the Chesapeake and Ohio Railroad in Maryland and those served by the Pennsylvania Railroad in central Pennsylvania, was disrupted in the mid-1880s by the shipment of low-volatile Pocahontas coal to Norfolk (Hampton Roads) on the Norfolk and Western Railroad. The resultant intensification of competitive price cutting generated efforts to organize tidewater competition through internal means. In 1887, the Seaboard Coal Association, a market-sharing and price-fixing organization, was organized. In that year, when demand was relatively high, and there was little incentive to cut prices, the cooperative prices were maintained, but in subsequent years the agreement collapsed, despite the presence of sanctions in 1889 and 1891. Commenting on one of the Seaboard Association's meetings, the *Engineering and Mining Journal* remarked that "the joke is somewhat old, but seems to stand repetition every year." After consistently failing to organize tidewater competition, the Association dissolved in 1894, its last act being an appeal to the railroads to assume the burden of organizing coal competition in the East.[40]

There were several ways in which the railroads could facilitate cooperation among coal operators. First, in the eastern market, at least, the railroads often took over the marketing of a district's coal, functioning as a joint sales agency and eliminating price competition among a district's operators. Thus, the Coal Producers' Contract, signed by all of the Pocahontas district operators in West Virginia and by the Norfolk and Western Railroad in 1886, designated a department of the railroad as the sole sales agent of Pocahontas coal. The railroad tied the freight rate charged to operators to the price it received for delivered coal, each

[40]Joseph T. Lambie, *From Mine to Market: The History of Coal Transportation on the Norfolk and Western Railway* (New York: New York University Press, 1954), pp. 88–109.

operator receiving 30 percent of the average delivered tidewater price obtained by the railroad, the railroad retaining the remainder as a freight tariff.[41] Railroads could also control output through the allocation of cars. The 1886 Pocahontas agreement included a clause giving to the railroad the authority to withhold cars should overproduction threaten the price level.[42] It was also possible for the carriers to use their allocation authority to punish individual operators. In the area of southern West Virginia served by the Chesapeake and Ohio (C&O) Railroad, operators who attemped to circumvent the C&O Coal Agency, the railroad's selling organ, "found it almost impossible to obtain railway cars."[43] Finally, by maintaining a standard freight rate, railroads could control a major element of the delivered price of coal. In the era before the ICC required railroads to observe published freight rates, coal-price and freight-rate competition were virtually indistinguishable. The typical practice was for the railroads and the operators to set a delivered price for coal that was sufficiently low to secure a buyer, then to divide the revenue in a mutually satisfactory manner. Tams, a West Virginia operator, recalls an occasion when the President of the New River Consolidated Coal Company and the freight manager of the C&O Railroad traveled to Detroit and sold 300,000 tons of coal to Detroit Edison, then spent two days wrangling in their hotel room over the division of the sales price.[44]

There were also drawbacks to having the railroads organize coal competition, however. In the first place, the railroads were interested in freight tonnage, not coal profits. Writing of the C&O Coal Agency, Tams notes that "the Agency, having no financial interest in the mines, cared little for the mines, but a great deal for the railway. The coal was sold, therefore, at a price that barely permitted the mines to survive."[45] In southern West Virginia, the Norfolk and Western Railroad intervened on behalf of workers on two occasions, offering to accept a lower proportion of the sales price for its freight rates if the additional operator revenue was used to increase wages, avert a strike, and avoid a cessation of the movement of coal. This "interference" was bitterly resented by operators and, in 1894, actually precipitated a lockout, which was di-

---

[41]Ibid., p. 47.
[42]Ibid.
[43]W.P. Tams, *The Smokeless Coal Fields of West Virginia: A Brief History* (Morgantown, West Virginia: West Virginia University Library, 1963), pp. 25–6.
[44]Ibid., p. 26.
[45]Ibid.

rected not against the workers, but against the railroad.[46] Second, when there was more than one producing district and more than one railroad involved in a market, the organization of coal competition by the railroads required the organization of the rail competition of the railroads. Each coal-transporting railroad felt the same incentive to reduce freight rates (and, hence, coal prices) as did the individual operator to cut prices. As Graebner notes, "price cutting initiated through cut-throat rail competition was just as harmful to coal operators as self initiated cutting."[47]

A study of the efforts of the eastern coal railroads to organize their competition would take us too far afield. Suffice it to say that their voluntary, internal attempts to control the coal market were unsuccessful.[48] However, between 1899 and 1901 the Pennsylvania Railroad (PRR) secured a controlling interest in its major competitors – the Norfolk and Western, the Chesapeake and Ohio, and the Baltimore and Ohio. According to the PRR's president, "it was hoped in this way to secure reasonable and stable rates and prevent the unjust discriminations which naturally resulted from conflicts between the railways and rival communities."[49]

Commentaries in coal-trade publications indicated that the railroad met with limited initial success in organizing coal competition.[50] However, the effectiveness of the railroads as an organizational mechanism declined as individual operators, rather than railroad-dominated district sales agencies, began to undertake their own marketing. As this occurred, the cooperation of coal-carrying railroads resulted only in the stabilization of a major item of delivered costs. It did not prevent cost cutting in other areas, such as wages, or price cutting.

There is also scattered evidence that coal-carrying railroads in Ohio formed rate pools in 1886, giving operators "the satisfaction that all fare alike as regards freight rates, and that every man will be compelled to sell coal on his own merits and the merits of the product he handles."[51] In its earlier form, the arrangement among the railroads was ineffective, for prices "jumped in all directions." So, in late 1897, a new, supposedly stronger pool was proposed. *Black Diamond* applauded it, and suggested

[46]Lambie, *From Mine to Market*, pp. 60–1.
[47]Graebner, "Great Expectations," pp. 52–3.
[48]Lambie, *From Mine to Market*, p. 188.
[49]Ibid.
[50]*Mineral Industry* 13 (1905): 91.
[51]*Black Diamond* 3 (October, 1886): 10.

that Illinois and Indiana operators would be wise to emulate it. "By the working of such a plan . . . the miners could be paid . . . and the operator could . . . secure a fair return for his product."[52] There is no evidence to indicate that the Ohio plan was implemented. If it was, it did not stop the decline of Ohio coal prices in the early twentieth century (see Table 4.3).

The rise of North–South competition: a second new competitive game

Coal operators in the Central Competitive Field accepted collective bargaining with their workers because they thought that the establishment of a floor under wages would limit price cutting and force themselves to maintain prices at a profitable level. The arrangement enjoyed some initial success but it soon became apparent that it would not achieve its original purpose. In part, this was due to the inherent weaknesses of collective bargaining as a mechanism to organize capitalists and to the presence of many loopholes in the joint agreements themselves. The main factor undermining the joint-agreement mechanism, however, was the entry of high-quality coal produced by nonunion mines in West Virginia and eastern Kentucky. This development produced another transformation of the competitive game played by operators and presented them with a new form of collective action problem.

In the first years after the 1898 joint conference, collective bargaining appeared to have fulfilled its promise. The average value of bituminous coal rose from its lowest point in history – $0.80 per ton in 1898 – to $1.04 in 1900, to $1.12 in 1902, and, in 1903, to its highest level since 1880 – $1.24 per ton (Table 4.3). The apparent strength of coal prices was attributed in part to the agreement with the miners. *Coal Trade Journal* described the price fixing that seemed to complement collective bargaining as the "natural consequence of the uniform mining scale."[53] And, in 1901, an officer of the Illinois Coal Operators Association testified that

severe as we find competition today in the bituminous coal field it has its foundations which it did not have before. The reason for this is plain. Relatively speaking, every operator knows substantially what it costs his rival to produce coal, and hence the selling price is more nearly uniform.[54]

[52]Ibid., 19 (December 4, 1897): 631.
[53]Quoted in Graebner, "Great Expectations," p. 54.
[54]Quoted in ibid.

However, this organization of capitalists by workers did not prove to be as successful as it first appeared. One reason for this lies in the very nature of a collective bargaining agreement as an organizational mechanism. A collective bargaining agreement prevents a firm from reducing its price below its present variable costs by reducing wages, but it does not prevent it from reducing costs in other ways or from accepting a smaller profit margin on each item sold. While it does place a floor on individual price reductions, then, it does not alter the logic of competitive relations which leads firms to lower their prices and their profit margins in order to increase sales and total profits. Nor does it guarantee that demand will be at a level such that individual firms will be able to sell enough goods at the reduced prices to yield a profit. This is especially true when considerable excess capacity exists, as it did in the bituminous coal industry during most of the pre–World War I period. The rise in the price of coal between 1899 and 1903 was accompanied by a 50-percent increase in output (Table 4.1). The underside of this boom was an expansion of capacity which, when production dropped off in 1904, left the industry in the familiar position of "too many mines and too many miners." In most of the major producing states, as Tables 4.1 and 4.2 show, miners in 1904 were producing twice as much coal as they had in 1892, the boom year from the previous decade, but were working several weeks less per year. In 1905, the Geological Survey estimated that bituminous coal capacity was 50 percent above consumption and that, if the industry had not experienced a car shortage, the glut of coal would have demoralized the trade.[55] Conditions improved in 1906, largely due to strikes in both the anthracite and bituminous fields, but the 1907 panic threw the coal industry into a depression that the Geological Survey likened to that of the mid-1890s.[56] Output declined from 395 million to 335 million tons. Ohio, Indiana, and Illinois, which had never fully recovered from the 1904 drop in demand, suffered especially. Beginning in 1910, there was some improvement in conditions, especially in the East, but this improvement was short lived. Production, average value, and working time in all of the major producing states declined sharply in 1914.

A second factor limiting the effectiveness of the organization of capitalist competition in the bituminous coal industry by workers was the particular form that collective bargaining took in the coal industry. In

---

[55]U.S. Geological Survey, *Mineral Resources*, 1905, pp. 516–18.
[56]Ibid., 1908, Part 2, pp. 5–8.

the first place, the Central Competitive Field agreements did not eliminate competitive wage reductions by operators. In theory, they established a differential wage floor that prevented price cutting, but, in
practice, the agreements allowed considerable flexibility to operators in
the determination of their labor costs. Not all types of mine labor were
included in the central- or district-level agreements. Thus, outside day
men, workers who labored above ground, were not covered by the joint
agreements until 1912, and then it was only their percentage increases
that were negotiated by the union, not their base wage rate. Even in
the case of the miners whose basic tonnage rate was included in the
contract, individual operators still possessed a considerable capacity to
reduce real wages through the practice of making deductions from a
miner's pay for dirty coal, supplies, living expenses, etc.[57] As late as
1915, a Kentucky operator wrote to *Coal Age* to complain about operators
who sold coal at a loss, making up for the deficit with sales from their
company commissary.[58] Also, rates for yardage – the cutting of entry
ways and passages – and for dead time – time spent timbering rooms,
laying track, or cleaning coal – were determined largely through individual negotiation.[59]

Second, the system of differentials that was supposed to preserve
competitive equality operated in an extremely haphazard way that was
a function more of the relative strength of different groups of miners
and operators than of any rational calculations of relative production
costs. Thin and thick seam distinctions were often arbitrary, and changes
in freight rates were not necessarily incorporated into wage rates. The
competition among operators which had formerly been carried out
through unilateral wage reductions was now carried out in the arena of
wage negotiations. One writer described the resultant system as "un-
choate – one is tempted to say unprincipled – . . . based on nothing more
defensible than competitive struggle."[60] More recently, it has been described simply as "total chaos."[61]

The most important factor undermining the organization of coal competition by a collective bargaining agreement, however, was another
shift in the structure of the coal market: the rise of nonunion coal pro-

[57]Alexander M. Thompson, *Technology, Labor, and Industrial Structure of the U.S. Coal Industry: An Historical Perspective* (New York: Garland, 1979), pp. 70–1.
[58]*Coal Age* 8 (June 19, 1915): 22.
[59]Lubin, *Miners' Wages*, p. 190; Thompson, *Technology*, p. 131.
[60]Berquist et al., *Economic Survey*, p. 367.
[61]Thompson, *Technology*, pp. 125–6.

duction in the southern Appalachian fields. In the late nineteenth century, when the agreement was first formulated, coal competition operated in an East–West pattern.[62] The major competitive development, we have seen, was the expansion westward of the market for Pennsylvania, and subsequently, Ohio, coals, into the "natural" Illinois and Indiana markets. In 1885, when the movement toward organization began, almost 80 percent of the Appalachian and Eastern Interior coal was produced in the four states that became party to the agreement. However, production in the South, particularly in weakly unionized West Virginia, boomed during the early 1900s. As early as 1896, West Virginia's output had surpassed Ohio's, and, by 1906, West Virginia had taken Illinois's position as the number two coal-producing state in the country. Kentucky was slower to develop into a major producer, but production in eastern Kentucky doubled between 1910 and 1915. At the beginning of World War I, less than two-thirds of the Appalachian and Eastern Interior output came from the Central Competitive Field states. As we saw in Chapter 3, West Virginia and Kentucky coals were directly competitive with Central Competitive Field coal in the tidewater and lake-cargo markets.

The emergence of the southern Appalachian fields transformed the competitive game played by operators into a wage–price game in which the players possess different capacities to select the defection strategy. There are three strategies in this game: (*a*) the cooperative strategy – maintain wages and maintain (at the very least) prices; (*b*) a defection strategy available to both unionized and nonunion firms – maintain the contract wage scale and reduce prices; and (*c*) the dominant strategy – reduce wages below the contract scale and reduce prices. This last strategy is available to the nonunion firms at all times. The union firms can pursue it only by renegotiating the wage differentials with the union.

This situation is slightly different from the typical, two-strategy Prisoner's Dilemma, where the elimination of the dominant defection strategy leaves the players no alternative but to cooperate. In the present game, there are two defection strategies, each of which is more attractive than cooperation. I will analyze this situation as two distinct games: a wage- *and* price-cutting game, and a price-cutting game. To avoid confusion, I will refer to the first game simply as the wage-cutting game. This analytic strategy makes sense because operators perceived themselves to be facing two separate problems. Moreover, the two

[62]Parker, *Coal Industry*, pp. 70–1.

problems did not affect all operators in the same way. Midwestern operators were not so seriously threatened by southern Appalachian coal,
and therefore were more concerned with price cutting than with wage
cutting, which, in their own markets, was effectively controlled by the
joint agreement with the UMWA. For the northern Appalachian operators, however, wage cutting was the principal competitive problem.
Only after they had achieved a cooperative wage level could they be
expected to be worried about price (as opposed to price and wage)
reductions.

The wage-cutting game has been discussed in Chapter 3. While unpunished defection (wage cutting) *would* be the dominant strategy for
all firms, unionized firms are prohibited from selecting that strategy by
their agreement with workers. In this game, we expect the following to
occur. First, the nonunion operators, located primarily in southern West
Virginia and eastern Kentucky, will select their dominant strategy and
press their competitive advantage by reducing wages and prices. The
unionized operators in the Central Competitive Field states will select
their dominant strategy – maintaining the wage levels embodied in their
contracts with the union. The outcome places the latter firms in a disadvantageous position. This position will be least endurable for those
operators whose production costs are relatively high and/or those operators – principally in Pennsylvania and Ohio – whose markets are
most accessible to the West Virginia fields, and who are therefore most
vulnerable to competition from West Virginia.

There are two ways in which this wage game between firms with
different capacities to defect can be transformed. Either cooperating firms
can successfully impose the cooperative strategy on defectors, or they
can win the capacity to defect, themselves. The former course of action
is most attractive because it imposes no additional costs on those firms
presently cooperating and because the alternative – breaking union contracts – is in itself costly and is likely to lead to the suboptimal universal
defection outcome. However, the attractiveness of an effort to impose
cooperation on defecting competitors declines along with its feasibility.
As union strength declines, and as the number of defectors increases,
it is probable that cooperating operators will try to protect themselves
by transforming the game in the other direction – by trying to defect.
The outcome will still be suboptimal, but the payoffs of the former
cooperators will be increased and, of almost equal importance, the payoff
differential between unionized and nonunion firms will be eliminated.
Before turning to the second stage of this game – price cutting among

firms at the same wage level, let us see how the wage-cutting game was played during the pre–World War I period.

Efforts to eliminate competitive wage cutting

Complaints of price cutting in the West Virginia fields began to be voiced less than six months after the 1898 agreement was signed, and continued as a persistent theme in statements by unionized operators.[63] As Table 4.3 indicates, these complaints had a basis in fact. Measured by average value of output, West Virginia coal prices were much lower than those of the other major producing states, although, in heat-producing terms, West Virginia's coal was more valuable to consumers.

The Central Competitive Field operators responded to this situation by urging the UMWA to impose cooperation on the southern Appalachian mines. Not only did these operators support the union's organizing efforts in West Virginia, but they blamed the union severely when these efforts didn't succeed. In the 1898 joint agreement, the miners' union agreed to "afford all possible protection to the trade . . . against any unfair competition," and the operators in subsequent conferences attacked the miners for not living up to the "pledge of 1898."[64] In 1906, when John Mitchell, the President of the UMWA, asked the operators why they did not bring the West Virginia operators to the joint conference, he received the following reply:

Why don't *you* bring them? If it was not for the check-off system granted you by the operators of these four states your organization would not last two years. *We* are giving your organization its strength here today. It is not you, . . . it is the gentlemen seated on *this* side of the hall that are making your organization what it is.[65]

The relationship between the unionized operators and the union was certainly not free of disputes, but it is important to note that in spite of the industry's hard times, operators did not contemplate breaking relations with the union and returning to the situation that existed before 1898. Apparently the level of nonunion defection was not so high as to make the universal defection outcome attractive to unionized firms. As Illinois operators repeated in 1908, "what is needed is not new relations with miners, but some check upon the progressive decline of Illinois

[63]*Black Diamond* 21 (July 23, 1898): 100.
[64]*Coal Age* 23 (January 18, 1923): 116; *Black Diamond* 22 (February 11, 1900): 156; ibid., 44 (March 12, 1910): 25; *Coal Age* 5 (July 26, 1913): 123.
[65]Ibid., 36 (January 27, 1906): 28, emphasis added.

coal prices."[66] It wasn't until 1914 that operators seriously began to attack the check-off, thereby questioning the basic structure of collective bargaining.

As predicted in Chapter 3, nonunion operators resisted unionization. Just as the structure of coal competition led the Central Competitive Field operators into a collective bargaining relationship with the union, it led the nonunion operators of West Virginia and Kentucky to reject a unionization of their mines that would deprive them of the price-cutting weapon that was leading them to dominate the industry and, in the case of the high-cost operators, that was keeping them in the market. The protracted, unsuccessful effort by the UMWA to organize the West Virginia and Kentucky coal fields was the bloodiest struggle in U.S. labor history. Miners had to fight against the state and federal judiciary and state and federal troops, as well as against company-financed private armies and local constabularies. The motives behind operator opposition included a fear that the union would take over the mines and that managerial discretion would be abolished.[67] However, a central theme in the statements of nonunion operators was the perception that unionization would raise their costs to the point that it would be impossible for them to continue to compete successfully against the Central Competitive Field operators. They perceived the unionization drive, and the parallel attempts by northern operators to increase the southern freight rates to northern consuming centers, to be two prongs of a concerted northern attack on their economic survival. They were right. The northern operators clearly supported the UMWA's efforts in West Virginia because they wished to force the southern operators to sell their coal at a higher, cooperative price. Those southern operators who mined in less than ideal conditions were also justifiably afraid that unionization – and universal cooperation – would leave them with negative profits.

Many West Virginia operators feared the union primarily because they saw it as a tool of their northern competitors. "Pennsylvania and Ohio operators are sending the union to action . . . . It is an operators' battle and the miners are being used as tools by the operators in competitive states."

[66] *Black Diamond* 40 (February 8, 1908): 17.
[67] David Alan Corbin, *Life, Work, and Rebellion in the Coal Fields: The Southern West Virginia Miners, 1880–1922* (Urbana: University of Illinois Press, 1981), p. 108.

It is charged by the northern operators that we are a mistake and have no right to an existence – and it is therefore legitimate for our rivals to drive us out of business if they can. The means selected for the accomplishment of this purpose are two-fold: first the pressure on the northern railroads to force exorbitant freight differentials against us; second the coercion of the miners' union to impose labor troubles of such magnitude that our mines cannot be operated successfully.[68]

The editors of *Coal Age* agreed with this assessment.

This unionizing of West Virginia means nothing more nor less than its ruin. . . . A readjustment of the wage would shut down the mines in many districts of the state. The industry is buttressed on the conditions which the Union and the Commerce Commission are trying to remove.[69]

Even in notorious Harlan County, Kentucky, which labor leaders feared to enter as late as the 1930s, the antiunionism of operators can be connected to their conflict with other capitalists.

Handicapped by disadvantageous fixed transportation costs, the [Harlan County] operators fiercely resisted any attempt . . . to achieve an industrywide standard for wages and hours as well. . . . [C]aught in a vise between higher freight rates and standardized wages and hours, the southern coal industry would face liquidation . . . .

The county's disadvantageous competitive position held the key to field-wide labor relations . . . . [T]herein lies most of the explanation for Harlan's vehement antiunionism.[70]

High-cost operators who could not afford to pay "cooperative" wages and prices were joined in their antiunionism by low-cost operators who could do so, but, because their low wages enabled them to undersell their unionized competitors, preferred not to.[71]

Aside from the encouragement that they gave to the UMWA in its efforts to unionize southern Appalachian coal miners, Central Competitive Field operators engaged in two other initiatives whose goal was to organize competition by eliminating the cost advantages enjoyed by operators in West Virginia and eastern Kentucky.

The first of these attempts to adjust perceived interdistrict competitive

[68] An official of the West Virginia Mining Association, quoted in *Coal Age* 3 (September 14, 1912): 361.
[69] *Coal Age* 3 (September 7, 1912): 330.
[70] John W. Hevener, *Which Side Are You On: The Harlan County Miners, 1931–1939* (Urbana: University of Illinois Press, 1978), pp. 8–9, 102–3.
[71] Baratz, *The Union*, pp. 103–4.

imbalances was the uniform mine-safety law movement. The back-ground for this effort was a resurgence of interest in mine-safety leg-islation in each of the major producing states between 1905 and 1911.[72] This legislation, which imposed substantial costs on coal operators, threatened to place further obstacles in the way of achieving competitive equality. "As coal operators competed for access to markets . . . , they were also forced to compete in their state legislatures by opposing safety and health measures which would add significantly to their production costs."[73]

Moreover, the burdens of mine-safety measures were generally great-est in the same states in which the UMWA was strongest, reinforcing the competitive disadvantage produced by wage differentials. If stan-dardized safety legislation could be enacted in all mining states, it would reduce the cost-cutting capacity of southern Appalachian operators. The movement for uniformity enjoyed some early success when, under the leadership of the American Mining Congress and the National Civic Federation, it achieved what William Graebner has described as "virtual uniformity" in workmen's compensation laws, but it ran aground when operators from West Virginia and Ohio failed to participate in a 1916 Uniform Mining Laws Conference.[74]

The other attempt by northern operators to raise the costs of southern competitors consisted of attacks before the Interstate Commerce Com-mission on the structure of coal freight rates, which they alleged were unreasonable and preferential to southern shippers. Beginning in 1909, northern operators competing in the lake, central western, and tidewater markets attempted to raise the costs of their West Virginia competitors to a cooperative level by attacking their low freight rates; which, we have seen, combined with their nonunion wages and the high quality of their coal to allow them to sell coal at prices competitive with operators from mining districts much closer to the markets. These rate controver-sies extended into the 1920s, past the period covered in this chapter, but the basic pattern of conflict was established in the pre–World War I cases.[75]

In each instance, operators from Pennsylvania and/or Ohio appealed

[72]William Graebner, *Coal Mining Safety in the Progressive Period: The Political Economy of Reform* (Lexington: University Press of Kentucky, 1976).
[73]Ibid, pp. 9–10.
[74]Graebner, "Great Expectations," p. 52.
[75]The most important of these cases are listed in the bibliography under "U.S. Interstate Commerce Commission." Also, see Harvey C. Mansfield, *The Lake Cargo Coal Rate Con-troversy* (New York: Columbia University Press, 1932).

to the ICC to reduce the differential between rates from the northern fields and those from the southern West Virginia and eastern Kentucky fields to Lake Erie and East Coast destinations. The latter fields, of course, vigorously resisted such increases, the effect of which would have increased their rates relative to their northern competitors. The lake-cargo cases began in 1901, continued through 1916, then resumed after World War I. In all of these cases, the objective of the Pittsburgh and Ohio complainants was clearly to impose a level of costs on their southern competitors that would, at the least, prevent them from undercutting the northern firms, and, at best, would force them out of the market altogether.

[C]omplainants' principal witness testified that they did not expect to keep West Virginia and Kentucky out of the lake-cargo market even if they secured the proposed differentials but that they undoubtedly could keep them out to an extent, adding "It will be merely a question of confining their growth as closely as we can." Upon cross examination he was asked: "This case then is really a commercial fight by your districts against West Virginia and Kentucky, and is not a rate case, is it?" He replied: "Any rate case I ever heard of was a commercial fight and this is just like the rest of them."[76]

This same basic conflict was repeated in the central western market in 1915 and 1923, when operators from Ohio sought to increase the differential between their freight rates and those from West Virginia to points in Ohio, Indiana, and Michigan; in the tidewater market, where, beginning in 1912, operators from central Pennsylvania and Maryland sought an adjustment in current rates that permitted "unnatural or abnormal competition" from West Virginia operators; and in the New England all-rail market, where, in the mid-1920s, Pennsylvania operators tried to prevent the introduction of through rates from West Virginia and Kentucky that would have greatly reduced the North–South freight differential.

The ICC exercised coercive capacity with respect to freight rates, but only within a relatively narrow range of rates. Consumers wanted the high-quality southern coal, and while the ICC did occasionally intervene on behalf of northern operators to make marginal adjustments in the North–South differential, it clearly lacked the inclination, the legal authority, or the political capacity to set the kind of rates demanded by northern operators – rates that would effectively bar further incursions into their traditional markets.

[76]U.S. Interstate Commerce Commission, *Rates, Charges, Regulations, and Practices Governing Transportation of Anthracite Coal*, 101 ICC 541, 1925.

Internal efforts to eliminate price cutting

It should be recalled that there are two defection strategies in the wage–price competitive game, one involving cost (wage) *and* price cutting, the other involving price cutting alone. So far I have focused on the wage-cutting game, which pitted nonunion firms possessing the capacity to reduce wages against unionized firms lacking this capacity. However, even if the wage-cutting strategy was not available to them, coal operators still faced a pricing Prisoner's Dilemma which generated price cutting and a suboptimal outcome. For operators in Ohio and Pennsylvania who were engaged in competition with nonunion operators from West Virginia, a solution to the pricing game was only meaningful after their principal collective action problem – the wage game – was solved. Operators whose low profits are perceived by them to be the result of a wage differential cannot expect to improve their situation until the wage differential is eliminated. Thus, eliminating price cutting among unionized firms will have a lower priority than eliminating wage cutting by nonunion firms. However, among firms less directly affected by low-wage competition, efforts to organize competition are likely to focus primarily on the elimination of price cutting (as opposed to wage cutting). In fact, as we shall see below, attempts to raise coal prices (again, as opposed to raising wages and costs) were centered principally in the midwestern states, which were least vulnerable to competition from West Virginia and eastern Kentucky. These efforts to organize out of the pricing game constitute another thread running through the history of the pre–World War I coal industry. They took several forms: a combination movement seeking the elimination of competition; informal internal efforts to restrict output and reduce price competition; more formal internal mechanisms, such as open price associations; and finally, efforts to secure federal legislation that would permit and, in some cases, compel operators to observe minimum prices.

During about the first decade of the twentieth century, the bituminous coal industry experienced a merger wave of sorts which paralleled developments in other sectors of the economy in its aspirations, but fell short in its achievements.[77] In 1899, *Mineral Industry* noted a "consid-

[77]Even before this period some major consolidations had occurred in the Pittsburgh district. In 1889, 104 operators combined into the Pittsburgh Coal Company, and another group of Pittsburgh-area firms joined to form the Monongahela River Consolidated Coal and Coke Company. In both cases, price increases of over 35 percent immediately followed consolidation (*Mineral Industry* 8 [1900]: 115–16).

erable tendency toward consolidation of interests."[78] Consolidation continued to be "evident" from 1901 to 1903.[79] The peak year appears to
have been 1905, when the Geological Survey was moved for the only
time to include a brief report on coal consolidations in its annual survey
of the industry. In that year, at least four major consolidations took place
in Illinois; there were five major consolidations in Indiana, where *Black
Diamond* observed that six or seven companies now controlled seventy-
nine previously independent mines; and important consolidations also
occurred in Ohio and West Virginia.[80] Regular reports of the formation
of large coal combinations continued from 1906 through 1910.[81] Between
1909 and 1911, J. P. Morgan was asked to undertake a massive consolidation scheme whose object was to create a midwestern coal trust in
the mold of U.S. Steel and Standard Oil, but the project failed to win
Morgan's support.[82]

As Chapter 3 has already indicated, this consolidation activity, which
was aimed at achieving price stability and restricting competition, had
little impact on the industry's market structure. Doubtless, some major
new firms did emerge, but, in most cases, they lacked the economic
power to dominate the markets in which they competed. Combination
continued to be a byword among some coal-industry spokesmen after
1910, but a few years of experience led most operators to adopt the view
articulated by one of their Ohio colleagues:

The last word in modern industrial life is "consolidation," but it is hopeless to
rely on any unifying system which does not bind the coal trade of all the states
in one, for the price cannot be raised in one district without the loss of entire
markets to another.[83]

The informal internal efforts to organize competition, reflected in the
exhortations of the trade journals, continued throughout the pre–World
War I period. The most persistent suggestion was to restrict output. In
1905, noting the demoralization of Illinois, Indiana, and Ohio prices,
Black Diamond told operators that "measures should be taken to coun-
teract the tendency to overproduction or the result will be drastic."

[78]Ibid., 8 (1900): 115–16.
[79]Ibid., 14 (1906): 75.
[80]U.S. Geological Survey, *Mineral Resources*, 1905, pp. 505–6; *Black Diamond* 34 (January 7,
    1905): 25; *Mineral Industry* 14 (1906): 83, 92.
[81]*Mineral Industry* 15 (1907): 131; *Black Diamond* 36 (February 10, 1906): 25; *Black Diamond*
    38 (April 6, 1907): 23; *Black Diamond* 40 (February 15, 1908): 17; *Black Diamond* 42 (February
    13, 1909): 16.
[82]Graebner, "Great Expectations," pp. 59–61.
[83]*Coal Age* 3 (August 2, 1912): 141.

The constant tendency to overproduce coal strikes us as extremely bad policy and our advice is that the operator get in touch with the market conditions and then shape his production to meet the exact needs of the consumers.[84]

While it attacked the illness – overproduction – *Black Diamond* also attacked the symptom – price cutting, criticizing operators for allowing competition to be carried out solely on the basis of price.

When coal men go to war, using cut prices as weapons, . . . it is a return to primitive conditions, where an existing overlord denies to all others the right to encroachments upon his domain . . . . Any battle waged with cut prices as a weapon does not result in the survival of the fittest; it terminates only in the victory of the man with the longest purse . . . . Reduced to its essence it is a question of savage retaliation, cloaking what seems to be a determination to protect a sacred property interest but really covering the barbarian principle of rule or ruin.[85]

Six months later, the same publication likened competition to a children's game whose object was to dislodge opponents from the corner of a room. Capitalists who cut prices were not playing the game fairly.

If one takes business away from another by cutting the price, there is not le-gitimate extraction; that simply is a matter of buying the other man's trade. We all have our price, you know, and any man can buy another man's trade if one only has money enough to keep up the spending. Giving a man a dollar to get him to shove another man out of the corner that you may slide in is not playing the game right.[86]

These exhortations did not have the desired effect, of course, and at the end of 1914, *Black Diamond* was repeating the familiar refrain.

For the last five or six years particularly, the bituminous coal trade has been calling attention at regular intervals to the deplorable state of disorganization into which the whole industry has fallen. . . . It is significant that almost the same identical conclusion has been reached . . . that the trade has been demoralized and made unprofitable by competitive tactics which are neither good business nor sane economy.[87]

Beginning in 1905, operators in the Midwest sought to move from informal exhortations to a more formal form of cooperation – a na-tional association of coal operators which would then form a joint tribunal with the miners' union.[88] The association would provide a

[84]*Black Diamond* 34 (January 14, 1905): 71; also see ibid., 41 (October 31, 1908): 20; and ibid., 45 (October 1, 1910): 25.
[85]Ibid., 42 (February 13, 1909): 21.
[86]Ibid., 45 (August 13, 1910): 20.
[87]Ibid., 53 (November 14, 1914): 383.
[88]Ibid., 35 (November 25, 1905): 26–8.

forum for the education of operators on conditions in the industry and through which an ongoing connection with the mine workers could be maintained. Proposals of this nature, which surfaced several times between 1905 and 1915, had a dual appeal; they attacked *both* defection strategies – cost cutting and price cutting.[89] However, the movement to establish such an association had no appeal for eastern operators. West Virginia operators were worried that participation in such a movement would constitute the first step toward unionization, while Pittsburgh and Ohio operators interpreted it as an effort to raise their own cost of production so as to benefit operators in Illinois.[90]

Appeals to the state to eliminate price cutting

Collective bargaining effectively eliminated wage cutting as a competitive weapon among unionized operators, but neither the joint agreement with the miners nor the various internal efforts discussed above succeeded in preventing self-destructive price cutting. The problem became worse in the wake of the panic of 1907, which increased the imbalance between capacity and demand, and put further pressure on operators to cut prices. Having failed to organize competition through internal and private external means, coal operators began to turn to the state.

Initially, they sought a passive state role. They wanted the government's antitrust policy to be modified so as to permit more formalized voluntary cooperation. *Black Diamond* argued repeatedly that the natural resource industries should receive special treatment in the government's system of trade regulation and that capitalists in these industries should be allowed to cooperate under government supervision so that they could combat the "predatory" tactics of large buyers and maintain a reasonable price level.[91] Unmodified, it was claimed, the Sherman Act will produce monopoly.

A system which seeks to procure the destruction, through excessive competition, of struggling young businesses can result only in one thing – the survival of the fittest. That is, in the destruction of all but the fittest some of the really fit are killed off.[92]

[89]Ibid., 44 (January 29, 1910): 221; Graebner, "Great Expectations," p. 56.
[90]Graebner, "Great Expectations," pp. 54–6.
[91]*Black Diamond*, 44 (May 21, 1910): 21.
[92]Ibid., 52 (June 13, 1914): 494.

In 1910 and 1911, there were several proposals to amend the Sherman Act so as to permit cooperation among coal operators.[93] Some operators called for the establishment of a federal commission, modeled on the Interstate Commerce Commission, that would set minimum and maximum prices and would sanction any trade agreements and joint selling arrangements that did not unreasonably restrict competition.[94] One Illinois advocate of such a plan pleaded that "we cannot continue as we are, we must be allowed to combine. If we are not allowed to combine the ruinous competition in which we are engaged will wipe the industry out of existence."[95] Although most proposals for legislation on the part of coal operators implied that the state would sanction agreements initiated and entered into voluntarily by operators, this was not always the case. Carl Schotz, the President of the American Mining Congress, urged that operators "be permitted, and perhaps *required to cooperate* in the sale of their coal" so that "a price be obtained . . . that would enable them to pay proper wages and still realize a profit on their investments."[96] And, when operators responded to a *Coal Age* survey on how to improve the coal industry, many of them submitted suggestions whose implementation required more than a passive state role. One operator proposed a government commission that would set the price of coal in every district and ensure a fair profit on every ton mined. Another would have granted a national commission power over output, prices, and distribution. A third would simply "get rid of the coal operators who insist on running their mines regardless of the price of coal in the market."[97]

The 1914 Federal Trade Commission Act was viewed by coal operators as the answer to their prayers. Although they did not succeed in their attempts to insert special amendments relating to the coal industry, they still believed that the Federal Trade Commission (FTC) would help them circumvent antitrust prohibitions. *Black Diamond's* prophecy was that the FTC would "sit . . . as an editor of the plans of business," reviewing them and "intimating" any of their illegal aspects before they were implemented.[98] *Coal Age* looked to the FTC to conduct a study of the bituminous coal industry "which, it is predicted, will lead to the tacit

[93]*Mineral Industry* 19 (1911): 1,105.
[94]*Coal Age* 1 (November 4, 1911): 109; ibid., 1 (November 11, 1911): 143–4; ibid., 1 (December 2, 1911): ibid., 1 (July, 1911): 15.
[95]Ibid., 1 (November 11, 1911): 144.
[96]*Coal Age* 6 (November 14, 1914): 798–9, emphasis added.
[97]Ibid., 10 (September 23, 1916): 505–6.
[98]*Black Diamond* 53 (December 19, 1914): 503.

or open sanctioning of suitable working agreements."[99] The beleaguered operators of Illinois and Indiana, represented by their respective state-wide associations, drafted an appeal to President Wilson, describing the ruinous competition characteristic of the midwestern coal industry and seeking his assistance in transforming the FTC into an instrument that could organize it. Coal operators, they said, "with the stringent antitrust laws . . . confronting them, . . . have not organized their business as many other industries have done." They "would not object to, but on the contrary, would welcome" FTC "supervision" of remedial plans worked out "through the agency of this commission, or upon the sanctioned initiative of the operators themselves."[100]

The Federal Trade Commission did not take the active role that midwestern operators wished on it. Nevertheless, the permissive attitude of Commissioner Edward Hurley to the plight of coal operators did lead them to pursue their cooperative efforts in a more formal manner. Operator associations were not new to the coal industry. They had been formed in many districts for collective bargaining purposes. But, in 1915 and 1916, these associations increasingly devoted themselves to open-price type activities designed to facilitate cooperation among operators. This was especially true in the Midwest, a fact which, in *Coal Age's* words, "was not by chance." "It was rather because of a competitive pressure from without so intense as to evoke an appeal for government intervention."[101] In 1915, operators in Illinois, under the benign eye of Commissioner Hurley, began organizing joint selling plans and open-price associations.[102] By the end of 1916, such associations had spread to almost every producing district.[103] However, Hurley's friendly attitude toward such ventures was not shared by his colleagues in the FTC and the Department of Justice. The latter agency investigated several associations in 1917 and 1918, and although no indictments were handed down, their questionable legality was clearly signaled.[104] By this time, however, the increase in the demand for coal produced by World War I had effected another transformation of the competitive game played by operators.

[99]*Coal Age* 6 (November 21, 1914): 844.
[100]*Black Diamond* 53 (December 19, 1914): 504–7.
[101]Ibid., 21 (February 16, 1922): 276.
[102]Johnson, *Politics*, pp. 29–31; *Coal Age* 7 (May 15, 1915): 865; ibid., 8 (November 6, 1915): 758; ibid., 10 (July 29, 1916): 189; *Black Diamond* 53 (November 28, 1914): 432.
[103]Graebner, "Great Expectations," pp. 63–4
[104]Ibid., pp. 68–9.

Conclusion

The premise of this chapter is that the behavior of individual capitalist firms can be understood as a rational response to strategic situations generated by capitalist relations of production. Firms select their best strategies *within* competitive games, and depending upon the outcomes and their evaluation of the outcomes, they may attempt to transform their competitive games.

During the 1880–1914 period, coal operators faced three distinct competitive games – a wage–price-cutting game produced by the "nationalization" of the coal market during the late 1880s; a wage-cutting game played among firms with different capacities to defect, generated by the development of a nonunion coal industry in the fields of southern West Virginia and eastern Kentucky; and a price-cutting game, played by operators who did not possess the capacity to reduce wages.

Within each game, coal operators behaved as we would expect them to. In the first game, their dominant strategy was to reduce wages and prices, and that is what they did. In the second game, firms again selected their dominant strategy, either high wages or low wages, depending upon whether they were unionized or not. And in the final price-cutting game, midwestern firms adopted their dominant price-cutting strategy.

A critical part of the argument so far has been the claim not only that firms would behave rationally within their competitive games, but that they would sometimes attempt to transform these games, and that it is possible to predict under which conditions that would occur. Here, our results are more ambiguous, in part because of the lack of firm-level data, both with regard to cost factors and so on, and with regard to behavior. In the first game, we predicted that efforts to reorganize the market would be led by operators from Ohio and the midwestern states of Illinois and Indiana. This appears to have been the case. In any event, Illinois operators were extremely prominent in the joint-conference movement. Our analysis of the overlapping wage-cutting and price-cutting game that structured the market in the early twentieth century led us, first, to suggest that unionized operators would seek to transform the game by raising the costs of their competitors; and, second, that the nonunion southern Appalachian firms would resist any further reorganization of the market. These hypotheses were confirmed by the data. We also suggested that the midwestern operators would be more interested in the price game than the wage game, and, in fact, it appears that most efforts to raise prices originated in Illinois and Indiana.

The analysis of the costs of market organization presented in Chapter 2 imply that attempts at market organization will begin with low-cost internal mechanisms, before proceeding to high-cost external and public mechanisms. Historical developments in the coal industry support this view. The initial attempts by operators to organize competition involved voluntary, internal means. It was only after the failure (a failure, by the way, that could be predicted from our previous analysis of the impact of market structure on cooperation in the Prisoner's Dilemma) that operators turned to external actors – the UMWA and coal-carrying railroads – and eventually to the state.

The most interesting findings of this analysis concern the pattern of labor relations in the coal industry. Here, the general deductive model has been greatly enriched by our attention to the coal industry, with its cost structure weighted toward labor costs and with competitive strategy consequently weighted toward wage cutting.

Because our general model directed our attention toward the competitive relations among individual capitalists, we were able to see how this aspect of capitalist relations of production – capital versus capital conflict rather than labor versus capital conflict – structured labor relations in the coal industry. While the formation of a national union of mine workers can only be credited to the struggle of miners, a struggle that often pitted them against capitalists, their achievement of an agreement with operators was motivated on the operators' side not by an unfavorable balance of forces with respect to workers, but by their desire to limit self-destructive wage and price cutting. Capitalists allied with workers in order to protect themselves against their own rational behavior. In 1898, operators agreed to strengthen the union by granting an eight-hour day and a wages–dues check-off in order to further the same goal. Within the unionized sector of the industry, the disputes between operators and workers that surfaced during wage negotiations were more often than not extensions of disputes among operators over the wage- differential system that cemented the different fields together. Operators agreed or refused to agree with workers in order to press their own competitive advantages or to eliminate those enjoyed by competitors. The bloody struggle to organize the West Virginia coal fields was, indeed, at one level, a struggle on the part of workers to deprive capitalists of some of their control over the production process. However, it was also part of a struggle to organize capitalists that was carried out by a set of firms who could not defect, in alliance with their unionized workers, against another set of firms who were unable or unwilling to cooperate.

The importance of the competitive relations among capitalists in structuring relations between capitalists and workers and, increasingly, between capitalists and the state, will continue to be driven home by the events of the 1920s and 1930s. Before we turn to this period, however, we must examine the impact of the World War I coal boom and the shortages it produced on the structure of coal competition and the behavior of operators.

5. The coal industry on the defensive: 1916–1922

Introduction

On the eve of World War I, bituminous coal operators, frustrated at continued low coal prices and their inability to reorganize the market so as to eliminate them, began to solicit state intervention. In 1915, they called for the establishment of a government commission to oversee cooperation in their industry. In their memorial to President Wilson, we have seen, the Indiana and Illinois operators "welcomed" publicity and supervision by the government. Five years later, this position was entirely reversed. In 1920 the National Coal Association, an organization of operators, went on record as being "unalterably opposed to the enactment of any legislation imposing additional regulation upon commerce and industry and as especially opposed to legislation which singles out any one industry for regulation by special commission."[1] A year later the same organization denounced a mild legislative proposal designed to secure data from operators as an attempt "ultimately to control every phase of the industry."[2]

In this chapter, I argue that the changed attitude of operators toward state intervention was the product of a change in the structure of their competitive game. The altered game generated different competitive behavior *within* the game, a different outcome, and different responses on the part of operators to that outcome. Factors on both the "demand" side and the "supply" side of regulation were involved. First, between 1916 and 1920, the sharp rise in the demand for coal produced by World War I and by the postwar industrial boom, along with temporary shortages caused by transportation problems and strikes, completely changed the competitive situation faced by bituminous coal operators. Because they could sell as much coal as they could produce and transport, operators no longer had any incentive to cut prices. Second, high coal prices and the experience of government regulation during the war transformed the political context of coal competition. In 1915, when the basic

[1] *Coal Age* 17 (June 3, 1920): 1,163.
[2] Ibid., 19 (June 23, 1921): 1,133.

model of federal regulation was the Interstate Commerce Commission, regulation was viewed by many operators as a benign prospect. In terms of the discussion presented in Chapter 2, the costs of state-enforced market organization were relatively low. This was no longer the case in 1920. Consumers who experienced a 500-percent increase in coal prices between 1915 and 1920 clamored for their own version of state-enforced coal market organization, one that would impose *maximum* rather than minimum coal prices. Moreover, the operators of 1920, unlike the operators of 1915, had had direct experience with government regulation, and possessed a greater appreciation of their vulnerability to hostile interests under such an arrangement. In short, while the transformation of their competitive game reduced their need for state intervention, the changed political context increased the perceived costs of state intervention. The result was an about-face in operator attitudes toward the state.

The World War I coal boom and the transformation of the competitive game

In late 1916, the increased industrial demand generated by the war finally caught up with the coal industry, leading eventually to another shift in the competitive game played by operators. Whereas before, operators had faced a pricing Prisoner's Dilemma in which the dominant defection strategy was to raise prices, bringing about suboptimally low profits, the defection strategy in the new game was to *raise* prices. The suboptimal consequence was a price level that might lead a hostile public to turn to the government to curtail perceived price gouging and profiteering.

Coal output in 1916 was at the highest level ever, and was exceeded in each of the two subsequent years. Production kept pace with demand through most of 1916, but, in the fall, a fear of a coal shortage and a shortage of railroad cars to transport coal led to a rush of buying that caused average spot prices to increase from $1.30 in August to $4.01 in December.[3] The extraordinary demand continued through the early months of 1917, increasing in April, when the United States entered the war.[4] Average spot prices peaked in February at $4.18, almost 300 per-

[3]U.S. Geological Survey, *Mineral Resources*, 1916, Part 2, pp. 902–3; ibid., 1922, Part 2, p. 554.
[4]Ibid., 1917, Part 2, pp. 904–11.

cent above their level twelve months earlier.[5] The increase in demand was aggravated by distribution problems, as increased shipments of other freight tended to push coal cars onto railroad sidings, where their cargo languished. Production stoppages attributable to car shortages increased from 6.8 percent to 30.0 percent of all stoppages. By October, consumers, worrying about their winter coal supplies and able to acquire enough coal only for their immediate needs, began to panic, demanding more coal than they needed in order to guard against future shortages. The result was a full-fledged coal shortage in the Northeast.[6] By the spring of 1918, government control over prices and distribution had restored a degree of stability to the coal market. However, while demand dropped off during the latter half of the year, production reached record levels in all of the major producing states.

Producing at capacity for consumers who couldn't buy enough coal, operators could increase profits most effectively by *increasing* prices. The collective action problem that had plagued them for thirty years was resolved willy-nilly "from above." There was a catch, however. High prices were certainly good for operators in the short run, but what if they generated dissatisfaction from consumers? It was conceivable, especially after the war, that consumer unhappiness would be translated into a government regulatory policy that would place lasting limits on operator autonomy and profitability. If operators could cooperate by keeping prices at a relatively low level, short-run profits might suffer, but the low prices would mollify the public and long-run profitability could be protected. This is a version of the intertemporal Prisoner's Dilemma discussed in Chapter 1, in which the optimal outcome is *long-term* high profits. Price gouging is the dominant strategy, since each firm can always win more profits in the short term in this market by raising prices. However, if all firms choose that strategy, they are likely to produce a demand from consumers for a form of government intervention that will limit their capacity to win high profits in the long run.

This situation differs from earlier competitive games in more respects than the labeling of the strategies. In their former pricing games, state compulsion was a *solution* to the problem of low profits. In this new game, it is not high prices, per se, but the possibility of resultant state intervention that is to be avoided. By definition, this problem cannot therefore be resolved by state intervention. State intervention *is* the

[5]Ibid., 1922, Part 2, p. 554.
[6]Ibid., 1917, Part 2, pp. 904–11; ibid., 1921, Part 2, pp. 451–3.

problem. Coal operators pursued a two-pronged effort to avoid state-enforced market organization. First, they tried, through voluntary means, to restrain themselves regarding the pricing of coal. Second, they dogmatically opposed any legislative initiative that at all limited their autonomy.

World War I regulation

The setting for the initial efforts of operators to keep prices at a reasonable level was the Committee on Coal Production, one of several industrial self-government committees formed under the auspices of a Cabinet-level Council of National Defense to promote the wartime mobilization of industry.[7] This committee was organized in May, 1917, and was headed by Francis S. Peabody, a prominent Illinois operator. Peabody's principal mandate was to increase production and improve distribution, but his attention was almost immediately turned to the question of prices. With the price of coal rising rapidly and with some consuming areas experiencing a shortage, coal operators came under increasing attack, both in and out of Congress. The month of June saw Senator Pomerene of Ohio introduce a bill that would give the president the power to fix coal prices and to take over the distribution of coal; as well as the publication of an FTC report on the bituminous coal shortage, which recommended that the production and distribution of coal and coke be placed under the control of a government agency.[8] On June 26, a meeting of representatives of the various coal fields convened in Washington to consider the situation. After receiving the go-ahead from the administration to set maximum coal prices, the operators agreed to set a maximum price of $3.00 per ton for mine-run coal in most of the major producing areas.[9] According to *Coal Age*, average spot prices during the month of June had been $4.00.[10] Most operators viewed this reduction as a considerable concession, but consumers and liberal politicians, mindful of the $1.26 average spot price of June, 1916, believed that they were excessively high. Secretary of the Navy Newton Baker immediately denounced the new prices as "exorbitant, unjust, and oppressive."[11] Meanwhile, the Senate Committee on Interstate Commerce began hear-

---

[7]Johnson, *Politics*, pp. 34–43.
[8]*Coal Age* 11 (June 23, 1917): 1,094.
[9]U.S. Geological Survey, *Mineral Resources*, 1918, Part 2, pp. 24–6.
[10]Ibid., 1922, Part 2, p. 554.
[11]*Coal Age*, 15 (January 30, 1919): 228.

ings on the Pomerene Bill, which was being considered as an amendment to the Lever Act, a measure designed to give the government authority to control the production and distribution of basic commodities during the wartime emergency period. *Coal Age* was justifiably worried: "The hearing develops the fact that members of the committee are not strongly averse to Government operation of the coal mines."[12]

The industry's fears were soon realized. In early August the Lever Act, along with the Pomerene Amendment, became law, empowering the president to set coal prices, to license operators, to force sales through a government- controlled pool, and to requisition the businesses of those firms who conduct their operations "in a manner prejudicial to the public interest."[13] President Wilson elected to use this new power to create a Fuel Administration, headed by Harry Garfield. Coal operations were to be left in private hands, but state power would be exercised over pricing and distribution.

The appointment of Garfield was preceded by Wilson's announcement of a revised price list that reduced the previous maximum price by one-third. These prices, in the words of *Coal Age*, "plunged the industry into the 'Slough of Despond.' A pall of uncertainty and foreboding hangs over the industry."[14] It feared that the new prices

will inevitably drive all but the larger and more efficient mines upon the rocks of bankruptcy. . . . The survival of the fittest has never been a satisfactory proposition when viewed from any other standpoint than that of the fittest. And there are not enough mines of the "fittest" class to produce the nation's coal.[15]

In fact, the Wilson prices failed to stimulate the desired level of production, and although prices were raised by $0.45 per ton in October to accommodate a new wage contract, production continued to lag behind demand through the fall of 1917. The coal shortage was compounded by railroad-car shortages in almost every producing district. When the winter of 1917–1918 brought unprecedented cold weather, consuming areas in the Northeast faced a serious coal famine.[16]

The government responded in two ways. On December 26, 1917, President Wilson announced that the state was assuming control over the railroads. Meanwhile, Fuel Administrator Garfield implemented a massive coal-conservation program, which culminated in January, when

[12]Ibid., 12 (July 14, 1917): 66.
[13]Johnson, *The Politics of Soft Coal* (Urbana: University of Illinois Press, 1979), p. 53.
[14]*Coal Age* 12 (September 1, 1917): 376.
[15]Ibid.
[16]Ibid., 15 (January 30, 1919): 228.

he ordered all businesses to close for a five-day period, and then to cease operations on every Monday for the duration of the winter.[17]

In the spring of 1918, the government's coal policy shifted from confrontation with operators to cooperation with them. Apparently, its experience during the fall and winter of 1917–1918 had convinced the administration that a policy built upon an attack on profiteering and the imposition of maximum prices was not achieving its goal of spurring output and improving distribution. By the end of the war, the government's friendlier stance toward operators, as well as the higher profits that it generated, led to a grudging acknowledgment from operators that state intervention could work. It did not eliminate their distrust of the state, however.

The shift in policy was signaled in late March, when Garfield began to shift his attention from prices to distribution. He announced a zoning plan that would force consumers to use coal from nearby producing districts.[18] This plan was accompanied by a new pricing policy, by which each district's prices were to be determined by the average costs of producing the "bulk" of its output. This allowed all but the highest-cost operations to enjoy a healthy profit.[19] Not only did the new policy provide more profits for operators, but it brought them into active cooperation with government officials, as local trade associations assisted in implementing the new distribution policy, serving as semiofficial agencies.[20] Not surprisingly, operators began to warm to the new approach.

Gradually the truth was borne in upon interested parties that the coal industry was being organized as it never was organized before. Many there were who believed that the production and distribution of the nation's entire coal output could not be systematized, but the Fuel Administration staff, under Dr. Garfield, was accomplishing the seemingly impossible.[21]

The threat of another shortage in the winter of 1918–1919 persisted, however, and in July the fuel administrator organized a Production Bureau to stimulate output. A month later, the Department of Labor, as part of an effort to keep mine workers from taking advantage of the higher wages offered in other industries and in order to combat the

[17]Ibid., pp. 227–8.
[18]Ibid., p. 229.
[19]Johnson, *Politics*, pp. 84–6.
[20]Ibid., pp. 73–4.
[21]*Coal Age* 15 (January 30, 1919): 230.

acute labor shortage suffered by many districts, classified coal mining as war work.[22]

As winter approached, Garfield seemed to have won over bituminous coal operators to his version of a state-organized coal industry. *Coal Age* wrote that "Even the most carping critic was forced to admit that the Fuel Administration had amply justified its reason for being . . . . In the face of apparently insurmountable obstacles and scathing sarcasm from many quarters Dr. Garfield and his assistant had labored steadily until chaos had given way to order."[23]

The postwar coal boom and the hostile state

We have seen how the World War I industrial boom transformed the economic context of coal competition and reduced the organizational need of coal operators. The political context of the industry also changed. This is already evident from our survey of coal policy during the war. Long accustomed to an absence of state intervention in their industry (with the notable exception of repression during strikes), operators suddenly found themselves in the middle of a debate about coal policy. Given the importance of coal in the economy and the fact of shortages and skyrocketing prices, it was scarcely surprising that the "public" character of coal production should be recognized.

However, it was not only the fact of a debate over coal policy but the tone of this debate that was decisive in shaping the attitude of operators toward state intervention. The high prices and distribution problems that had generated such public outrage at the onset of the war persisted in the immediate postwar years. Although demand for coal decreased slightly during the beginning of 1919, after the record levels of the previous year, a strike threat in November gave added impetus to both demand and production.[24] Whatever slackness the coal market showed in 1919 was eliminated in early 1920, as a postwar industrial boom caused production to approach the 1918 level and, when price controls were removed in April, led prices to skyrocket. In August, the average spot price of bituminous coal reached $9.51.[25] The spurt in industrial activity began to end in late 1920, and coal consumption was down 24 percent in 1921. According to one publication, the increased competition for the

[22]Ibid., 14 (August 15, 1918): 322.
[23]Ibid., 15 (January 30, 1919): 231.
[24]U.S. Geological Survey, *Mineral Resources*, 1921, Part 2, pp. 451–3.
[25]Ibid., 1922, Part 2, 554.

shrinking pie "threatened to upset all traditions of the trade."[26] This augured ill for the industry, whose numbers were greatly augmented by entry in recent years, particularly in 1920. However, major strikes in both the bituminous and anthracite fields reinforced the boom/bust pattern of the industry, bolstering the relative power of sellers and supporting a continued high price level.

Consumers blamed the high coal prices on the greed of operators. The bituminous coal industry's sister industry – anthracite – was clearly and correctly perceived by the public to be a combination controlled by a few railroad companies, and consumers who felt equally victimized by high anthracite prices and high bituminous coal prices suspected that a handful of "coal barons" was at fault in both cases. Even observers who had a clearer understanding of the coal situation began to lose faith in the ability of the operators to meet the basic coal needs of the nation under a system of relatively unrestricted private ownership. A 1919 proposal by the United Mine Workers that the coal mines of the United States be nationalized was not as divorced from mainstream political debate as it would have been seventy years later. As Coal Age noted, "The spirit of our national as well as state and local legislators is not any too friendly to the coal industry just now."[27] In July, 1920, Coal Age reported that "disinterested economists" saw the coal industry as "moving rapidly toward out-and-out classification as a public utility."[28] A few weeks later there were rumors that the wartime powers granted by the Lever Act would be invoked, prompting Coal Age to note that the industry is "struggling hard to justify its existence as private enterprise."[29] In September, "representatives of the coal operators were frankly expressing fear of the nationalization of the country's coal mines."[30]

It is idle to pass lightly over the evident signs of danger threatening the political and economic freedom of the coal industry. The storm signals have been displayed and all have been warned that when Congress assembles in December the coal troubles of the nation will be aired in a way that will not help the industry.[31]

George Cushing, the managing director of the Wholesale Coal Association, began plans to undertake a national speaking tour to warn the

[26]Mineral Industry 30 (1922): 97–122.
[27]Coal Age, 17 (April 22, 1920): 789.
[28]Ibid., 18 (July 29, 1920): 252.
[29]Ibid., 18 (August 12, 1920): 322.
[30]Ibid., 18 (September 9, 1920).
[31]Ibid., 18 (October 21, 1920): 835.

public against the nationalization of the coal industry, which he viewed as imminent.[32] And in late 1920 the editors of *Coal Age* received a notice from a civic and oratorical league representing twelve midwestern colleges which proposed to debate the proposition that "the United States should own and operate the coal mines."[33]

The fear of operators had more concrete foci, however. In August, 1920, the state of Indiana enacted a law establishing a commission to set the price of coal, and empowering the governor to confiscate the mines of any uncooperative operators. The operators won an injunction against the law at the end of November, about a month after the first price list was published, but still, there was a justifiable feeling among operators that the "spread of the Indiana idea . . . is certain to result in a national feeling that better than that were national control."[34] The general suspicion of coal operators also emerged in a federal grand jury indictment, returned in February, 1921, of 226 Indiana coal operations, the National Coal Association, and the principal officers of the United Mine Workers of America. This remarkable document not only alleges that the operators, through their trade association, engaged in the traditional antitrust violations, but also that the joint conferences between mine workers and operators constituted agreements between both parties to increase wages, increase prices, and to create shortages. The miners and operators were charged, according to *Coal Age*, with agreeing "that the miners and the operators were partners in mining, producing, and distributing coal."

It is charged that the agreements entered into between the miners and operators provided that coal should not be sold at any time for a price that did not yield a profit to the operator; that increases of wages to miners should be added to the price of coal; that the competition among operators should be eliminated; that no coal should be sold below cost of production and that the means of increasing cost and production in the price of coal should be by closing and keeping idle the coal mines.[35]

The operators were also accused of refusing to collect penalties from the mine workers for wildcat strikes, thereby encouraging strikes, and contributing to the production of shortages and consequent high prices.[36]

Times clearly had changed since 1915, when operators from Indiana

[32]Ibid., 18 (September 2, 1920): 5–7.
[33]Ibid., 18 (December 9, 1920): 1,171.
[34]Ibid., 18 (July 22, 1920): 188; ibid., 18 (August 19, 1920): 414; ibid., 18 (October 21, 1920): 864; ibid., 18 (December 2, 1920): 1,155; ibid., 18 (October 21, 1920): 835.
[35]Ibid., 19 (March 3, 1921): 420.
[36]Ibid.

and Illinois had formally requested federal government intervention to regulate coal prices. Now, the state of Indiana *was* regulating coal prices, but to what effect! The costs of state intervention had escalated, and the willingness of operators to incur those costs had declined accordingly. The common interest of operators was now to avoid state intervention and, as they had earlier, they tried to do so with a dual strategy of attempting to moderate their prices and by vigorously resisting all state initiatives.

Once again, then, we find spokespersons for the coal industry urging operators to keep prices low and to improve distribution. The editors of *Coal Age* wrote that "in the long run coal men will injure themselves most by charging outrageous prices and are certainly inviting early trouble by permitting such practices as overshipping on permits and abusing every privilege given them by the government."[37] A leading coal retailer, J. E. Lloyd, warned that unless distribution was improved and unless a plan was worked out "to prevent a repetition of recent price evils, . . . a public clamor through the press will force the government to take drastic action . . . . "

Must we admit our failure as practical business men and allow the government to step in and manage the coal business for us? [The coal trade] is in the shadow of at least some kind of government supervision, if not . . . government control [because of certain] selfish interests.[38]

In October, 1920, the efforts of coal operators to keep prices down took a more definite shape when Attorney-General Palmer requested that they take up the question of fair prices at the National Coal Association's annual meeting. The participants resolved that where "unreasonably high prices" and "unwise practices" existed in the industry, they should be "eliminated"; and toward that end, each district should establish fair-price or fair-practice committees which would cooperate with the Department of Justice. Apparently, such committees were established in most producing fields.[39]

The second aspect of operator strategy during this period was to oppose all proposals that would impose any form of government regulation on the coal industry. They had several opportunities between 1920 and 1922 to put this position into practice. During the winter of 1919–1920,

---

[37]Ibid., 18 (October 21, 1920): 836.
[38]Ibid., 19 (January 20, 1921): 109.
[39]Ibid., 18 (October 21, 1920): 867; ibid., 18 (October 28, 1920): 915; ibid., 19 (November 4, 1920): 963.

a subcommittee of the Senate Committee on Interstate Commerce headed by Senator Joseph Frelinghuysen conducted hearings on coal prices. The outcome was two legislative proposals – a bill to impose seasonal freight rates to stimulate off-season production, and a bill that would establish a fact-finding commission to evaluate the industry.[40] The reactions of operators to the freight-rate bill, which would reduce summer rates and raise winter ones, varied according to their immediate interests. Apparently, shortage conditions led a number of operators to change from "warm advocates" to "vigorous opponents" as they saw an opportunity to exploit seasonal disjunctions in supply and win large profits. It was also opposed by operators from Ohio, who feared that it would stimulate long-haul traffic and damage their competitive position.[41] The commission bill found few friends among operators.

The coal industry sees it as an opening wedge for Federal interference with the coal business, and we have no doubt that once such a commission were in action there would be increasing meddling with the coal industry, not all of which would be harmful, but some of which would be distasteful to coal men.[42]

These first Frelinghuysen bills died a quiet death.

It was similar fact-finding proposals, however, that were the major stake in the conflict over postwar coal industry regulation. During the war, the Federal Trade Commission had collected data on costs and prices. However, in 1920, the National Coal Association, in *Maynard Coal Co. vs. FTC*, succeeded in challenging the FTC's legal authority to collect such data on anything other than a voluntary basis. As a result, the public's access to the data that would enable it to evaluate the reasonableness of coal prices and profits was removed.

Some profiteering in coal there certainly is. How much there is nobody knows. There is a vast deal of inefficiency, but here again nobody can say just how much. Nobody knows what the coal miner of average efficiency is actually making, or what it really costs him to live. Ask almost any serious question you wish about the industry, and the one truthful reply will be, nobody knows . . . . Why have we not the facts . . . ? Because the coal operators will not let us have them . . . . But why do not the operators' associations waive their rights to secrecy and offer free access to their books? If they have nothing to hide, why do they act as if they had everything to hide?[43]

---

[40] These proposed bills had their origin in testimony by an atypical operator named Eugene McAuliff [*Coal Age* 17 (March 11, 1920): 490–2].

[41] Ibid., 17 (April 29, 1920): 864–5.

[42] Ibid., 17 (June 17, 1920): 1,241.

[43] A 1922 *New Republic* editorial quoted in Julia A. Johnsen, ed., *Selected Articles on Government Ownership of Coal Mines* (New York: H.W. Wilson, 1926), pp. 28–9.

While coal operators continued to maintain that shortages were not their fault, these assurances did not satisfy the industry's critics, who began to press in Congress for some form of fact-finding legislation that would reestablish the government's authority to collect cost and profit data.

The first legislative effort to resolve this problem was undertaken by Senator William Calder, whose Reconstruction Committee's hearings on the building industry turned into a highly publicized attack on alleged coal profiteering. The Calder hearings took place in the latter part of 1920, and when the new Congress was convened in 1921, the Committee reported that

it would be a gross dereliction of duty for Congress to shut its eyes to such possibilities or probabilities [as a return of the conditions of 1920] and to fail to take some steps to prevent the control in such recurring emergencies from being left in the hands of those whose conduct during the last year amounted to a national scandal.[44]

The bill that Calder introduced in January called for mandatory monthly reports by operators to the FTC, an investigation of car supply and mine ratings by the ICC, weekly reports by the Geological Survey, the licensing of all operators and dealers, the exercise of control over production and distribution by the president in case of emergency, the prohibition of coal sales to affiliated concerns except under conditions of competitive bidding, a tax on coal brokers, investigations of shortages, inspection and grading by the Bureau of Mines, and an investigation of miner welfare by the Department of Labor.[45]

Operators opposed this legislation vehemently. They argued, first, that the problems that the bill was trying to address – coal shortages and high prices – were attributable to poor transportation, on the one hand, and, on the other, to the workers, whose poor work habits and frequent strikes kept output at a low level. Their major argument, however, was not that the Calder bill was unnecessary, but that, in principle, it was undesirable. The provisions of the Calder bill were identified with "federal control over business," which invariably produces "stagnation, failure, and an increased cost to the public." "If federal control is assumed over the coal business, initiative will be destroyed, incentive removed, and high costs and short supply will result."[46] *Coal Age* called the Calder bill a "drastic form of control for the coal industry."[47] J. D. A.

[44]*Coal Age* 19 (March 31, 1921): 597.
[45]Ibid., 19 (January 20, 1921): 109; ibid., 19 (January 27, 1921): 195.
[46]Ibid., 19 (January 27, 1921): 200.
[47]Ibid.

Morrow, representing the National Coal Association, testified that the collection of price and cost data, which the operators viewed as their "private business," would "revolutionize the conduct of government and industry."[48]

When the Calder bill was reported out of the Committee on Manufacturers, the licensing, taxing, and emergency control provisions were dropped. The resultant bill was renamed by this committee, chaired by Senator Robert LaFollette, as "a bill providing for current publicity of information concerning the coal industry and trade."[49] However, even this relatively mild measure was denounced by *Coal Age* as giving "sweeping powers" to the FTC and was seen by coal operators as establishing the foundation for further federal control, beginning with an FTC-mandated system of cost accounting.[50] This bill died with the end of the 66th Congress.

In the spring of 1921, Senator Frelinghuysen introduced another fact-finding bill. This new measure had the Secretary of Commerce collecting data on production, stocks, distribution, and prices; the Bureau of Mines collecting data on storage, inspection, sampling, analysis, purchasing, classification, and utilization methods; and appointed the Director of the Geological Survey (later the Secretary of the Interior) as the Federal Coal Commissioner. This individual was to make recommendations to Congress on the legislative formulation of standard grades of coal and on the desirability of some kind of market-zoning plan.[51] Frelinghuysen went to great lengths to assure the operators of his good intentions. In May, he wrote to the National Coal Association, expressing his opposition to any legislation "which would regulate or restrict the private operation of any industry."[52] However, he argued, some form of coal regulation was inevitable if and when prices rose again. He claimed that his own bill would forestall more drastic and less friendly proposals.[53] Initially, at least, coal operators responded to this latest piece of coal legislation with more restraint than had been their custom. Apparently, although they continued to oppose any form of government intervention for the same reasons as before, they were sensitive enough to their public-relations problems that they did not wish to be viewed as un-

[48]Ibid., pp. 198–9.
[49]Ibid., 19 (March 3, 1921): 418.
[50]Ibid.
[51]Ibid., 19 (April 21, 1921): 725.
[52]Ibid., 19 (May 26, 1921): 962.
[53]Ibid., 19 (June 16, 1921): 1,067.

reasonable "negativists." Thus, J. D. A. Morrow, the leading spokes-
person for the National Coal Association, tried to approve of data
collection in general, while declaring his opposition to "regulation," or
compulsory data collection.[54] *Coal Age* reported that this was the position
of many operators, who saw the value of data collection and of the
increase in and centralization of information pertaining to the industry,
but thought that this end should be achieved through "education," not
"compulsion" or "regulation."[55] When the National Coal Association
issued its official view of the Frelinghuysen bill, however, such subtle
distinctions were absent.

"Stabilization" of an industry necessarily means control of that industry. That
the purpose of this legislation is not merely information but the ultimate regulation of the coal industry, is clearly indicated by many of its provisions. Private
industry cannot voluntarily submit to legislation in which the deliberate purpose
is announced, as it is here, to control ultimately every phase of the industry.
. . . The bill, if passed, would be a forerunner and precedent for similar paternal
and regulatory legislation with reference to every line of private business.[56]

Frelinghuysen, who considered himself a friend of business in general
and of the coal industry in particular, bitterly blamed the bituminous
coal operators for the eventual demise of the bill. "The coal lobby effectively tied the government's hands and poked out its eyes."[57]

Similar coal bills were introduced in 1921 and 1922, but these met the
same fate as the Calder and Frelinghuysen bills. The only other proposal
in this period to draw much attention from operators was made by
Secretary of Commerce Herbert Hoover. Attempting to arrive at an
agreement with Attorney-General Harry Daugherty on the type of activities which trade associations could engage in, Hoover proposed,
among other things, that trade associations should be permitted to collect
trade data, including past prices, which would be disseminated only
through the Department of Commerce. Even this mild proposal was
greeted with an absence of enthusiasm by coal operators. According to
Coal Age, "the conversational verdict among [Chicago coal men] is that
it would amount to government control of business . . . ." In staking out
this position, operators showed a clear understanding of the indeter-
minacy of democratic politics. "While this program may work fine while
Mr. Hoover is head of the department, what happens when somebody

[54]Ibid., 19 (May 21, 1921): 877.
[55]Ibid., 19 (June 16, 1921): 1,068.
[56]Ibid., 19 (June 23, 1921): 1,133.
[57]Quoted in Parker, *The Coal Industry*, p. 90.

else takes Mr. Hoover's place? We know he is fully in sympathy with honest big business, but think of the trouble that could be caused by a man who wasn't!"[58]

Conclusion

In Chapter 2, I argued that a capitalist firm's response to a proposed organizational mechanism will depend on its organizational need and on the costs associated with the mechanism. Between 1915 and 1918, changes in the economic and political contexts of bituminous coal competition caused a reduction in the need of coal operators for outside intervention in their market and an increase in the costs associated with such intervention. The economic change was produced by a combination of war-induced demand and distribution problems that resulted in a seller's market for bituminous coal. Rational individual economic behavior no longer generated self-destructive price cutting and suboptimal profits. In fact, the opposite occurred. Individual operators took advantage of the novelty of "too little coal, too few mines" and pushed the market price to unprecedented levels.

The changed political climate was largely a product of the high coal prices, which generated vocal public hostility. It was easy to translate such disaffection into effective demands for government action during and after the war, when relatively drastic forms of state intervention in the economy were an accepted fact of life.

Government regulation to quell high coal prices was clearly not in the long-term best interests of coal operators. The problem was that their unbridled economic behavior was likely to generate such an outcome. Operators responded to this Prisoner's Dilemma by trying voluntarily to "cooperate" by moderating prices and by employing all of the political means at their disposal to prevent high coal prices from issuing in government regulation. In this, they were successful, beating back even the most moderate forms of state intervention.

Their prosperity, and the choices it presented them, did not last, however. A renewal of familiar competitive pressures was felt even in 1922, and, for the next decade, operators were thrown again into their price- and wage-cutting games, which generated new patterns of labor versus capital and capital versus capital conflict and eventually led operators again to seek state intervention to organize their competition.

[58]*Coal Age* 21 (March 20, 1922): 541.

6. Labor–capital conflict and the disorganization of the coal market, 1921–1928

Introduction

When the World War I bituminous coal boom came to an end in the early 1920s, the structure of the competitive game played by operators changed again. Competition resumed the form of a price–wage game played among firms with different capacities to defect. The postwar version of this game differed from the earlier version in two important respects, however. First, the proportion of industry output produced in union mines was significantly lower than it was before the war. Second, the range of feasible ways to transform the game had narrowed. The experience of the previous twenty years had demonstrated both that it was virtually impossible to secure the cooperation of nonunion firms without recourse to state intervention, and that state intervention was an overly costly and dangerous option. These changes altered the way in which unionized operators responded to the outcome produced by the price–wage game. In the pre-war context, they had accepted the constraints on their own price and wage cutting as constructive and necessary and had sought to impose similar constraints on defecting firms, either through unionization or through a variety of other measures. Now, they effectively gave up such efforts as hopeless and sought, instead, to transform the game so that they, too, could select the defection strategy.

Their efforts to accomplish this proceeded in two stages. First, in an attempt to maintain the positive aspects of unionization – the limitation on unrestricted wage cutting – while seeking a greater capacity to meet nonunion wage cuts, unionized operators tried to achieve increased flexibility and autonomy *within* the framework of the collective bargaining relationship. They did this by attempting to negotiate district-level, rather than interstate, contracts with the UMWA. It was only when this strategy was defeated by workers in the 1922 strike that they attacked the very existence of collective bargaining and succeeded in winning the dubious privilege of meeting their competitors' low wages. Of course, this was a hollow victory, since it only served to *disorganize* the market,

reimposing the self-destructive wage and price competition that operators had been struggling to escape for forty years.

Along with Chapter 4, this chapter demonstrates the importance of
the capital versus capital conflict in structuring relations between workers and capitalists, as well as relations among capitalists. In attacking
industrywide collective bargaining, bituminous coal operators behaved
the way in which most people would expect capitalists to behave: They
attacked the union of workers and, when it was weak, effectively destroyed it. However, in their assault on collective bargaining, as well as
in their earlier acquiescence and defense of it, capitalists in the coal
industry were responding to a situation produced by the logic of their
competitive relations. Their attack on workers was derivative of their
efforts to survive against competing capitalists in an environment of
competitive wage cutting. This conclusion is reinforced by the willingness of operators to turn toward the union in the 1930s, a development
that is considered in Chapter 8.

The "new" competitive game: price cutting and wage cutting revisited

In contrast to the period lasting through World War I, competition in
the bituminous coal industry during the interwar period took place
against a background of stagnating demand. The industry's 5.5 percent
rate of average annual growth between 1900 and 1920 dropped to 0.1
percent during the period from 1920 to 1940 (see Table 4.1). To a large
extent, especially during the 1930s, the reduction in the demand for coal
was a function of the drop in industrial activity connected with the Great
Depression. However, there were two other influences at work, both of
which were felt well before the stock market crash of late 1929. The first
of these was increased competition from fuel oil and natural gas. In 1920,
bituminous coal supplied 64.9 percent of the energy requirements of the
United States; by 1935, this figure had dropped to 46 percent, while the
combined contribution of fuel oil and natural gas rose from 15 percent
to 37.9 percent during the same period.[1] The new fuels were cleaner,
more convenient, and less subject to the irregularities in supply that had
long plagued the coal trade. Moreover, in many cases, the technologies
that employed oil and gas were more efficient than those that used coal.
Second, in those sectors in which coal still predominated, increased

[1]Schurr and Netschert, *Energy*, p. 500.

efficiency in its consumption was a further brake on demand. Railroads, electric-power plants, and iron and steel mills experienced reductions ranging from 18 to 50 percent in the amount of coal that they required to do equivalent amounts of work.[2]

The impact of this leveling off of demand was aggravated by the phenomenal entry that occurred during the World War I period. The number of bituminous coal mines in the United States, which had remained constant from 1909 through 1916, increased by over 50 percent from 1916 to 1918. In 1910, 5,818 mines produced 417 million tons of coal. In 1921, 8,038 mines produced 416 million tons.[3] Moreover, by the 1920s, the distribution and transportation difficulties that had served to keep marginal operations in the market had been substantially corrected. In the words of one commentator, the coal industry had been transformed "from a speculative venture dependent upon external conditions for large short term profits into a business which must rely on regular movement, low costs and modern merchandising methods for its future financial success."[4]

The new reality of coal competition was first evidenced in 1921, when the effect on coal demand of the industrial boom of 1920 had worn off and output had experienced its biggest drop in history – from 569 million tons in 1920 to 416 million tons in 1921 (Table 4.1). However, coal strikes in both the anthracite and bituminous fields in 1922 kept output down and prices at a relatively high level during that year. The crunch came in 1923, which in spite of a 565-million ton output, *Black Diamond* could describe as "the most disastrous in the history of the trade."[5] The two subsequent years were just as bad, if not worse. The Geological Survey noted that the coal industry "had experienced hard times before, but never, so far as reflected in the statistical record, as hard as those of 1924 and 1925."[6] An anthracite strike, a lengthy British coal strike (that sent U.S. coal to Newcastle), and strong industrial demand brought a short-term improvement in 1926, but the following year brought a return to depressed conditions, and, in 1928, output, spot prices, and values continued their downward slide (Tables 4.1 and 4.3).

[2]U.S. Bureau of Mines, *Minerals Yearbook*, 1939, p. 807; Schurr and Netschert, *Energy*, p. 80.
[3]Baratz, *The Union*, pp. 40–1.
[4]*Coal Age* 41 (October, 1936): 394–5.
[5]*Black Diamond* 72 (January 5, 1924): 7.
[6]U.S. Geological Survey, *Mineral Resources*, 1927, Part 2, p. 396.

Once again, operators faced the wage-cutting/price-cutting Prisoner's
Dilemma that we discussed in Chapter 4. Again, for analytic purposes,
it is useful to subdivide this game into two components – a wage- *and*
price-cutting game (the *wage game*), and a price-cutting (but *not* a wage-
cutting) game (the *price game*). In the present chapter, I focus on the
wage game. (I consider the price game in the next chapter.) The dominant strategy is to reduce prices and wages. The data indicate that this
is what in fact occurred. Except for 1926, when eastern coal prices increased slightly, the 1922–1927 period was one of declining average
values in all of the major producing states. Nationwide, average value
declined from $2.38 in 1923 to $1.99 in 1927 (Table 4.3). The *Coal Age*
average spot price dropped from $2.77 to $1.99 during the same period.
Those nonunion operators who were able to reduce costs by reducing
wages did so. In 1921, nonunion operators reacted to the fall in demand
by reducing average wages for tonnage men by over 21 percent.[7] In
1925, *Coal Age* estimated that average labor costs per ton in the predominantly unionized Pittsburgh district were $1.50, while in the nonunion
Logan field of West Virginia, they were $0.90. Similarly, unionized Hock-
ing Valley, Ohio, labor costs were $1.65 per ton, while nonunion Hazard
County, Kentucky, labor costs were only $1.20 per ton.[8] As Table 4.3
indicates, these lower wages translated into consistently lower prices in
the nonunion states of West Virginia and Kentucky.

In this game, the presence of a sizeable number of nonunion, defecting
firms means that the unionized firms will receive suboptimal payoffs.
Recall that there are two ways in which the position of a cooperating
firm can be improved in such a situation. First, the payoff structures of
defecting firms can be transformed so that these firms are led to cooperate. As the level of cooperation increases, so do the payoffs of all
cooperating firms. Second, cooperating firms can win the right to defect.
We have seen that during the period before World War I, union operators
responded to their suboptimal payoffs by attempting the first type of
transformation. Rather than try to defect, themselves, they sought to
force their nonunion competitors to cooperate by raising their labor and
transportation costs. The postwar game differed from the earlier game,
however, in two key respects. First, there was a significant increase in
the level of defection. Between 1923 and 1925 alone, the proportion of

Fisher and Bezanson, *Wages*, pp. 42–3, 74–5.
Coal Age 28 (July 2, 1925): 8.

coal produced in nonunion fields increased from 47 percent to 70 per
cent.[9] Once a sizeable majority of the industry, the unionized cooperators
were reduced to a minority.

Such a reduction in the level of cooperation is likely to have several
important effects. First, it increases the organizational need of cooper
ating firms. When cooperators are a majority, they receive suboptima
profits but their profits are still at a relatively high level. Thus, in Figure
1.7, as long as the level of cooperation remains above k percent of output
the market position of cooperators is secure. When cooperation drops
below k, however, cooperating firms begin to receive negative profits
and have a much greater incentive to transform the market in one way
or another. An increase in defection is also likely to affect the kind of
transformation that they prefer, increasing the appeal of the second type
of transformation described above, in which they gain the capacity to
defect, relative to the first, in which their competitors are forced to
cooperate. There are three reasons for this. First, as the level of defection
increases, the difficulty of forcing defectors to cooperate increases. Co
operation increasingly becomes a question of creating a new organiza
tional mechanism rather than extending the coverage of an existing one
a considerably less costly and less risky alternative. Second, at the cog
nitive level, it is likely that as the level of defection increases, cooperators
will increasingly blame their position on the agency responsible for their
cooperation, rather than on the defectors. They will be more inclined to
view themselves as victims than to view defectors as irresponsible free
riders. They will thus tend to see their own defection, rather than the
cooperation of others, as the "natural" way to improve their position
Third, as the level of cooperation reaches very low levels, defection
becomes a more attractive strategy for cooperating firms. As we have
seen, it is likely that the fear that one firm's defection will lead to the
defection of others and will eventually generate the universal defection
outcome, which leads some firms to refrain from defecting. This motive
can only be effective, however, as long as the cooperative payoff is
greater than the universal defection payoff. As figure 1.7 indicates, at
very low levels of cooperation, the unilateral cooperation payoff is less
than the universal defection payoff. In this situation there is no reason
for cooperating firms to fear that their defection will set off a bandwagon
effect, since the outcome of such a rush to defection will be an improve
ment in their payoffs.

[9] Ibid., p. 9.

A second difference between the pre- and postwar situations is the fact that operators in the more recent period had a greater appreciation of the difficulty of effecting a transformation of the market that would force nonunion firms to cooperate. By 1922, efforts to impose cooperation of southern Appalachian operators had a long history of failure. Moreover, the costs of the most effective means of imposing cooperation – state intervention – had increased dramatically as a result of the industry's experience between 1917 and 1921.

In short, as the increase in nonunion production was pushing unionized firms to do something about their low payoffs, it was also pushing them away from a continuation of their earlier efforts to impose cooperation on defecting firms and toward an attempt to join the ranks of the defectors themselves. We would expect this movement to be led by high-cost firms and firms most vulnerable to nonunion competition (i.e., firms located in Pennsylvania and Ohio).

The context for this struggle over the reorganization (or, more accurately, the disorganization) of the postwar coal market was the negotiations with the union over the content and extent of their joint agreements with operators. Initially, unionized operators sought to have their cake and eat it too – to maintain a collective bargaining agreement and the associated constraint on competitive wage cutting, but to limit the scope of those agreements to individual districts and thereby provide relief to those operators most victimized by nonunion wage cutting. By the latter half of the decade, however, collective bargaining itself became the stake, and the whole notion of union-enforced wage levels came under attack. The point it is essential to emphasize is that the unraveling of collective bargaining in the coal industry flowed from the logic of capitalist collective action generated by the wage-cutting game, rather than from the logic of labor–capital conflict. Operators understood the consequences of fully free (no union) competition and broke their agreements with the union reluctantly. They did so because they felt that their competitive position vis-à-vis other operators gave them no choice.

The 1922 coal strike

The issue over which the nation's coal miners struck on April 1, 1922 was whether collective bargaining should be on an interstate basis, as had been the case since 1898, or on a district-by-district basis, as operators now demanded. District-level negotiations would give operators more flexibility in meeting competitive wage rates, while still affording them some protection from unrestrained mutual wage cutting.

The 1921 recession and resultant wage cuts in the nonunion fields brought home with greater force than ever before the vulnerability of the union operators – particularly those in Ohio, Pennsylvania, and West Virginia – to nonunion competition. To most Appalachian operators, the villain in the piece was the interstate joint agreement, which tied them to a collective bargaining framework and wage structure more attuned to the market of the 1890s than to contemporary conditions.

At the beginning of January, just before the mine workers and operators were scheduled to meet in joint conference to negotiate the 1922 contract, operators from southern Ohio and Pittsburgh announced their refusal to attend the joint conference and to negotiate anything more extensive than district-level agreements. They were joined by operators from eastern Ohio. Operators from Indiana and Illinois both notified the UMWA of their willingness to attend a joint conference, but UMWA President John L. Lewis canceled the meeting in the wake of the opposition from Pennsylvania and Ohio.[10] A *Coal Age* editorial explained this opposition.

In all this land there are no truer friends of the union coal miner, no stauncher advocates of collective bargaining, than among the operators of the southern Ohio fields. Yet it was the southern Ohio operators who to a man first took the stand that has prevented a central field conference. With hands tied behind their backs by wage scales and working conditions dictated . . . by a national labor union and by operators in larger fields to the north and west with which it is not now and has not for a score of years been competitive, southern Ohio has had to submit to having its throat cut by non-union fields to the south. With this field it is not a question of how its wage scales and costs compare with eastern Ohio or Indiana but how they compare with West Virginia.[11]

The Central Competitive Field movement to meet southern Appalachian competition moved forward another step at the end of January, when unionized operators from southern Ohio, Pennsylvania, northern West Virginia, Indiana, and Tennessee all announced that the new wage scales that would be effective on April 1 if no contract was signed would embody pay cuts of about 30 percent.[12]

As the March 31 strike deadline approached, operators from Indiana,

[10]Ibid., 21 (January 15, 1922): 21; ibid., 23 (January 18, 1923): 100.
[11]Ibid., 22 (July 6, 1922): 1.
[12]Ibid., 21 (February 2, 1922): 219; ibid., 261 (February 9, 1922): 21; ibid., 21 (February 16, 1922): 300.

southern Ohio, Pittsburgh, and central Pennsylvania all attempted un-successfully to engage their workers in district-level negotiations, while eastern Ohio, central Ohio, and West Virginia Panhandle operators joined the Illinois operators in expressing a willingness to enter an interstate conference, but only if operators from other districts did so.[13]

The operators were in a difficult position. On the one hand, they were highly aware of the benefits of collective bargaining. "All the Central Competitive Region feels to a degree that it would like a contract for the stability of wages and prices it affords."[14]

Those who have been in intimate touch with coal operators in union territory in recent weeks declare there is no desire to get rid of the miners' union. The advantages of collective bargaining are in such contrast with the confusion of other days that most of these operators would not cripple the union if they could.[15]

The Central Competitive Field operator ... does not like the union. ... That organization does not keep its bargains; it does not assure peaceful operation; it is not reasonable; it does not give the operator ... his due. It opposes the introduction of new and better machinery. As you listen to the operating man you wonder that he ever signed up with such a treacherous, unfair, and unfaithful antagonist. And yet! The union has one advantage. Its far-reaching biennial agreements, broken though they often are, have done something for permanence in operation.[16]

Similar sentiments were expressed by Phil Penna, a leading Indiana operator, who told a gathering of Illinois operators that the 1898 joint convention was a "declaration that the open shop had been tried and was a despicable, miserable failure. Lots of you don't like that, but you cannot gainsay it. ... "

This open shop proposition is only a fad. ... What would you do if you had it? If you had a union of the mines, a little union at each mine, or if you didn't have any union ... , you would make a scale of wages and over there would be the other gentleman doing the same thing ... and all along the line in the same district and interdistricts you would all make scales of wages and you would all make them different. ... Then what happens? Well, I would go out and have a meeting with my men, ... and say, "John and Bill, my trade is gone; that fellow over there, Harry Taylor, went out and talked to his men the other night and they took a 5¢ reduction from their wages. I've got to have a 7½¢ reduction to

[13]Ibid., 21 (March 23, 1922): 505.
[14]Ibid., 21 (January 12, 1922): 37.
[15]Ibid., 21 (March 23, 1922): 545.
[16]Ibid., 21 (January 12, 1922): 37.

get back that business or I can't get along. . . . Now you take the reduction and I have got my 2½¢ to the good. I will go out and take his trade then." As foolish as that may sound to you, this was actually the rule of life in the coal fields in Indiana, Ohio, Pennsylvania, and your great state of Illinois. . . . That is the way it would be again tomorrow, but we can't live that way, and you know it. We must have uniform costs of production, as near as physical conditions will permit.[17]

The problem is that unionization can only contribute to stability if all firms pay comparable wages. District-level agreements may prevent competitive wage cutting *within* the confines of individual regions, but the organization of the interdistrict wage-cutting game requires inter-district collective bargaining.

Unless the whole Central Competitive Region makes a scale and the rest of the unionized areas follow it, there will be no assurance that some important regions will not obtain lower wage scales and the area signing be obliged to close down. It seems clear that the whole Central Competitive Region or a still larger region must sign or it will not be safe for any section to make any kind of a contract.[18]

Operators from Illinois and Indiana, who were less concerned than eastern operators about competition from the South, did respond favorably to the UMWA call for an interstate conference, but could not commit themselves to a contract in the absence of similar agreements in the other Central Competitive Field states. In essence, all of the Central Competitive Field would have preferred a contract, as long as their competitors would also be bound by it. Unfortunately, a major set of competitors would not be bound by a contract negotiated under the old Central Competitive Field framework. And, within this framework, eastern Appalachian operators would not be able to prevail and to secure a wage scale competitive with what was in place in southern West Virginia. "Sitting with Illinois and the miners, Pittsburgh and Ohio, having but two votes in eight, have no chance in the Central Competitive conference to adjust their differentials to meet the more potent competition of West Virginia."[19] A second-best option for the Pennsylvania and Ohio operators would have been district-level negotiations. In such a context, they may have had a better chance of winning concessions from the union, which would be weakened by the absence of a faction of operators (those from Illinois) willing to settle for a higher wage scale. The union wasn't buying this proposal, however, and the Pennsylvania and Ohio operators were faced with a choice between signing a union contract and

[17]Ibid., 21 (February 23, 1922): 330–1.
[18]Ibid., 21 (January 12, 1922): 37.
[19]Ibid., 22 (July 27, 1922): 120.

locking themselves into a unilateral cooperative strategy that would result in a further decline in their position, or not signing, and risking the
unraveling of collective bargaining and an eventual universal defection
outcome. They chose the latter path.

"Shout with the crowd," said Mr. Pickwick. "But if there are two crowds?,"
asked Mr. Snodgrass. "Then shout with the largest." Apparently the operators
on the banks of the Allegheny and the Ohio are taking Mr. Pickwick's time-
honored advice and have decided that the non-union areas constitute the larger
crowd. . . . And that being the case, they cannot make a contract with the union.[20]

Illinois operators, who were willing to negotiate on an interstate basis,
found themselves in a similar dilemma.

Illinois knows that the Middle West cannot endure to be alone under the bond.
If it can only put the rest under the same yoke, well and good, but if not, Illinois,
Indiana, and Iowa must be free and if the eastern operators will not bind them-
selves there can scarcely be an agreement of any kind anywhere.[21]

The strike was unexpectedly successful in shutting down production,
both in the unionized fields and in some important nonunion fields
located in southwestern Pennsylvania. By June, however, there were
signs that the union was weakening, and operators were beginning to
taste victory when President Harding unexpectedly intervened to convene a conference of miners and operators at the White House on July
1.[22] When the two sides failed to come to an early agreement, Harding
presented them with his own plan for resolving the conflict. The miners
would resume work at the present wage scale while a tripartite commission would recommend within thirty days a new scale that would
be effective until March 31, 1923. Meanwhile, the commission would be
empowered to investigate the industry and make recommendations toward the establishment of industrial peace and the elimination of
waste.[23] Most operators accepted this plan unconditionally, although
some Pennsylvania operators still pressed for district-level wage negotiations, and operators from Indiana wanted an arbitration mechanism
that, unlike the president's, would not include representatives from the
two contending sides. On the other hand, the miners rejected any form
of arbitration.[24]

This was where matters stood until the beginning of August, when

[20]Ibid., 21 (January 12, 1922): 38.
[21]Ibid., p. 37.
[22]Ibid., 23 (January 23, 1923): 102; ibid., 21 (June 22, 1922): 1,059.
[23]Ibid., 22 (July 13, 1922): 63.
[24]Ibid., 22 (July 20, 1922): 103–4.

Lewis, again with the participation of some eastern Ohio operators, convened a joint interstate conference in Cleveland. Shortly after the skeleton conference commenced, a new plan surfaced on the UMWA side, calling for a return to work at the old wage scale until March 31, 1923, and the appointment of a bipartite commission to recommend a method for negotiating the next contract. The conference was kept in session while this plan was examined and while Lewis tried to attract more operators from western Pennsylvania, southern Ohio, Illinois, and Indiana.[25] By August 15, enough operators were represented at the conference to legitimize it and an agreement was signed. By the end of the month, most remaining Central Competitive Field operators had joined the bandwagon. The agreement called for an October 1 meeting of operators and miners to appoint both a reorganization committee to devise a method for carrying out future wage negotiations and a fact-finding commission to study the industry. On January 3, operators and miners would meet to act on the reorganization committee's findings and to determine a new format for wage negotiations. These negotiations would then commence on January 8.[26] Lewis thus succeeded in winning an interstate agreement in part by offering operators the prospect of a new, possibly more flexible, bargaining framework in the future.

Coal legislation in 1922

Although the coal strike of 1922 was largely a product of the wage-cutting Prisoner's Dilemma, its immediate effect was a coal shortage that quickly threw operators into a very different situation, one that was reminiscent of the World War I period. By generating a seller's market, the strike presented operators both with the opportunity to raise prices and the danger that consumers would seek state intervention to prevent profiteering and price gouging. Because of public sensitivity to the level of coal prices, then, coal operators were placed in the perverse position of having to fight off government intervention aimed at shortages and high prices at the same time that they were seeking to expand their capacity to *reduce* prices by transforming their relationship with the union.

Prices were stable in the first weeks after the strike began, but they began to rise in early May. Secretary of Commerce Herbert Hoover

---

[25]Ibid., 22 (August 10, 1922): 215.
[26]Ibid., 22 (August 17, 1922): 253; ibid., 23 (January 23, 1923): 184.

responded with a program that sought the voluntary cooperation of nonunion operators to keep prices at a moderate level.[27] When the strike drew to a close at the end of the summer, there was a renewal of public concern about coal shortages and profiteering in the coming winter months. *Coal Age* warned in late July that if, as seemed the case, operators were not able to prevent the price increases that were generating so much hostility, the government would be "more than warranted in stepping in. Whether some producers like it or not, they must be protected from themselves."[28] The administration responded to the impending danger of a coal shortage by drafting emergency legislation that would place the distribution and pricing of coal under government authority. In spite of the fact that the Cabinet-level presidential fuel committee found the exercise of such government powers "highly distasteful," two bills were sent to Congress in late August. One would have established a federal agency that would buy, sell, and distribute coal. The other, which was favored by the administration as being "less cumbersome," would expand the powers of the Interstate Commerce Commission so that that agency, by controlling car supply, would be enabled to alleviate shortages and punish profiteers.[29]

Coal operators appear to have universally condemned this legislation. J. D. A. Morrow, representing the National Coal Association, told the House Committee on Interstate Commerce that, in the words of a reporter who was present, "it would accomplish no purpose . . . , but would hamper operations by governmental interference with legitimate channels of trade."[30] The Illinois Coal Operators' Association wrote to their congressional delegation, opposing the bill, denying "that any arbitrary action of the government through bureaucratic organization can handle any situation of emergency for a major industry, as well as it can be handled under private ownership." They blamed the coal problem on inadequate transportation and on an absence of "law and order" in labor relations, and urged that, instead of regulating the distribution of coal, the government should appoint a fact-finding commission.[31] Aside from this general opposition to "bureaucratic interference," some high-cost operators, remembering their unhappy experience with government maximum-price fixing under the Lever Act, feared that gov-

[27] Ibid., 23 (January 19, 1923): 102; ibid., 21 (May 25, 1922): 895.
[28] Ibid., 22 (July 17, 1922): 119.
[29] Ibid., 22 (September 7, 1922): 373.
[30] Ibid., 22 (August 31, 1922): 335.
[31] Ibid., 22 (September 7, 1922): 373.

ernment prices would be too low to cover costs. As *Coal Age* remarked, "no price can be set for the product of a particular field that is within reason as respects the majority that is not below the cost of a small portion of production."[32]

This opposition did not halt the progress of the emergency-distribution bill through Congress, however, and it appeared that the coal industry was finally about to experience "the kind of regulation it has been fearing and opposing since 1922."[33] As it finally passed, the bill declared that a "national emergency exists" and, to meet it, enlarged the powers of the ICC to issue priority orders and embargoes to provide for equitable distribution and to prevent the sale of coal at prices that are "unjustly or unreasonably high." This authority was to last until the president declared that the emergency was over, and not longer than twelve months.[34] The operation of this law – the 1922 Coal Distribution Act – was uncontroversial. At the "instance and request" of the Federal Fuel Distributor, operators in most of the major eastern and midwestern fields voluntarily lowered their prices by amounts varying from $3.00 to $1.00 per ton. Few priority orders were issued and few complaints about profiteering were received.[35]

Another piece of legislation that came out of the 1922 strike created the U.S. Coal Commission, a fact-finding group of seven members who were mandated "to investigate and ascertain fully the facts and conditions and study the problems and questions relative to the coal industry" in order to aid Congress in drafting legislation that would ensure an uninterrupted coal supply.[36]

Meanwhile, the Central Competitive Field operators and the UMWA still had to implement the agreement that they had signed in August. Aside from the wage provisions, it called for the appointment of a fact-finding commission and the appointment of a bipartite commission to develop a new collective-bargaining framework. The passage by Congress of a fact-finding bill for the coal industry obviated the need for the operators and miners to implement that aspect of their own agreement. As for the reorganization committee, whose mandate was to recommend a new collective-bargaining framework, it met on November 14 and heard operators from the outlying districts propose a national wage

[32]Ibid., 22 (September 21, 1922): 439.
[33]Ibid., 22 (September 14, 1922): 388.
[34]Ibid., 22 (September 21, 1922): 461.
[35]Ibid., 23 (January 4, 1923): 21.
[36]Ibid., 22 (September 28, 1922): 503.

agreement, variations to which could be negotiated at the district level. The operators failed to unite behind any single proposal, however.[37] The committee met again a month later, with the operators proposing district-level agreements and arbitration, neither of which was acceptable to the miners.[38] When the full joint conference convened in January, it was without a recommendation from this committee. Following a suggestion put forward by the U.S. Coal Commission, the UMWA and the operators from the three participating states – Illinois, Indiana, and Ohio (Pennsylvania had dropped out) – agreed to extend their current contract until March 31, 1924.[39] This agreement represented a de facto reestablishment of the Central Competitive Field, and insofar as the subdivision of that field was the major operator issue, a victory for the UMWA.[40]

The Jacksonville agreement and the breakdown of collective bargaining

The resolution of the 1922 strike did not alleviate the position of the union operators. Their position in the market continued to deteriorate and the proportion of national output produced in union mines continued to decline. We have seen that as the level of cooperation declines in the wage game, cooperating firms increasingly need to transform the game; and as the feasibility of imposing cooperation on defecting wage-cutting firms decreases, it becomes more likely that cooperating firms will seek to transform the game by throwing off the constraints that prevent them from defecting – in this case, their collective bargaining agreement with workers.

As reflected in *Coal Age*, coal industry spokesmen were clearly worried throughout 1923 that the combination of frustration on the part of unionized operators and continued price cutting by nonunion operators would lead to a fatal attack on collective bargaining that would leave everyone worse off. *Coal Age* urged nonunion firms to discipline themselves so as to maintain their wage scales against destructive wage and price cutting.

Apparently the application of any constructive principle must await the time when the non-union operators will pledge themselves jointly to maintain some

---

[37]Ibid., 22 (November 23, 1922): 843–4.
[38]Ibid., 22 (December 24, 1922): 963.
[39]Ibid., 23 (January 25, 1923): 195.
[40]Ibid., 23 (February 1, 1923): 207–8.

reasonable, proper and constant relationship between their wage rates and those in effect in the union fields.[41]

Similarly, one month later, *Coal Age* welcomed the news that nonunion operators were attempting to act collectively to stabilize wage rates.

The fact that the non-union operators are acting in groups on this question is held by some to indicate that they have discovered what the Central Competitive Field operators learned long ago – that the adjustment of wages by individual operators without reference to the rate of pay in the field as a whole has a demoralizing effect. When one operator is not entirely certain as to the wages paid by his competition, frequent changes in the rate, with their unsettling tendencies result.[42]

Fairly confident that the UMWA would be demanding a continuation of the present scale at Jacksonville, *Coal Age* also warned the unionized operators not to try to break the union in order to free themselves from nonunion wage cuts. Rather than make an "ill-advised" commitment to a wage cut, which would probably lead to a strike, *Coal Age* advised union operators to reduce costs in other areas and to meet nonunion wage cuts with greater efficiency in production.[43] *Coal Age* also argued against the dissolution of the United Mine Workers. While it castigated that organization's postwar policies as "militant, arrogant, and unreasoning," it still concluded that

unionism is an important and necessary factor in the coal industry. It has brought the mine worker to an advantaged position, has stabilized wages and prevented in large areas a form of cut-throat competition of by-gone times that made operators sell their men rather than their coal. It has even stabilized conditions in the nonunion fields – put those districts on good behavior . . . . No, the coal industry does not want the union dissolved – not even the nonunion operators wish it – nor would it be in the public interest.[44]

This sentiment was certainly shared by many operators. In July, 1923, John L. Lewis received a letter from a Pennsylvania operator saying that "many operators – both 'outlaws' [nonunion] and 'inlaws' – are wishing more power to your union."[45]

These arguments, in conjunction with a relatively high demand for coal in 1923, apparently had their desired effect. As the Jacksonville

[41]Ibid., 24 (October 18, 1923): 605.
[42]Ibid., 24 (November 22, 1923): 788.
[43]Ibid., 24 (November 29, 1923): 801.
[44]Ibid., 24 (September 16, 1923): 345.
[45]Melvyn Dubofsky and Warren Van Tine, *John L. Lewis: A Biography* (New York: Quadrangle, 1977), p. 106.

conference approached and the participants began to state their cases to the public, it appeared that most Central Competitive Field operators would be willing to accept a continuation of the same wage rate. Having lived through a long strike in 1922 which had cut production and brought on state intervention, union operators were evidently attaching greater importance to uninterrupted production than to wages.[46] In late 1925, a *Coal Age* writer looked back two years to reflect that

for the most part, . . . little serious consideration was given to the question of operators in organized fields severing their alliance with the United Mine Workers of America. Those producing companies with up-to-date plants and alert merchandising organizations carried on with profit. Another large group of operators, who are constitutionally opportunists, held on in the hope that some dislocation of supply would intervene to curtail output and run up the prices on their tonnage to sky-rocket figures. And a third group of constitutional optimists hung on in the belief that conditions with the coming of the New Year would justify the maintenance of the 1920 bases of pay or, if not, that the new wage agreement to be negotiated would relieve the organized fields of their burdens.[47]

The negotiations at Jacksonville proceeded smoothly. The main stumbling block was the length of the contract. The final agreement called for the continuation of the present scale for three years.[48] Both operators and union officials viewed the Jacksonville agreement as a means to eliminate the excess capacity that all agreed was the industry's major problem. It was assumed (rightly) that a significant percentage of operators would be unable to pay the relatively high Jacksonville wages during an extended period of uninterrupted competition. Phil Penna, a leading operator, stated at the Jacksonville conference that "both sides realize that a process of elimination through the operation of economic laws is the only salvation."[49] Likewise, *Coal Age's* Washington correspondent wrote that "all are agreed that the next three years will be ones of strenuous competition and painful readjustment. . . . The elimination of high cost mines will proceed at a much more rapid rate from this time forward."[50] However, both Lewis and the leading unionized operators assumed that the "surplus mines and surplus labor" were to be found primarily in the nonunion fields or on the margins of the unionized fields. They apparently believed that the nonunion operators

---

[46]*Coal Age* 25 (January 3, 1924): 19.
[47]Ibid., 28 (September 24, 1925): 419–20.
[48]Ibid., 25 (February 21, 1924): 284.
[49]Ibid.
[50]Ibid., 25 (February 28, 1924): 329.

would continue to be kept on "good behavior," that the union mines were operated more efficiently than the nonunion mines, and that the high demand of 1923 would be typical of the next three years.

None of these assumptions was valid. The 1923 level of demand did not persist. Between 1923 and 1924, national output dropped from 565 million tons to 484 million tons (Table 4.1). Nonunion operators reacted to the shrinking of the pie not by exiting from the market but by reducing wages in a struggle to maintain their position. Whether the supposed greater efficiency of the union firms was a fiction or whether it was simply overshadowed by the depth of the nonunion wage cuts is less important than the fact that shortly after the Jacksonville scale went into effect, it became apparent that the "medicine of supply and demand" was acting on the established unionized operators, not the allegedly marginal nonunion ones.

Within weeks after the signing of the Jacksonville agreement, reports of wage cuts in the nonunion areas of Pennsylvania began to appear.[51] In the Kanawha, West Virginia, field, a union toehold in West Virginia where union strength had declined significantly since 1922, the last 26 union operations closed their mines and attempted to resume operations under the 1917 wage scale.[52] *Coal Age*, meanwhile, published three editorials in June and early July urging operators to stabilize wages and refrain from attacking the union.

To all appearances the wage rate in nonunion fields tends to decline and will continue to do so unless the nonunion operators meet together and decide to stabilize the wage. The present cut-throat competition cannot fail to have an unfavorable reaction on the nonunion regions.[53]

There would be chaos in the coal industry were there no such unit [as the UMWA]. Let us hope that the union will not break, for the system of checks and balances which exists between unionism and nonunionism in coal is a healthy though oftimes painful thing for the industry.[54]

In its July 3 editorial, *Coal Age* took a new tack, supplementing its usual argument with a warning that if the South persisted in ruthlessly exploiting its wage advantage, the effect might be to make unionization more attractive to its employees.

[51]Ibid., 25 (May 18, 1924): 696; ibid., 25 (June 5, 1924): 850.
[52]Ibid., 26 (July 10, 1924): 55.
[53]Ibid., 25 (June 12, 1924): 865.
[54]Ibid., 25 (June 26, 1924): 933.

A few weeks ago a coal operator obtained a contract from a railroad company by ruthlessly underbidding his competitors. . . . No sooner had he obtained the contract than he went down to the mines and notified his employees that the price for which he had sold his coal would not permit him to pay the former rate of wages. . . .

No wonder that operators have at times advocated unionism, arguing that such unfair competition was making the operation of coal mines an industry in which few well-meaning men would care to engage. Such behavior has convinced some operators and is fast convincing others that the beneficence of the employer is not a sufficient pledge that mine workers will receive honorable treatment. . . . With a few men playing their hand unfairly it becomes increasingly necessary for their competitors to be equally callous of the needs of their employees. . . .

Many times in the past has competition in the reduction of wages argued for unionism and its recognition by employers. Beware lest it argue again so forcibly that the expression the "solid South" will be applied to its unionism instead of its politics.[55]

In late August the unionized central Pennsylvania operators began to appeal to the union to grant them wage cuts, arguing that nearby non-union mines were paying wages that were $.50 to $1.00 below the union scale.[56] Meanwhile, in western Kentucky, which, like central Pennsylvania, was another area in which unionization was incomplete, existing primarily in the western half of the region, operators continued to refuse to pay the Jacksonville wages and attempted unsuccessfully to reopen their mines at the 1917 scale.[57] Complaints from central Pennsylvania continued through October and November, and in late November *Coal Age* observed that "prices have fallen to levels which restrict profits to the lowest cost producers."[58] Data published in *Coal Age* showed that these low-cost producers were mostly nonunion operations. The unionized Pittsburgh district, for instance, worked an average of 51.6 percent of its full-time hours during the week of October 5, while the nonunion Tug River district of West Virginia worked 82.6 percent of full time.[59] By the end of 1924, 43 percent of the nation's coal mines were shut, the UMWA's small presence in southern West Virginia and eastern Kentucky had been eliminated, and its positions in central Pennsylvania and

[55]Ibid., 26 (July 3, 1924): 2.
[56]Ibid., 26 (August 28, 1923): 299.
[57]Ibid., 26 (September 4, 1924): 339.
[58]Ibid., 26 (November 20, 1924): 729.
[59]Ibid.

northern West Virginia were considerably weakened.[60] Again, *Coal Age* expressed concern over the implications of a weak union.

The more the union shrinks the more the non-union districts will find themselves in the condition that the whole country experienced during the nineties, when there was no agreement on wage rates and every man's hand was raised against his neighbor.[61]

The new year saw no improvement in the situation in central Pennsylvania. During the month of January, nonunion production exceeded union production for the first time in that district since it was organized by the UMWA, and there were reports that union operators and miners were subverting their contract by using 2,800-pound tons as the basis of payment and by working six days per week for a four-day paycheck.[62]

At the beginning of March, operators from western Pennsylvania and Ohio attempted to convene a meeting of operators from the four Central Competitive Field States to formulate a joint wage-reduction proposal to present to the union. However, operators from Indiana and Illinois, who were not suffering as much from nonunion competition, preferred to continue with the present contract until the UMWA proposed an alteration.[63] A month later, operators from western Pennsylvania and Ohio did convene a meeting to seek a way to find relief from the Jacksonville scale.[64] At about this same time, Secretary of Labor James Davis reported to President Coolidge that operators were shifting their operations to nonunion districts, that employers in the outlying union districts were openly repudiating the Jacksonville agreement, and that there was a possibility that no union mines would be in operation anywhere after April 1.[65]

As bituminous coal mining became increasingly nonunion and competition correspondingly less organized, *Coal Age* predicted that the fruits of the victory of the nonunion competition may not be so sweet.

The nonunion shipper has had an easy time of it in recent years; with his hands free he has been fighting the union producer, whose hands have been tied. The nonunion producer probably will find the fight a more gruelling one from this time forward. He now faces an antagonist whose hands also are free. The bout

[60]Ibid., 26 (December 11, 1924): 837.
[61]Ibid.
[62]Ibid., 27 (February 6, 1925): 224.
[63]Ibid., 27 (March 5, 1925): 365; ibid., 28 (October 8, 1925): 437; ibid., 27 (March 19, 1925): 437.
[64]Ibid., 27 (April 2, 1925): 508.
[65]Dubofsky and Van Tine, *John L. Lewis*, p. 135.

is catch-as-catch-can. There is practically no limit to the extent that the slashing of prices and wage rates may go.[66]

Warnings from *Coal Age* about the dangers of a competition unregulated by collective bargaining notwithstanding, unionized operators, particularly those in coal districts contiguous to nonunion fields and in direct competition with them – those in northern West Virginia, Ohio, western Pennsylvania, and central Pennsylvania – increasingly felt that they could not afford to cooperate, and their appeals to the UMWA for a revision of their wage contract having been repeatedly rebuffed, they began both openly and surreptitiously to violate their agreements. The importance of this decision by a growing number of operators to operate outside of the long-standing collective bargaining framework was noted by *Coal Age*.

The quarter of a century... following the signing of the joint interstate agreement of 1898 has not... been free from strikes. ... But even in the most prolonged of struggles, ... there was no real attempt upon the part of the operators to challenge the control of the United Mine Workers over their destiny. ... It is only in the present year that growing resentment over the unqualified refusal of the international [union] officers to recognize post-war economic readjustments and to meet the operators to discuss downward revisions in wage rates ... has flared into open rebellion. Up to this year it has been a question of making the best bargain possible with the union. There was no suggestion that, if a satisfactory bargain could not be made with the union, the operators could dispense with the union. Even the abortive attacks made by producers of Ohio and western Pennsylvania in 1922 were attacks upon the Central Competitive Field system of making contracts – not attacks upon the principle of making contracts between the operators and the United Mine Workers of America.[67]

In mid-1925 this principle did come under attack. In June, two months into a UMWA strike against open-shop production in West Virginia, Consolidation Coal Co., the most important union operation in the northern portion of the state, announced that some of its mines would operate on an open-shop basis. Several other operators indicated that they would follow suit.[68] At the end of August, Pittsburgh Coal Co., the leading Pittsburgh-district producer, opened two mines at the 1917 wage rate, initiating an open revolt against the union in western Pennsylvania.[69] A few weeks earlier the Pittsburgh Chamber of Commerce hired an "industrial aide" whose function was to organize a union of

[66]*Coal Age* 27 (March 26, 1925): 479.
[67]Ibid., 28 (October 1, 1925): 459–60.
[68]Ibid., 27 (June 1, 1925): 877.
[69]Ibid., 28 (August 27, 1925): 288.

jobless miners that "will make an agreement with the operators in order that the mines may operate."[70] In an article published in July, a month before Pittsburgh Coal abrogated the Jacksonville agreement, C. E. Lesher, its vice president, appealed to the union to modify its wage scales. He had expected the Jacksonville scale to drive some firms out of business, but had not reckoned on Pittsburgh Coal being among them. It was not "fair."

All know that some, many in fact, must be forced out through sheer inability to compete. This is American business. The struggle of the fittest to survive must be governed by rules of the game that will equalize the opportunity. Other things (such as quality of coal) being equal, it is cost of production and freight rates to consumers that fix the limits of competition. There is a fair tribunal before which the coal operator may take his questions of freight rates. This tribunal, the Interstate Commerce Commission, has constantly before it the complaints of coal operators. With respect to the other largest item in cost of putting coal to the consumer, the labor cost of mining, there is no such fair tribunal.[71]

By the beginning of the new year, the situation in Pennsylvania had deteriorated to the point where the Pittsburgh Coal Producers' Association, the principal Pittsburgh-district collective bargaining agent for operators, was dissolved.[72]

While defections continued through the early months of 1926, a protracted British coal strike, which began on May 1, had begun to push prices up in the fall. In early September, operators in Ohio, once again unsuccessful in their efforts to reach an agreement with the union to revise wages, resolved to stick to the Jacksonville scale rather than cut wages and risk a shutdown. In early November, meanwhile, in an instance of what *Coal Age* referred to as "Lewis luck," wages in Pittsburgh, central Pennsylvania, and northern West Virginia were actually raised to the Jacksonville scale, so that operators could take advantage of the prevailing high prices.[73] Most of these increases did not survive the new year, however.[74]

As the preliminary jockeying preceding the commencement of the 1927 wage negotiations began, the operators adopted positions roughly corresponding to their relative vulnerability to nonunion competition. Operators from Ohio, "firmly convinced that [the continuation of the

[70]Ibid., 28 (August 6, 1925): 189.
[71]Ibid., 28 (July 2, 1925): 9–10.
[72]Ibid., 29 (January 14, 1926): 54.
[73]Ibid., 30 (November 4, 1926): 641–7.
[74]Ibid., 31 (January 6, 1927): 20.

present scale] will mean the elimination of Ohio operators from the competitive field," were most adamant in their refusal to discuss anything but wage reductions with the UMWA. They were joined by those less efficient Pittsburgh-district operators who needed both low wages and high prices to sell their coal at a profit. It was rumored that these Ohio and Pennsylvania operators would be quick to withdraw from the negotiations if the union did not meet their demands. Operators from Illinois, on the other hand, were "rather cheerful over the mildness of the wage demands of the miners" for a two-year extension of the Jacksonville scale, and were prepared to negotiate on the basis of that demand. Operators in these states preferred accepting union demands and paying high wages to interrupting their output and struggling with the union.[75]

Operators and miners failed to reach an agreement at the Miami joint conference and on April 1 the miners left the mines. This strike was disastrous for the union for, in 1927, unlike 1922, operators from Ohio and Pennsylvania would not settle for anything less than a wage cut, even if it meant the end of collective bargaining. Just before the strike deadline, Lewis conceded the issue that precipitated the 1922 shutdown and authorized district-level union organizations to sign interim agreements with district-level operator groups.[76] This did not stem the open-shop tide. In the first week of April, operators in the Pittsburgh district, led by the Pittsburgh Terminal Coal Corporation, the largest union operator, commenced open-shop operations.[77] Elsewhere in the Central Competitive Field, operators continued to demand a wage reduction, although there were continual reports of dissension from this policy from Illinois, where some operators continued to prefer signing with the union under any terms offered.[78] Union operators from central Pennsylvania negotiated intermittently with the UMWA until the end of June, when open-shop production began there.[79] In late June, operators from Ohio issued an ultimatum to their miners, then, in July, commenced open-shop operations.[80]

Predictably, the UMWA fared better in Illinois and Indiana. In Illinois,

---

[75]Ibid., 31 (January 27, 1927): 175; ibid., 31 (February 2, 1927): 203; ibid., 31 (February 10, 1927): 235; ibid., 31 (February 17, 1927): 267; ibid., 31 (February 24, 1927): 302–3; ibid., 31 (March 10, 1927): 370–1; ibid., 33 (January, 1928): 56–7.
[76]Ibid., 31 (March 31, 1927): 472.
[77]Ibid., 31 (April 7, 1927): 506–7.
[78]Ibid., 31 (April 28, 1927): 609.
[79]Ibid., 33 (January, 1928): 41–2.
[80]Ibid.

an agreement was signed between operators and miners on October 1, referring negotiations to a commission of operators and miners that would report its recommendations in February, 1928. In the meantime, work would proceed at the old rate. A similar truce was signed on October 7 in Indiana.[81] Miners from Illinois and Indiana eventually signed contracts reducing basic wages from $7.50 per day to $6.10.[82]

However, the most important result of the 1927 strike was the virtual elimination of the UMWA from their remaining footholds in the Appalachian coal fields. By 1928, membership in the UMWA had declined from its 1921–1922 peak of 500,000, to 80,000 miners, two-thirds of whom were in Illinois.[83]

Conclusion

Not only is the cooperative outcome difficult to *achieve* in Prisoner's Dilemma situations, it is also difficult to *maintain*. Regardless of how many other players are cooperating, the single-play payoff of the individual player can always be improved if he or she chooses the defection strategy. Thus, the Prisoner's Dilemma simultaneously provides individual firms with a motive to organize their competition and an incentive to evade that organization themselves. In the 1920s, as a result both of the rapidly weakening position of the unionized firms and of their consistent failure to win the cooperation of southern Appalachian operators, this latter temptation increasingly prevailed among unionized firms. The result was the *dis*organization of the bituminous coal market and its effective return to the conditions that prevailed during the 1880s, except that the earlier East-West competition had been replaced by North-South competition.

During the 1920s, as well as during the pre-war period, the nature of labor–capital relations in the bituminous coal industry continued to be determined principally by the relations among competing capitalist firms. Although the decade of the 1920s did, in fact, see capital versus labor conflict over the shape and, ultimately, the very existence of collective bargaining in the coal industry, this capital–labor conflict was structured by the capital–capital conflict inherent in economic competition. Coal operators did not attack the miners' union out of any natural antipathy toward labor organizations but because it had failed to organ-

[81]Ibid.
[82]Parker, *Coal Industry*, p. 72.
[83]Dubofsky and Van Tine, *John L. Lewis*, p. 147.

ize competition among operators by preventing wage cutting and, in its failure, had left unionized operators in a position that became increasingly untenable as their market share dwindled. It was the *failure* of the union, not its success, that offended operators into opposing collective bargaining. Operators had seen in industrywide collective bargaining a way to escape the self-destructive wage and price cutting that had so harmed workers *and* capitalists, but the union had ended up placing unionized operators in a worse position than the one that they had escaped originally. The union had organized East–West competition among northern operators, but had left them vulnerable to southern competition. "Created in the first instance out of common necessities, . . . [the Central Competitive Field] appears to have outlived its usefulness. The internal competition which moved the operators of this field to unite to save themselves from themselves no longer dominates."[84] It was replaced by competition from an *external* source, West Virginia. Having failed to force West Virginia operators to raise their costs to the Central Competitive Field level, these latter operators competed with nonunion mines by moving against the union.

They were led by the Ohio and Pennsylvania operators, who were most vulnerable to southern Appalachian competition, as our model suggests. This confirms that the competitive position of operators vis-à-vis operators was the major determinant of their relations with the union. The relatively insulated Illinois and Indiana operators continued to support interstate collective bargaining and stuck with the union through the 1927 strike because their internal competition, which the union had helped to stabilize, was more important than competition with distant nonunion wage cutters. In the Midwest, the union had not "outlived its usefulness," but continued to assist in providing the "common necessities" of competing capitalist firms.

[84]*Coal Age* 31 (April 28, 1927): 591.

7. From free competition to state intervention

Introduction

While the breaking of the union by northern Appalachian coal operators constituted a solution to their short-term problem of not being able to meet the wage and price levels of their southern competitors, it did nothing to solve the industry's long-term collective action problem of achieving a cooperative wage and price level that would yield satisfactory profits. On the contrary, without a national labor union to enforce the cooperative wage rate, operators were no closer to organizing their competition than they were forty years earlier, when the problem had first arisen. The absence of collective bargaining, which had provided a check on at least one form of competition, combined with the continued depression, which worsened in 1930, generated persistent wage- and price-cutting pressure, and unsatisfactory, suboptimal outcomes. This chapter examines the response of operators to this new situation. Even as they were dismantling one organizational mechanism – the collective bargaining framework – they were seeking to escape the consequences by trying to reorganize themselves by other means. As the depression deepened, some operators showed a renewed willingness to accept external intervention to transform their competitive game and to enforce their collective action. The positions of operators toward market organization were not uniform, however. As was the case during earlier periods, operators weighed the benefits and risks of market organization differently, depending on their competitive positions. Once again, the "logic of capitalist collective action" generated by the various competitive situations faced by operators played the principal role in determining their political and economic behavior.

Four separate competitive situations can be distinguished. The first was a price game played by operators during the mid-1920s while the process of market disorganization analyzed in the preceding chapter was in progress. At the same time that they were seeking to reduce their labor costs so that they could lower their prices, operators were also trying to stem the downward slide in coal prices through cooperative action. These efforts, which involved internal mechanisms and consolidation, were unsuccessful.

The second period begins with the end of the Central Competitive Field collective bargaining framework. Between 1927 and the spring of 1933, operators in the Appalachian fields faced a price–wage game in which the dominant competitive strategy was unchecked by wage agreements. Only in Illinois and Indiana were operators still constrained by collective bargaining contracts. As our model leads us to expect, operators reacted to the suboptimally low profits generated by this game by trying to transform it. Operators in the South, whose financial position was slightly better and who were extremely distrustful of any industry-wide form of organization that would limit their independence and place them at the mercy of their northern competitors, were the principal advocates of internal mechanisms such as district sales agencies and fair trade codes. Midwestern and northern operators, whose organizational need was higher and whose prior experience with the UMWA made them less wary of external intervention, drifted toward renewed support for unionization and state intervention. The passage of the National Industrial Recovery Act (NIRA) in March, 1933, altered the terms of the debate between these two groups of operators over the appropriate form of market organization in the coal industry. As one of the nation's most important and most competitive industries, there could be little doubt that the bituminous coal industry would be organized under a state-sponsored code of fair competition. The question was what form this code would take. Nonunion Appalachian operators favored a decentralized code leaving each district a great deal of autonomy in setting prices and wages, while midwestern operators, along with the UMWA, tended to favor a more centralized mechanism. The final outcome was a centralized, industrywide collective bargaining agreement appended to a decentralized code of fair competition. Once again, it was the union of workers that organized capitalist firms in the coal industry.

The period of the code's operation constituted a third distinct competitive situation, one in which competition among individual operators was supplanted by competition among groups of operators – the twenty-two autonomous district code authorities created by the Bituminous Coal Code. As it did in the pricing game among individual operators, the Prisoner's Dilemma logic prevailed in this new game as well, and soon operators were responding to the suboptimal outcomes produced by their rational behavior by advocating new measures to transform the game and to organize competition.

The final period begins with the demise of the NIRA and the movement of operators toward a form of market organization that, unlike the relatively weak coal code, would actually be enforced by the state. Here, again, the debate was marked by a cleavage between the UMWA–northern-operator coalition and operators in the South, the latter struggling to maintain district-level autonomy. This period ended with the onset of World War II, which returned the bituminous coal industry to prosperity.

Internal organization and consolidation during the mid-1920s

The wage cutting that was the focus of the previous chapter was the symptom, not the cause, of the competitive pressures felt by coal operators, and while the elimination of collective bargaining left some operators better able to compete and therefore caused a short-term improvement to their position, the elimination of an imperfect organizational mechanism and the consequent disorganization of competition in no way constituted a satisfactory outcome to their collective action problem. Whether operators were unionized or not, they still felt the pressure to cut prices generated by the Prisoner's Dilemma structure of price competition. Moreover, as operators succeeded in breaking the union, they pushed down the payoff received by all wage- and price-cutting firms, thereby increasing their need for a further organization of the market. The wage- and price-cutting game played by coal operators during the mid-1920s, then, generated two types of behavior among operators. At the same time that unionized firms sought successfully to win the capacity to cut wages and prices and to meet the competition of nonunion firms, both unionized and nonunion coal operators sought to escape the suboptimal outcomes that were generated by competitive price cutting. They did so by turning to internal organizational mechanisms and by attempting to consolidate their properties.

The principal arena for their internal efforts was the National Coal Association (NCA), a trade association formed in 1917 to undertake publicity for the industry, to collect statistics, to promote uniform contracts, and, in *Coal Age*'s words, to "promote harmonious feeling and conduct."[1] In its early years, the NCA's efforts to promote collective action in the market focused on the promotion of standardized cost

[1] *Coal Age*, 12 (July 17, 1917): 32.

accounting and data collection. As the organization's secretary pointed out, "the man who through an adequate cost accounting system knows his cost of production will most likely prove a fair competitor, since he will insist on getting a fair price for his product."[2] These efforts never really caught on, in part because the coal boom of 1920 temporarily eliminated the problem of sales below cost, but also because there was a fear, reinforced by the Calder committee's "raid" on the NCA's offices in 1920, that the data collected by operators would be used against them by the industry's enemies.[3]

The depression that began in 1924 led to a renewal of the association's data-collection activities. *Coal Age* wrote that "in view of the existing situation, all agree that comprehensive and accurate statistics are more important to the coal industry at this time than any other activity."[4] One reason was that better data could help to curb the industry's expansion.

In many industries the financing is so centralized that a careful check is kept on expansion. Most new coal companies are financed in the immediate locality. The backers, as a rule, have no conception of the number of properties being opened in similar fashion.[5]

Fearing that hard times would lead to a retrenchment that would weaken the industry's associations and hamper their activities, which were "most needed in this troublesome time," *Coal Age* urged operators to solidarity. "The coal digger is willing to stick to his union even if it means going hungry. . . . More of the same spirit is needed among operators."[6] In 1925, nudged by the specter of more fact-finding legislation as well as by the continuation of the depression, the NCA appointed a committee to cajole operators into cooperating with its data-collection program.[7]

Even before this committee was organized, several regional statistical agencies were organized in the spring of 1925.[8] Noting that a "principal fault with the coal business is that it is a business conducted in the dark," *Black Diamond* applauded the formation of these bureaus as the "most concrete thing that is being done to help conditions in the bituminous coal industry."[9] However, a year later, the hesitancy of many

---

[2]Ibid., 18 (October 7, 1920): 761.
[3]Ibid., 18 (July 29, 1920): 252.
[4]Ibid., 25 (March 13, 1924): 399.
[5]Ibid., 25 (February 28, 1924): 329.
[6]Ibid., 25 (May 15, 1924): 735.
[7]Ibid., 28 (July 23, 1925): 125.
[8]*Black Diamond* 74 (April 18, 1925): 451; ibid., 74 (June 13, 1925): 694–5.
[9]Ibid., 74 (June 13, 1925): 694–5.

operators to submit reports to such agencies had not been overcome. One operator blamed the industry's negative attitudes on a "vocal minority" who thought "more in terms of price psychology than of the good of the industry."[10] However, it is possible that operators declined to participate because they had come to realize that the price cutting that was eating away at their profits was not the result of "psychology" or ignorance about costs, but was a product of their competitive social relations. As I pointed out in Chapter 2, internal organizational mechanisms are attractive to capitalist firms from the point of view of costs, but do not generally effect a transformation of the payoff structure of defecting firms of sufficient magnitude to promote cooperation. *Coal Age* noted in 1916 that "correct cost accounting

will only show the need for high prices of coal. It will not show how to secure them when the demand for coal is at a low ebb. ... It is not cost accounting, but cooperation alone that can prevent the cutting of prices to the unprofitable level."[11]

Like the renewal of the cooperative efforts of the National Coal Association, the merger movements experienced by the coal industry in the mid–1920s were clearly motivated by the industry's depressed condition and the corresponding desire to reduce competitive pressure. Consolidation was a way of reducing output and eliminating the competitive relationships that pushed operators to mine coal at unrenumerative prices.

The failure of the coal industry's earlier, turn of the century, merger movement to eliminate competition appears to have had no impact on the enthusiasm with which consolidation was embraced in the 1920s. *Coal Age* and *Black Diamond* continually pressed consolidation as the way out of the industry's troubles. " 'Consolidate' has been the cry. 'Let economic pressure squeeze these excess mines either out of business forever or else into big, well operated groups.' "[12] Several months later *Black Diamond* claimed that "if each district will convene itself, confront its situation and adopt a somewhat broader attitude than coal operators usually assume, it can consolidate itself into one or two companies."[13] "There is no economic justification for five to fifty mining companies in each district."[14]

[10]*Coal Age* 30 (August 12, 1926).
[11]Ibid., 10 (November 25, 1916): 891.
[12]Ibid., 24 (October 25, 1923): 617.
[13]*Black Diamond* 72 (March 1, 1924): 239.
[14]Ibid., 73 (August 23, 1924): 214–15; also, see ibid., 74 (February 7, 1925): 159.

These exhortations reflected developments in the coal fields. In February, 1924, *Coal Age* announced that

feverish movement toward consolidation of mines in various bituminous coal fields is gaining headway daily. Operators both strong and weak turn their thoughts upon it – the former in the hope that it will improve conditions of operating and marketing; the latter in pure desperation. In some regions the proposal is overshadowing almost every other subject except wages.[15]

Eight months later, the same journal's Washington correspondent wrote optimistically that

consolidations have been effected and are in course of consummation almost sufficient to constitute evolution. . . . Before the end of the year, it is predicted, enough mines will have been acquired in this manner to give a new degree of stability to the entire bituminous industry.[16]

Coal Age's predictions did not come true. Major mergers did occur during 1924, but they involved less than 30,000,000 tons of annual capacity, far below what would have been necessary to have a significant impact on the structure of competition.[17]

Enthusiastic discussion of mergers continued in 1925, when *Black Diamond* reported that "seldom does the day pass . . . that . . . does not bring some word of a consolidation of coal producing companies" and suggested hopefully that the "era of consolidation" in the coal business had begun.[18]

Coal Age reported only one merger in 1926, a year when the organizational need of bituminous coal operators was temporarily reduced by shortages produced by coal strikes in the anthracite fields of the United States and in the English coal industry. However, when depressed conditions returned in 1927 and 1928, mergers again became a major topic of discussion. In *Coal Age's* first issue of 1928, the editors asked a number of leading operators to name the biggest problem facing the industry and the way in which it could best be solved. For most respondents, the problem was overproduction, and for many, the best solution remained more consolidation "so as to get the coal industry into fewer hands, as it would likely be handled more intelligently." "If several consolidations could be made . . . it would be possible to maintain a price for coal which would at least return to the property the cost of production . . . , and in addition to

[15]*Coal Age* 25 (February 21, 1924): 268.
[16]Ibid., 26 (August 21, 1924): 262.
[17]Ibid., 27 (March 19, 1925): 423.
[18]*Black Diamond* 75 (August 29, 1925): 229.

that a reasonable margin of profit would be expected."[19] In March, the outgoing President of the American Institute of Mining Engineers stated that "rumors of mergers are now thick" and the editors of *Coal Age* observed that "mergers are a staple topic of conversation when coal men meet these days."[20]

As in the earlier merger wave during the first decade of the twentieth century, the obstacles in the way of eliminating competition in the coal industry through consolidation outweighed the desire of operators to do so. Far more mergers were planned, proposed, or on the verge of realization than were actually effected. And by the beginning of 1930, *Coal Age* was forced to conclude that "large scale combinations have not been effected with the rapidity many looking for a quick way out hoped."[21] The 1923–1928 period was a transitional one in the bituminous coal industry. As we saw in Chapter 6, it marked the collapse of the Central Competitive Field collective bargaining framework and with it the end of a forty-year effort on the part of operators to organize their own competition by agreeing to a wage floor enforced by the union of their workers. However, it can also be seen as the start of another "cycle" of efforts to organize the market. Breaking the union may have caused a temporary relative improvement in the competitive position of northern Appalachian operators, but it did not solve the problem of self-destructive competitive price cutting. The efforts on the part of operators to tackle this problem internally, through voluntary efforts to cooperate and through consolidations, reminded them of the magnitude of the structural obstacles in the way of a reorganization of their market. When the Great Depression further deepened the hard times faced by operators, they continued along the path begun during the preceding years. First they sought salvation in more "organized" internal mechanisms – fair-trade codes and district sales agencies; then they once more turned to the union and to the state.

The Great Depression: the "unorganized" price and wage game revisited

Beginning in late 1929, the coal industry's own depression was compounded by the general industrial depression precipitated by the stock market crash. The full brunt of the depression did not hit the coal in-

[19]*Coal Age* 33 (January, 1928): 6–17, 42–3.
[20]Ibid., 33 (March, 1928): 141, 183.
[21]Ibid., 35 (January, 1930): 8.

dustry until 1931, but, even in 1930, output and working time were at their lowest level since 1924 (Tables 4.1 and 4.2). However, by 1931 and 1932, the bituminous coal industry was experiencing an unprecedented crisis. Working time, which is generally viewed against a 280-day capacity, was at 160 and 146 days. Output in 1932, the industry's nadir, was at its lowest level since 1904. Between 1928 and 1932, the bituminous coal industry experienced the largest aggregate losses of any U.S. industry.[22]

The immediate impact of the industrial crisis on coal operators was to increase competitive pressure. With demand dropping off, operators could maintain their sales only by reducing prices. What was new in the competitive game of the early thirties was the absence of a union-enforced wage floor in the northern Appalachian districts. This meant, of course, that the competitive advantage enjoyed by nonunion southern districts had largely been eliminated. In the Appalachian region, then, the game was a wage–price Prisoner's Dilemma played among firms with different costs but possessing similar capacities to reduce costs by cutting wages.

We expect that this game will generate wage and price cutting, leading to suboptimal outcomes. This expectation is borne out by the data. Prices declined from $1.78 in 1929 to $1.54 in 1931 and to $1.31 in 1932 (Table 4.3). Price cutting was accompanied by wage cutting. Berquist writes that "during this period the intense competition was basically one of wage rates, non-union workers being obliged to accept what the successive price cuts permitted operators to pay them."[23] One central Pennsylvania operator stated that "wage cutting had become so prevalent in the industry that it was difficult for anyone to know exactly what any other operator was paying. It had become a matter of individual slashing of prices and individual slashing of wages in order to meet the prices and try to keep in business."[24] Even in the unionized fields of Illinois and Indiana, wages fell from $6.10 to $4.58 (IN) and $5.00 (IL) between 1931 and 1932.[25]

The willingness of operators to organize out of the suboptimal outcome produced by such a game depends, we have seen, on their organizational need, and on the perceived costs of the organizational

[22]N. H. Leonard, "The Bituminous Coal Industry," in *The Structure of the American Economy*, ed. Walter Adams (New York: Macmillan, 1950), p. 40.
[23]Berquist et al., *Economic Survey*, p. 418.
[24]Ibid., p. 279.
[25]*Coal Age* 38 (February, 1933): 35.

mechanism in question. In the present context, the southern operators, whose lower wage level brought them relative prosperity during the 1920s, probably entered the 1930s in a more secure position and with less of an organizational need than did their northern competitors. The northern Appalachian operators shared the advantage of freedom from a wage contract with their southern competitors, but the losses that they sustained during the 1920s, when they were prevented from cutting wages by the Jacksonville Agreement, probably left them in a weaker competitive position and with a greater organizational need. Unionized midwestern operators were protected to some extent by geography from competition from the Appalachian region. Still, their contract with the UMWA prevented them from cutting wages competitively and thereby placed them in a disadvantageous position. We would therefore expect them to be most desirous of securing the cooperation of other firms in the industry.

With respect to the perceived costs of most organizational mechanisms, the relative position of these three groups of operators is reversed. Since they were already partially organized by an external actor – the UMWA – the midwestern operators had little to fear from an extension of an external mechanism across the industry. The increased loss of autonomy that they would suffer would be relatively small. The southern Appalachian firms, on the other hand, had the most to fear from industry-wide market organization, since every attempt to organize coal competition across the northern and southern fields in the past had been directed against their competitive advantage with respect to wages and freight rates. The northern Appalachian operators occupied a middle position. They might risk losing their capacity to cut wages and prices but, on the basis of their past experience, they would probably gladly do so if they could at the same time limit the flexibility of their southern competitors. In general, then, we would expect the midwestern firms to be most willing to go beyond relatively low-cost, internal forms of market organization, followed by the northern Appalachian firms and the southern Appalachian firms. The resistance of all firms to paying the costs of organizing competition will decrease as the low profits brought on by the economic crisis persist.

Internal efforts to organize competition

We saw in Chapter 7 that the desire to eliminate price competition during the 1920s led to small spurts of mergers in 1924–1925 and 1927–1928.

Even before the industrial crisis of late 1929, however, consolidation had proven to be an ineffectual solution to the industry's competitive problems.

Large scale combinations still seem to many the ideal, if not the only, way out of the destructive competitive situation sapping the strength of the bituminous coal industry. Prospects for an early realization of that ideal . . . , however, are not bright. The collapse of the merger movement in southern West Virginia last year demonstrated anew how difficult it is to reach a basis for combination acceptable to conflicting groups in a highly personalized business. The general disinclination on the part of investment bankers to underwrite soft-coal consolidations puts a definite check upon the probabilities of lessening ruinous competition by outright cash purchase. . . . The fact that one door has been closed outright ought to be a challenge to leadership to find another way out. Obviously if the industry is to be denied the quick advantages inherent to mergers in their familiar guise, the problem before it is how the industry may best and most speedily win like benefits under its existing form of organization.[26]

The industrial collapse and the resultant wage and price cutting gave a further impetus to the search for alternative solutions to the problem of market organization. As we might have expected, operators first turned, again, to internal means – district sales agencies and fair-trade codes. Southern firms appeared to be the prime movers behind both efforts. Meanwhile, firms in the North began to reassess their relationship with workers and to rediscover the capacity of organized workers to organize capitalist competition.

We have seen that coal operators frequently viewed price cutting by their competitors as "sales below cost." This behavior, which had long been criticized as "unbusinesslike" and "unreasonable" began to be described at the end of the 1920s as "unfair," an adjective that made it more amenable to collective remedies under the antitrust laws. Beginning in 1929, this concern with sales below cost, along with the increase in competition in general, was reflected in the formulation of many district-level codes of fair trade practice, which outlawed sales below cost and various other "unfair trade practices." Compliance to these codes was voluntary. This movement apparently originated in Tennessee in January, 1929, when the Southern Appalachian Coal Association, a local operators' association, named a trade practice committee.[27] Two months later, the Southern Appalachian Coal Exchange was organized as an auxiliary to the association.[28] The exchange later promulgated a

[26]*Coal Age* 34 (February, 1929): 73.
[27]Ibid., p. 66.
[28]Ibid., 33 (April, 1929): 248.

code banning the shipment of coal on consignment, an adjunct of the practice of mining coal before it was sold; and selling coal below the cost of production in order to injure a competitor or to control competition.[29] The idea of a code of ethics spread to other districts during 1929 and 1930.[30] In the spring of the latter year, the National Coal Association entered the picture, establishing a committee to put the fair trade code movement on the "highest plane possible."[31] During the next year, the movement continued to gather steam. In January, 1931, representatives from the National Coal Association, the National Association of Purchasing Agents, the National Retail Coal Merchants' Association, and the International Railway Fuel Association approved a code of ethics to govern the buying and selling of railroad fuel.[32] In February, representatives from seven southern coal bureaus met to resolve that "the trade practice movement be established and strengthened in every producing field in the country . . . ," and a month later, forty-two representatives of operator organizations met in Cincinnati to discuss the trade practice movement and to develop a plan to extend it throughout the industry.[33] Again, there is no evidence that these codes had any effect on individual competitive behavior. They certainly did not halt the downward slide of coal prices.

By late 1931, bituminous coal operators were beginning to seek to organize competition through an even more effective internal organizational mechanism: the district selling agency. The notion of district-wide selling agencies, a form of pooling in which the output of the entire field would be marketed by a single agent, cropped up on several occasions during the 1920s. In 1924 and 1925 *Coal Age* ran a series of articles pushing for some form of cooperative marketing of coal, citing the success that similar practices had enjoyed in American agriculture, and in the German and British coal and coke industries; and in 1928, district selling agencies, along with consolidation by merger, were the solutions to overproduction most frequently mentioned by operators who responded to *Coal Age's* survey on the problems of the coal industry.[34] Perhaps because there was a general perception among operators that the Sherman Act would have to be modified in order to proceed with

[29]Ibid., 34 (November, 1929): 667.
[30]Ibid., pp. 704–5; *Mineral Industry* 39 (1931): 183.
[31]*Coal Age* 35 (May, 1930): 183.
[32]Ibid., 36 (February, 1931): 115.
[33]Ibid., 36 (April, 1931): 205.
[34]Ibid., 27 (February 19, 1925): 293; ibid., 26 (October 9, 1924): 516–17; ibid., 25 (May 8, 1924): 695; ibid., 33 (January, 1928): 6–17, 42–7.

any cooperative marketing arrangements, something that most operators were not willing to risk attempting at this time, no concrete steps were taken to formulate district selling plans until 1931. The impetus was provided by a meeting of Appalachian governors convened by Governor Flem D. Sampson of Kentucky, at which a recommendation was made that the National Coal Association develop a plan to ease the depressed condition of the bituminous coal industry.[35] The latter organization appointed a committee on stabilizing the industry, and on December 3, 1931, the committee issued a report recommending, among other things, that each producing field be divided into districts, each served by a district selling agency. Within two months operators in northern West Virginia, western Kentucky, western Pennsylvania, central Pennsylvania, and southern West Virginia had each met to begin planning selling agencies.[36] This first one to reach the actual organization stage was Appalachian Coals, Inc., which comprised operators from Virginia, Tennessee, and Kentucky. In exchange for a 10-percent commission, Appalachian Coals assumed all marketing functions for its members. Control was based on common stock issued to operators on the basis of production. The governing board was composed of two members from each producing district and nine at-large members.[37] Before Appalachian Coals had a chance to commence operations, however, a U.S. District Court in Richmond, Virginia, ruled that it was in restraint of trade. The Supreme Court dismissed this decision in March, 1933, and by the end of June operators in eastern Ohio, Alabama, northern West Virginia, central Pennsylvania, western Pennsylvania, western Kentucky, and southern Ohio had organized district selling agencies of their own. However, only Alabama Coals, Inc. and Northern Coals (eastern Ohio) were actually at the operational stage when the National Industrial Recovery Act went into effect, creating an alternative basis for district-level cooperation.[38]

Even if they had not been eclipsed by subsequent legislation, there is every reason to doubt whether the district sales agency mechanism would have been sufficient to transform the coal market. This conclusion, which follows from our analysis of the structure of coal competition, matches *Coal Age*'s own evaluation of the district sales agency idea, published in 1924.

[35]Parker, *The Coal Industry*, p. 163.
[36]*Coal Age* 37 (February, 1932): 85.
[37]Parker, *The Coal Industry*, p. 164.
[38]*Coal Age* 39 (February, 1934): 42.

The natural desire to bunch together for mutual protection has led operators to consider some grotesque schemes for business groupings. Most such schemes are hopeless. For instance, in a field where many . . . producers have worked their own undoing time and time again by mutual distrust and stealthy price cutting what hope would there be in a "consolidation" which consisted only in the various companies selling through a common agency? There would be no reduction of costs through central management. There would be much opportunity for discrimination as between members. The cohesion of the group would be weak. It would fly apart on any provocation and upset the market and conditions generally. It would be no consolidation at all. Any half hearted plan for weakly linking up mines or partially pooling properties is a futile dream.[39]

Demands for external intervention to organize coal competition

I argued above that the organizational need of southern operators was generally lower than that of their northern counterparts at the beginning of the Great Depression. While no section of the coal industry can be said to have been prosperous, nonunion firms expanded their market share during the 1920s, and therefore entered the new decade in a slightly stronger position than the unionized operators, who had suffered severely under the Jacksonville regime. This means that we would expect southern firms to be more reluctant to turn to high-cost organizational mechanisms. Rather, they would support low-cost internal mechanisms, turning to higher-cost alternatives only when the internal mechanisms had failed. Things were different in the North. First, the organizational need of northern operators – and hence their willingness to pay the costs of organization – was greater. Second, they had a clear understanding of the benefits of collective bargaining and were therefore less threatened by the prospect of collective bargaining than their southern competitors. On both demand (organizational need) and supply (cost of organization) grounds, we would expect northern operators to be more willing to risk higher-cost forms of market organization.

These rough predictions are borne out by the facts. As we saw in the previous section, while northern districts did participate in them, the fair-trade code and district selling agency movements drew most of their momentum from the South, where they originated. In this section I analyze the movement for the return of some form of external intervention – either from the union or the state – which got under way in the

[39]Ibid., 25 (February 21, 1924): 268.

early 1930s and which received most of its support from operators in the North.

It would be an exaggeration to say that the operators who had so successfully broken the United Mine Workers' strength in the Appalachian fields in 1927 had, en masse, become staunch advocates of collective bargaining during the next five years, but there is evidence of a growing perception among operators that the union's role in stabilizing wages had contributed to the organization of competition that operators had been trying to achieve for decades, and that, for this reason, conditions without a union were worse than conditions with the union. A second factor in this shift toward the United Mine Workers was a fear that workers would turn to a more radical organization, the National Miners' Union. As early as 1928, John Jones, a Pittsburgh district operator, told the Senate Committee on Interstate Commerce that the wage agreements with the UMWA had been a stabilizing force in the coal market and that if some arbitration body could enforce agreement between miners and operators when strikes threatened, then he would prefer to work under a union contract.[40] This position was considerably less isolated by 1931. In June of that year, the Pittsburgh Terminal Coal Co., the second-largest Pittsburgh-district operation, caused a major splash in bituminous coal circles when it signed a contract with the UMWA. Pittsburgh Terminal's President, Frank Taplin, explained this move in a letter that is worth quoting at length.

For the past four years these operators who have dispensed with union agreements have had plenty of time to view the experience of running without any fixed wage scale or without having any labor organization to deal with. It must be admitted that the situation is even worse than when we dealt with the union. Many operators try to keep their properties operating by cutting prices to ridiculous figures, then go back and cut the wages of the miners. . . . Personally, I would much prefer to deal with the United Mine Workers than with these ruthless, price-cutting operators who are a detriment to the industry.

The southern high volatile fields have been cutting wages as well as the northern fields, and they are likely to get into trouble with the communistic element of miners, and before we get through we may find that the only way to solve the wage problem is to put all competitive fields under a well managed union with a fixed living scale, to which the miners are entitled, but which never can be

[40]Ibid., 33 (April, 1928): 247.

done without a union because the operators will not stick to any decent fixed wage if they are left to their own devices.[41]

A month later, *Coal Age* took up the same argument.

When district after district in the bituminous fields parted company with organized labor a few years ago, they embarked upon an experiment in internal regulation without precedent for success in the history of American industry. Today the results of that experiment are finding expression in widespread labor disturbances.... Their inevitability was foretold when a major part of an overdeveloped and disorganized industry exchanged the restrictions of contractual labor relations for unlicensed indulgence in ruinous wage and price competition.... Alliance with the National Miners' Union is unthinkable because the ultimate aim of that organization is the destruction of our present capitalistic civilization. District unions without national affiliations are handicapped by the same limitations as company unions.... Elimination of these organizations from consideration naturally raises the question whether the reestablishment of the United Mine Workers, or some other national union, to the position of dominance held by the Indianapolis group prior to 1920 is the only way out.[42]

In September, 1931, *Coal Age*, in recognition of the fact that "while the law of the jungle is driving out some of the inefficient, it is also draining the resources of many producers who richly deserve to survive," published a major stabilization plan, calling for the relaxation of the antitrust laws, sound merchandizing by operators, increased mechanization, improved safety, increased consolidation, coordinated research, and stabilized industrial relations.

Direct labor charges are such a major part of the cost of production that it is obvious that there can be no hope for price stability and for long term planning without stabilization of wages and standardization of working conditions. In an industry compelled to carry the idle-capacity load of bituminous coal, such stabilization without the interposition of some outside agency representing the workers presents almost insuperable obstacles. During periods of sharp competition, individual companies and districts seeking to maintain what they conceive to be proper industrial relations find themselves isolated from their logical markets because competing districts have cut wages, increased the hours of labor or by otherwise changing working conditions have reduced out-of-pocket costs of production. Inherited prejudices in some fields and bitter personal experiences in others have made the idea of the revival of unionism obnoxious to many employers. Nevertheless, unless some new formula can be found, the conclusion seems inevitable that the desired stabilization of wages and working conditions must come through a recognition and an acceptance of outside labor organization by a sufficiently large percentage of operators.[43]

[41]Quoted in Berquist et al., *Economic Survey*, pp. 184–5.
[42]*Coal Age* 36 (July, 1931): 345.
[43]Ibid., 36 (September, 1931): 471.

The difference in the attitudes between the northern operators, who were increasingly willing to accept external intervention, and the southern operators, who were reluctant to do so and who continued to prefer such low-cost internal mechanisms as district sales agencies, is reflected in the debate over the Davis–Kelly bill. In 1928, at the conclusion of an extended Senate investigation of labor conditions in the Appalachian coal districts, Senator James Watson introduced a bill, sponsored by the UMWA, that would license those operators who permitted their employees to organize to engage in various cooperative activities. Licensing and oversight would be carried out by a five-member Bituminous Coal Commission.[44] When this measure was introduced in 1928, it was received with no enthusiasm at all on the part of the operators. By 1932, however, four more years of depressed conditions and continuous wage and price cutting had led to a more receptive attitude, and when the Watson bill was revived, with few changes, as the Davis–Kelly bill, it received some operator support. These operators saw state intervention as the logical extension of the industry's failure to organize itself by nonstate means. One operator testified that "innumerable" efforts had been made to stabilize the coal industry, but that none had succeeded.

And the explanation . . . is and always has been the disloyalty and treachery of the membership who, as soon as a price fixing arrangement had been signed . . . , would hurriedly leave the meeting for a telephone booth, where they would secretly call up a coal buyer and propose to sell him sufficient coal to supply his needs at less than the price agreed upon . . . and each member of the organization, suspecting every other member of resorting to these tactics, seemed to join the rush for lower prices and more rapid methods of precipitating insolvency. . . . After so many years of unhappy experiences and fruitless efforts to stabilize the industry by those in it, does it not seem a strain on optimism to believe that the bituminous coal industry is going to become profitable under existing conditions or through any plan or organization which the operators may propose unaided by some outside stabilizing force? Some new and different plan must be sought and adopted. Those who mine coal must be required to conform to uniform standards and regulations both as to production and as to marketing, and these must be inaugurated and supervised outside the industry itself.[45]

For this same operator, one effect of state intervention must be the standardization of wages which, it was hoped at one time, the United Mine Workers could achieve.

[44]Ibid., 31 (June, 1928): 389.
[45]U.S. Congress, Senate, Committee on Mines and Mining, *To Create a Bituminous Coal Commission*, Hearings on S.2935, 72nd Congress, 2nd Session, 1932, p. 131.

There will be – human desire for business and profits will not let it be otherwise – no enduring stabilization of coal sale prices unless and until there is a uniformity of wage scales in each district upon which a uniform cost of production may rest; and any marketing plan is a visionary dream . . . that does not take into consideration the cost of production and especially a fair wage to the mine workers, standardized throughout each district.[46]

One central Pennsylvania operator testified that the attitude of coal operators toward government intervention was undergoing a "transformation."

The attitude has been taken in the past that they did not want government regulation, and a great many operators to-day are bitterly opposed to any form of regulation, upon the general principle that the Government should not be in business. But I think that with every day that goes by and every month that goes by the men who are seriously studying the problems of our industry realize that there is no apparent remedy that will come by voluntary action of the operators, and that unless regulation or control or guidance comes from Washington we are simply going to drift into greater chaos than we are in at the present time.[47]

However, most operators who testified at the Davis–Kelly hearings opposed the bill. Operators from the Southwest, who were in direct competition with natural gas and fuel oil, feared that minimum prices would be imposed upon them that would drive them out of their regional energy market. For Appalachian operators, opposition centered around two issues: "compulsory unionization" and the alleged vagueness of the Coal Commission's powers, both of which concerned the costs of organization. While *Coal Age* had been arguing for the past year that the stabilization of wages was desirable and that it could only be achieved by a national labor union, it clearly envisioned more employer input in the definition of the role of such a union than was provided in the Davis–Kelly bill.

Unionization by legislative fiat is vicious in principle and dangerous in practice. Instead of economic penetration of unorganized fields, it invites industrial strife. Moreover, the bill as drawn affords no protection to the public. . . . Nowhere is any curb placed upon labor drunk with new power.[48]

Operators were also worried about the uncertainty surrounding the exact powers of the Coal Commission. One West Virginia operator stated simply that "we do not know what these five men will do." He was

[46]Ibid.
[47]Ibid., p. 127.
[48]*Coal Age* 37 (March, 1932): 91.

particularly worried that they would have the capacity to keep West Virginia coal out of the lake market; or to put it another way, that they would be influenced by his northern competitors.[49] A Pittsburgh operator argued that

this bill requires the owners and operators of coal to agree to obey rules and regulations for the conduct of their business before they know what these rules and regulations are to be. It is the equivalent of asking the operators to sign a blank check.[50]

The Davis–Kelly bill's legislative history was cut short when the Senate Mines and Mining Subcommittee determined that it was unconstitutional. Meanwhile, shortly after the 1932 election, another coal bill was introduced – the Lewis–Hayden bill, which would have established production quotas, and which was modeled after British coal legislation.[51] Consideration of this bill, which was preempted by the National Industrial Recovery Act, took place against a background of continued economic distress in the coal industry and an increase in interest among operators, particularly in the North, for state intervention to organize competition.

In May, 1933, in the early days of the Roosevelt administration, delegations of operators from Indiana, Illinois, western Pennsylvania, and Ohio met with administration officials, urging their support for coal legislation. According to Secretary of the Interior Harold Ickes, the midwestern operators "wanted the Government to set up a minimum wage, fix minimum and maximum prices . . . , and if necessary limit the production of coal and prorate such production among the different states and coal fields." The Ohio and Pennsylvania operators asked for a coal "czar." And a group of operators who met with Secretary of Labor Frances Perkins asked the government to relieve them of the burden of competition by purchasing their mines "at any price."[52] Another group of bituminous coal operators, working with representatives from the anthracite, oil, copper, and lumber industries, were planning legislation modeled after the Capper–Volstead Act, which would exempt the mining industries from the Sherman Act and would permit cooperative marketing arrangements.[53] Southern operators continued their opposition to any form of legislation beyond that necessary to legitimate private

[49]U.S. Congress, Senate, Committee on Mines and Mining, *Coal Commission*, p. 256.
[50]Ibid., p. 464.
[51]Johnson, *Politics*, pp. 132–3.
[52]Ibid., p. 140; *Coal Age* 38 (June, 1933): 216.
[53]*Coal Age* 39 (February, 1934): 42.

district sales agencies such as Appalachian Coals, which, while receiving the imprimatur of the Supreme Court, were still thought to be on a slightly shaky legal foundation.[54] Meanwhile, President Roosevelt had met with UMWA officials to discuss coal legislation and an administration coal bill was "said to be very much in the picture" up until the passage of the National Industrial Recovery Act (NIRA), which forestalled any further discussion of legislation.[55]

The Bituminous Coal Code: external organization returns to the coal industry

The legislative history and background of the NIRA have been described in detail by other writers.[56] What captured the interest of coal operators, as well as most other American capitalists, was Title I, which gave to each industry the power to organize codes of fair competition, which, once approved by the president, were not subject to the antitrust laws and were binding upon all members of the industry. Violations of these codes were punishable by fines of up to $500 and/or imprisonment of up to six months. The only rub was Section 7a, which gave workers the right to organize and bargain collectively through representatives of their own choosing, free from employer interference, and which freed workers from any compulsion to join a company union or to refrain from joining the organization of their choice.

Representatives of the coal industry joined the National Association of Manufacturers in condemning the collective bargaining provisions of the act and asking for more industry representation in its administration, but the industry's general attitude was one of wary acceptance. Thus, while *Coal Age* disapproved of "the shadow of compulsory unionization" cast by the bill, it was willing to admit that the industry's need for organization warranted paying a higher price to achieve it. It noted that even "the most enthusiastic exponents of rugged individualism" must admit that "social and economic standards have broken down" and there was little chance of building them "without the government support and sanctions implied in this bill."[57]

[54]Johnson, *Politics*, p. 140.
[55]*Coal Age* 38 (June, 1933): 216; James P. Johnson, *A "New Deal" for Soft Coal* (New York: Arno, 1979), p. 14.
[56]Ellis Hawley, *The New Deal and the Problem of Monopoly* (Princeton: Princeton University Press, 1966); Robert F. Himmelberg, *The Origins of the National Recovery Administration* (New York: Fordham University Press, 1976).
[57]*Coal Age* 38 (June, 1933): 173–4.

The National Industrial Recovery Act was based largely on the principle of "industrial self-government." The members of each industry
were given the opportunity to develop their own codes of fair competition. We have seen that, for each individual player, the preferred solution to a Prisoner's Dilemma situation is one that produces cooperation
among one's competitors, while preserving one's own freedom of action.
This basic ambiguity was reflected in the attitude of operators as they
entered the process of developing a code of fair competition in the
bituminous coal industry. "They wanted both stable minimums and
control over their business. Effective minimums could help the industry
as a whole, but no . . . operator wished to relinquish his opportunity to
cut prices . . . ."[58] Operators, of course, could not have it both ways. We
would expect that their willingness to "pay for" increased industrywide
cooperation by accepting constraints on their own behavior would be
determined by the way in which they weighed the costs and benefits
of market organization. According to our previous analysis, then, we
would expect the midwestern operators to be most willing to accept a
form of market organization that would guarantee industrywide cooperation, and the southern Appalachian firms to be most resistant to such
an outcome. The northern Appalachian firms would probably join their
erstwhile allies in the Midwest. The history of the code-writing process
in the bituminous coal industry partially supports these predictions.
Unionized operators from Illinois and Indiana pressed for a centralized
code that would stipulate wages and prices, while the Appalachian operators, both North and South, attempted to minimize external control
over their operations and argued for weaker, decentralized codes. This
would have meant that instead of the single coal code which the National
Recovery Administration (the NRA – the administrative arm of the
NIRA) expected, there would be several district-level codes, each setting
its own price and wage level. "Cooperation" under a single code came
only under pressure from the state, reinforced by the renewed clout of
the United Mine Workers.

The debate over the coal code began in mid-June, 1933, at the National
Coal Association meeting, where a committee appointed earlier in the
month presented the so-called model code. This document called for
the "sale of all coal at such price or prices as will realize . . . the cost of
production, plus a reasonable margin of profit" and empowered each
district to achieve this through the setting of minimum prices. Besides

[58]Johnson, *Politics*, p. 143.

providing for standard size classifications and standard sales contracts, it also identified eleven categories of unfair methods of competition in addition to cutting the minimum price. However, it contained no administrative provisions and its labor provisions, besides failing to provide for standard hours or wages, appeared to qualify Section 7a by recognizing that some operators "employ their labor under satisfactory individual relationship between the employer and employee." As envisioned by the proponents of this code, it was to serve as a model to be followed by each district in the development of its own code.[59] Operators from Pittsburgh, western Kentucky, and Appalachian Coals, Inc., favored the adoption of the model code so that district codes could be drawn up that would meet local conditions and preserve local autonomy. Midwestern unionized operators, on the other hand, wanted to extend the model code to include hours, wages, and prices. Not surprisingly, these operators, who could expect the union to enforce district-level agreements, were hesitant to commit themselves to a cooperative agreement without knowing the terms of the codes developed by competing districts. "I don't see how it is possible for us people who are working under contracts to present any code fixing hours of labor until we know what our competition is going to be from other sources."[60] In spite of a radioed plea from General Hugh Johnson, the NRA Administrator, for a meaningful industrywide code, coal operators voted to accept the model code.[61]

When the official bituminous code hearings opened on August 9, at least twenty-eight separate codes had been proposed by various groups of operators. Most of them were in agreement as to their ultimate aim – the elimination of "unfair competition" – and their lists of unfair practices were almost all adaptations of the model code's proscriptions. They also provided for minimum-price fixing. However, operators were also in agreement over excluding external actors from the administration of their codes. With the exception of the code worked out by the UMWA and a group of union operators, each code was an affirmation of industrial self-government, and even the UMWA-sponsored code possessed decidedly weak administrative provisions.[62]

Just as competition in the coal market had long been dominated by wage cutting, so the hearings on the coal code were dominated by the

[59]*Coal Age* 38 (July, 1933): 234.
[60]Ibid., 38 (July, 1933): 233; Parker, *Coal Industry*, pp. 108–9.
[61]*Coal Age* 38 (July, 1933): 233–4; Johnson, *"New Deal,"* p. 15.
[62]*Coal Age* 38 (August, 1933): 280–3.

question of interdistrict wage differentials.[63] "The operators, who had competed by lowering wages, fought tenaciously to keep another district from successfully arguing for a lower rate."[64] Virtually all bituminous operators were willing to agree to abide by minimum prices fixed at the district level, but there was a fundamental conflict between those who drew the line at such purely internal mechanisms and those who desired a more effective correlation of interdistrict wages and prices, one that would be enforced by a combination of operator committees and organized workers. This was a conflict between those who were willing to accept the escalating organizational costs of submission to operators from competing fields, to workers, and possibly to the state, and those who were not. Again, this cleavage divided the unionized midwestern operators from their nonunion competitors.

That the bituminous coal operators eventually submitted to a single code of fair competition was the result of several factors: the success of the UMWA organizing drive, which generated a solution to the sticky problem of wage differentials independent of the NRA code negotiations; the intervention of the Roosevelt administration, which pressured the operators to negotiate a contract with the union and to agree to a single code; wildcat strikes in western Pennsylvania, which provided each party involved in the code-formulation process with an added incentive to produce quick results; and the content of the code, which turned out to be almost as decentralized as operators first demanded.

Probably the most lasting success story to come from the whole NRA experience was the 1933 UMWA organization drive, to which John L. Lewis committed the remaining resources of his dwindled organization, and which quadrupled the union's membership within a few months. While the operators were trying to fiddle with Section 7a of the NIRA and were arguing over centralized control of wages and prices, the UMWA was making such issues obsolete by eliminating open shop from the coal fields and by constituting itself into an instrument with the capacity to centralize and stabilize wage rates. The story of this movement has been retold many times. What is of particular interest to us is the relationship of operators to it. I have noted already that there was a visible softening of operator attitudes toward the union in 1931 and 1932. It is not taking any credit away from the UMWA leadership, its field organizers, or the rank and file miners to point out that in the

[63]Berquist et al., *Economic Survey*, pp. 90–4; Johnson, "*New Deal*," p. 32.
[64]Johnson, "*New Deal*," p. 32.

context of bituminous coal labor relations of the late 1920s, the UMWA in the words of an NRA analyst, faced "surprisingly little opposition from operators."[65] There were exceptions, of course – the notorious antiunion bastion in eastern Kentucky and the captive mines in western Pennsylvania, whose operators were steel companies – but, on the whole, an increasing number of operators came to accept stabilization of wages by the UMWA, even while they were submitting codes calling for a district-by-district determination of wages. "Operators in the former union fields realized that a national union would help reduce the wage differentials which had given the South an advantage," and, even in the South, operators underwent a change of heart.[66] W. Tams, a prominent southern West Virginia operator, wrote in his memoirs that "the experience of 1929–1933 had shown that some method of preventing wage cutting was necessary, and the union contract appeared to be the only dependable device to secure this end."[67] In the words of another analyst, the "relaxation of sentiment among employers against dealing with an outside organization of workers . . . came as the result neither of a change in employer ideology nor of a greater or lesser approval of trade unionism *per se*, but of the economics of the industry."[68] Plagued by continual price competition and the resulting suboptimal profits, unable to achieve a cooperative solution to their wage–price game, and with the depletion of their financial resources increasing their organizational need, coal operators came to accept intervention by the "moderate" UMWA as the next-less costly alternative.

Meanwhile, back in Washington, where the process of writing the code of fair competition was in progress, wage differentials continued to be the major stumbling block. The Roosevelt administration's strategy was to deflect this issue into collective bargaining. As *Coal Age* pointed out, if the administration "could bring the Appalachian operators and the United Mine Workers together, its task of fixing wage minimums would be greatly simplified, since it could then write into the new code the wages agreed upon."[69] On August 24, after some nudging by the president, the Appalachian operators met representatives of the UMWA at the first joint conference since the 1927 strike.[70] The conference took

[65]Berquist et al., *Economic Survey*, p. 302.
[66]Johnson, *Politics*, p. 169.
[67]Tams, *Smokeless*, pp. 70–1.
[68]Grant W. Farr, "The Origins of Recent Labor Policy," *University of Colorado Studies*, Series in Economics, No. 3, 1959, pp. 31–2.
[69]*Coal Age* 38 (October, 1933): 316.
[70]Ibid., pp. 293, 316.

place under the watchful eye of the administration – "by the direction of the President under supervision of the NRA, which will lay down the program of negotiations and act as a mediator throughout."[71]

While the joint conference was in session, the administration continued to press operators to agree on an industrywide code of fair competition. Finally, pushed by administration threats, as well as by a strike in western Pennsylvania protesting the absence of a coal code, the operators came up with a code that met administration approval. On September 19, the day after the code was approved, the president reconvened the joint conference of operators and workers, and their contract, signed on September 21, was appended to the code as Schedule A.[72]

The final, approved version of the code was a relatively weak organizational mechanism. It declared that "the selling of coal under a fair market price is hereby declared to be an unfair competitive practice and in violation of this code," but it provided no further indication of how these "fair market prices" would be determined, leaving this to the divisional and subdivisional code authorities (eventually numbering twenty-two), each of which would set prices for its own members.[73] The only interregional administrative organ was a National Bituminous Coal Industrial Board, whose main purpose was to make recommendations relating to the amending of the code or the promulgation of further stabilization measures.

The Appalachian wage agreement and the NRA code reflected a greater willingness on the part of operators to accept higher costs to increase the level of cooperation in their market. While this was in part a continuation of the steady drift of operators toward more effective organizational mechanisms as their competitive position declined, it also reflected pressure from administration officials and mine workers. What is notable in the context of the opportunities provided by the NIRA is the reluctance of operators to relinquish pricing authority to an outside actor. Their willingness to sacrifice autonomy in order to achieve cooperation was limited. Thus they were willing to sacrifice control over price making to code authorities, but only to code authorities dominated by other operators, and, most importantly, by other operators from their own districts. While desiring stable prices, operators were unwilling to

[71]Ibid., p. 316.
[72]*Coal Age* 38 (October, 1933): 293, 316–18, 327, 351; Johnson, *"New Deal,"* pp. 39–40;
Berquist et al., *Economic Survey*, p. 303.
[73]Ibid., p. 351.

create a mechanism with the capacity to organize interdistrict competition, a mechanism that, by necessity, would subordinate the price-making capacity of a district's operators to an actor that might be controlled by operators from competing districts. As J. D. A. Morrow, now an official of the Pittsburgh Coal Co. and a leading participant in the code negotiations, later put it,

we deliberately wrote it up to preserve competition. Now, the reason why we did that, we were afraid. True, we have a code here all right, but that was in the back of our minds. We didn't put any authority in the Division or into this Board for the same sufficient reason. We didn't want it there. Each of us wanted to be there to act to take care of his own business, to protect his interests. In other words, to compete.[74]

Confronted with the UMWA organizing drive, and the rapid unionization of the coal fields, many operators, particularly those who had dealt with the union in the pre-Jacksonville period and who were aware of its beneficial stabilizing capacity, were willing, under a little pressure, to accept the additional costs of a wage agreement. However, there appeared to be no growth in the number of operators who wanted to strengthen and centralize the administrative features of the code to limit further interdistrict competition. With the exception of the midwestern operators, few operators needed the cooperation of their competitors badly enough to submit their pricing decisions to operators from competing regions. The result was a single national code that was, in effect, twenty-two autonomous, potentially competing regional codes. State intervention at this stage was directed toward permitting operators to set minimum prices and toward forcing them to enter into a cooperative agreement in which enforcement remained in private hands – those of the United Mine Workers of America.

The operation of the code: interdistrict competition

By establishing a floor under labor costs and by facilitating communication among operators, particularly at the district level, the Bituminous Coal Code could be expected to have some stabilizing effect on the price structure. However, its solution to the critical problem of interdistrict competition was simply to replace the pricing Prisoner's Dilemma among individual operators with a pricing Prisoner's Dilemma among divisional and subdivisional code authorities.

[74]Johnson, "New Deal," pp. 164–65.

Under the NRA the twenty-two divisional and subdivisional code authorities felt the same pressures to compete among themselves that operators as individuals had experienced in the years before. Each local code authority sought to press its region's markets by under-pricing a neighboring code authority.[75]

The code authorities playing this pricing game responded to it exactly as we would predict individual firms to behave: They selected their rational defection strategy, cutting prices. Then, when their joint behavior had produced a suboptimal outcome, they attempted to transform the game and to organize their competition.

Almost immediately after the code went into effect in October, 1934, interdistrict conflicts over price cutting appeared. The most prominent of these was between Indiana and Illinois. Rather than setting f.o.b. prices, at the mouth of the mine, therefore excluding delivery costs, as most code authorities were doing, Indiana's code authority set delivered prices, which, because they included freight-rate absorptions, allowed Indiana to extend its market into the territory normally covered by western Kentucky, Iowa, and, especially, Illinois. The latter state retaliated by abandoning its price lists altogether and selling its coal for whatever price it could get. The breakdown of midwestern prices was seen as a threat by eastern operators, who issued a formal complaint against Illinois's price cutting, threatening to retaliate in kind if a loss of their own markets resulted. Repeated efforts by the NRA to resolve the Indiana–Illinois conflict proved unsuccessful and it wore on throughout the life of the code.[76] In the Appalachian region, meanwhile, subdivisions in western Pennsylvania, central Pennsylvania, and West Virginia competed by reclassifying their coals, so that consumers could purchase high-quality coal for the same price for which a neighboring district was selling mediocre coal. Again, this controversy lasted during the entire NRA period.[77] There were also conflicts between the Alabama and southern Appalachian (Tennessee) code authorities.[78]

Besides its failure to control interdistrict competition, the code was not entirely successful at organizing competition *within* districts. *Coal Age* reported that in November, the second month of code operation, there were reports of chiseling both by large companies and by fly-by-night "wagon mines," marginal operations which needed reduced prices

[75]Ibid., p. 142.
[76]*Coal Age* 38 (November, 1933): 390; ibid., 38 (December, 1933): 428–9; ibid., 39 (February, 1934): 8; ibid., 39 (January, 1934): 32; ibid., 39 (September, 1934): 364; Johnson, *Politics*, p. 202.
[77]Johnson, "New Deal," p. 148.
[78]*Coal Age* 39 (June, 1934): 254.

to carve out a market. Sales by these latter operations "at lower than code prices and the absence of a definite ruling on truck quotations by the NRA were reported to be disturbing factors of serious proportions in a number of divisions."[79] Understandably in this context, *Coal Age* editorialized that small units should not be exempt from the code: "There is no sanctity in sizes: a small unit can wreck a structure of fair wages and fair trade practices as effectively as its bigger competitor."[80]

By December, 1933, its concern over the failure of the code to prevent the deterioration of the "structure of fair trade practices" had led *Coal Age* to call for more effective government enforcement.

Announcement that the NRA would invoke the penal provisions of the law against willful violators of codes and agreements has unloosed a suspicious flood of protests bewailing this proposal to destroy the "purely voluntary basis" upon which the new self-government in business has been reestablished. But not from the coal industry. Responsible leaders in this industry know that more than moral persuasion is needed to induce the persistent chiseler in prices and wages to abandon practices which have threatened the very existence of those elements in business that desire to play the game fairly and squarely. Opposition to enforcement is not in their minds; on the contrary, they will welcome the governmental action to compel strict and impartial adherence to the rules laid down.[81]

Such enforcement never materialized.

The code mechanism suffered a further setback in March, 1939. After the Appalachian Agreement between operators and the UMWA was amended to reduce the wage differentials enjoyed by some southern operators, one group of affected operators – those in Western Kentucky – sought a District Court injunction, not just against the implementation of this contract, but against NRA jurisdiction over wages and hours.[82] The injunction was granted by Judge Charles Dawson, presiding at the U.S. District Court at Louisville. Basing his opinion on the claim that the mining of coal was not interstate commerce, Dawson called NRA interference in "local" affairs the "boldest kind of usurpation."[83] For once, *Coal Age* did not savor a set of arguments used to evade government intervention.

Commercially mined coal operators, however, will be less interested in these . . . legal distinctions than in the practical effects which may follow if the Louis-

---

[79]Ibid., 38 (December, 1933): 428.
[80]Ibid., 39 (January, 1934): 1.
[81]Ibid., 38 (December, 1933): 395.
[82]Ibid., 39 (April, 1934): 152; Berquist et al., *Economic Survey*, pp. 109–18, 318.
[83]*Coal Age* 39 (June, 1934): 254.

ville injunction is sustained on appeal. . . . If, after fair hearing, no power resides in NRA to establish minimum wages, then, except as organized labor may be strong enough to impose its will upon reluctant employers, the whole system of regulation envisaged by NIRA falls. Such a collapse would foreshadow an inevitable return to the vicious competition from which the bituminous industry has so lately emerged – a competition under which neither labor nor capital has profited.[84]

That the code created by the operators was ineffective in organizing interdistrict competition, or, in the language of the time, in correlating interdistrict prices, was apparent by the spring of 1934. While some operators advocated government price fixing and the allocation of output, the first concrete steps taken to organize intercode-authority competition were internal measures. The earliest of these was the setting of market-zone prices. When the code first went into operation, most prices were f.o.b. mine prices. As I noted in the Chapter 2 discussion of basepoint pricing, f.o.b. pricing greatly increases the difficulty of comparing the prices actually paid by consumers for the delivered product and, in the words of an NRA coal analyst, leaves "room for abuse in trade practices."[85] Beginning in the spring of 1934, code authorities began to set delivered prices for market areas.[86] This produced some improvement by eliminating abuses that were the result of confusion or misunderstanding, but it did not eliminate the relationships that were at the base of interdistrict conflicts. During this same time period, several competing code authorities established "joint market committees" whose purpose was to negotiate a satisfactory correlation of prices before the prices were actually announced.[87] These informal arrangements were strengthened somewhat in June, 1934, when, after a meeting of the Appalachian and midwestern code authorities, NRA Deputy Administrator Charles E. Adams addressed a letter to the divisional and subdivisional authorities in these regions declaring that "an emergency exists which warrants prompt action." According to the new plan, all prices would have to be filed with the NRA and with the various code authorities ten days before their effective date. Affected code authorities would have five days to study the new prices and, if necessary, could attend a meeting in Washington five days before their effective date in order to discuss differences. Any unresolved conflicts would be referred to the NRA for a final de-

[84]Ibid., p. 209.
[85]Berquist et al., *Economic Survey*, p. 512.
[86]Ibid.
[87]*Coal Age* 39 (February, 1934): 80; Berquist et al., *Economic Survey*, p. 502.

cision.[88] Moreover, July production quotas, based on 1929–1933 market shares, were introduced in Division I (the Appalachian region), although Ohio refused to participate in this because it rejected the 1929–1933 period as an unfair standard.[89]

None of these measures halted the breakdown of the NRA price structure in the fall of 1934. With compliance remaining on a voluntary basis, "each man was confronted with the question which he asked himself: This cannot last; here is this tremendous quantity of production pressing on the market and I am not getting my share. . . . I must act now to protect myself."[90] The deterioration was hastened by the departure of Johnson as NRA administrator and the ensuing doubt over future NRA policy on minimum-price fixing. In October, some public statements by key administration officials led many people to believe that NRA price fixing would be banned. The resultant "buyers' strike" of coal consumers put more pressure on the already beleaguered coal operators to reduce prices below the code minima or to sell coal for delivery after the code expired at subcode prices.[91] One operator stated that "price chiselers may drop the tool that takes off shavings and substitute the axe."[92]

It is not surprising that the latter half of 1934 saw many expressions of support for NRA price control and for more effective and costly methods of achieving it. As *Coal Age* wrote in July,

The essential point is that no sane operator wants to contemplate reverting to the chaotic and ruinous condition which prevailed less than a year ago. To prevent such a return some sacrifice of individual preferences and advantages for the general good and even some surrender of cherished local autonomy may be necessary. But that is not too high a price to pay for profitable stabilization.[93]

In October, a special legislative committee of the National Coal Association issued a report declaring that the emergency which led to the NIRA still existed, as did the necessity for continuing price controls. Moreover, the NCA committee went on to say that "some control of overexpansion of productive facilities should be established," something which can be done "only by the United States Government."[94] *Coal Age* applauded the NCA's acceptance of the committee's recommendations.

[88]*Coal Age* 39 (July, 1934): 291.
[89]Berquist et al., *Economic Survey*, p. 124.
[90]Testimony of J. L. Steinbugler, U.S. Congress, Senate, Committee on Interstate Commerce, *Stabilization*, p. 58.
[91]Johnson, *Politics*, pp. 208–10; Berquist et al., *Economic Survey*, p. 522.
[92]Quoted in Parker, *Coal Industry*, p. 118.
[93]*Coal Age* 39 (July, 1934): 257–8.
[94]Ibid., 39 (November, 1934): 415.

"Cold realities and a keen desire to forestall a return to the chaos of recent years have triumphed over deep seated predilections for untrammeled freedom of action."[95]

In January, 1935, after western Pennsylvania had dropped out of Division I's voluntary allocation scheme, the federal government intervened; but, again, as was the case in 1933, it did so only to force operators to create an internal mechanism, not to enforce the agreement produced by this mechanism. The NRA called a meeting of the National Bituminous Coal Industrial Board (NBCIB) in order to consider an NRA proposal that the National Industrial Relations Board, an organ that would not necessarily have much sympathy for coal operators, investigate coal costs and set prices. The implication was clear: Unless the operators took some positive steps toward organizing competition, the government was prepared to do so, and in a not so friendly fashion. According to Berquist, operators who testified at the NBCIB hearings wanted more-centralized price fixing with the government enforcing the prices set by operators. There were exceptions, though. One West Virginia operator stated that "we are very much in favor of the government's fixing the prices. We do not feel that the government or any other group could make such a colossal blunder in fixing prices and carrying out price fixing arrangements as these Code Authorities have done."[96] The eventual outcome of these deliberations was Code Amendment 6, which established a five-member National Coal Board of Arbitration, which would be empowered to settle any disputes arising between individual operators, subdivisional code authorities, and divisional code authorities.[97] Arguing for the amendment, J. D. Francis, President of Appalachian Coals, Inc., told his fellow operators that

during this past year and a half, you producers of coal throughout this country have been taken far enough on the mountain side to look back and see a small acreage that represents the kingdom of the earth and the valley of fruitfulness therein, and you are about to pass it all away by reason of your inability to regulate the rapacity of some individuals and curb the selfishness of others.[98]

Amendment 6 came too late, however, and although it is doubtful whether the National Coal Board of Arbitration could have halted the slide in coal prices, it never received much of a chance. In May, 1935, the Supreme Court declared the NIRA to be unconstitutional and, once

[95]Ibid., p. 409.
[96]Berquist et al., *Economic Survey*, pp. 525–6.
[97]Ibid., p. 525.
[98]Johnson, "*New Deal*," p. 159.

again (but, wisened by the NRA experience, and held somewhat in check by the UMWA), bituminous coal operators were exiled to a competitive state of nature.

Most analysts agree that because it stabilized the wage level, the Bituminous Coal Code did have a beneficial effect on the organization of the bituminous coal industry. Whatever stabilization was achieved, however, was achieved by the United Mine Workers, not the state. The NRA, at least as it operated in the bituminous coal industry, was not a state-enforced cartel, but a group of loose pools held together by the enforcement capacity of a national labor union. The state promoted the organization of competition only indirectly, by pressuring operators to sign the Appalachian wage agreements in 1933 and 1934.[99] This role for the union was anticipated by an Ohio operator who wrote Lewis a congratulatory telegram after the code was established.

I want to congratulate you on getting a code... which puts the United Mine Workers in every bituminous mine in the country which I am sure will do more to stabilize the... coal industry than anything which has been done in its history.[100]

Not only did the mine workers enforce a uniform wage level, but, in some instances, they actually struck to prevent price cutting before it generated wage cuts. In June, 1934, when it was reported that some eastern Kentucky and Tennessee operators had made sales to the Louisville and Nashville Railroad at subcode prices, "miners at some of the operations walked out, claiming the sales were in violation of the code."[101] Workers in Alabama also struck against operators who were cutting code prices.[102] *Coal Age*, which rarely found a reason to praise John L. Lewis, also credited the union with serving as the foundation of the code.

A strong and independent labor organization to protect both employers and employees from the degradation of jungle competition was advocated by Coal Age in its proposed bituminous stabilization program back in 1931, when union influence was at low ebb. Far more than NRA itself, Mr. Lewis and his associates have been the front line defense against assaults upon the code.[103]

[99]Cf. Johnson, "New Deal"; Baratz, The Union.
[100]Dubofsky and Van Tine, John L. Lewis, p. 191.
[101]Coal Age 39 (June, 1934): 254.
[102]Johnson, "New Deal," pp. 166–7.
[103]Coal Age 40 (May, 1935): 181.

State intervention to organize the coal industry

The breakdown of the NRA Bituminous Coal Code and the invalidation of the NIRA by the Supreme Court in May, 1935, left coal operators once again in a situation where the struggle for economic survival in a depressed market was generating wide-scale price cutting and suboptimal profits. Many operators felt that a control on prices more direct than was provided by the UMWA contract was required in order to protect their market position from the behavior of competitors. Beginning in 1934, they appealed for state enforcement of minimum prices through the agency of, first, the Guffey–Snyder bill, passed in 1935; and, second, the Guffey–Vinson bill, passed in 1937. The conflicts among capitalists and between capitalists and workers which surrounded this legislation were largely a reproduction of the conflict surrounding the formulation of the Bituminous Coal Code. Northern operators, in alliance with the United Mine Workers, sought to impose a cooperative strategy on the industry that would eliminate the pressure to engage in self-destructive price and wage cutting and would limit the capacity of the southern districts to make further inroads on their market shares. These measures were opposed by southern operators, who, while they cherished the right to make district-level price agreements among themselves, feared any mechanism that would restrict their capacity to set prices lower than competing districts in the North.

Even before the NIRA was invalidated, the breakdown of code prices had led the United Mine Workers and some operators to seek a more effective, state-enforced, organizational mechanism. During the spring of 1934, John L. Lewis and J. D. A. Morrow, of Pittsburgh Coal, began an effort to obtain a coal-stabilization bill that led to a series of meetings between UMWA and NCA representatives that continued through the fall. This movement never came to fruition, however. According to Johnson, "they all wanted a . . . commission with power to stabilize prices, . . . but the age-old regional differences among operators – primarily the sharp North–South cleavage – and the operator–union split prevented agreement."[104] In January, 1935, Senator Joseph Guffey introduced legislation drafted by the United Mine Workers that would have created a National Bituminous Coal Commission that would set minimum prices in each of twenty-four producing districts on the basis of average mining costs, along with a National Coal Producers' Board that would set dis-

[104]Johnson, *Politics*, p. 218.

trict-level output quotas, which would then be translated at the district level into quotas for individual mines. These quotas would be based on production records over the past fifteen years. Cooperation would be enforced by a 25-percent tax on all coal sold. Most of the tax would be refunded to operators who abided by the provisions of the act. This bill also guaranteed the right of workers to bargain collectively and made any wages and hours agreements that were agreed upon by operators representing a majority of a district's tonnage and workers representing a majority of a district's miners valid for all workers and operators in the district.[105]

Senate hearings on this piece of legislation were held in February and March, before the Supreme Court's invalidation of the NIRA. The bill's advocates – the UMWA and a group of operators who were primarily from Pennsylvania and Ohio, pointed to the inability of the industry to organize itself under any type of less stringent system. Charles O'Neill, who was representing operators in central Pennsylvania, testified that whatever disagreements they might have concerning the details of legislation, they were agreed that "federal control of the coal industry is essential. . . ."[106]

As to why the coal industry needs regulation by the Government, the answer is that it has demonstrated its utter inability to govern itself. The bituminous coal industry was given the broadest powers of perhaps any industry under the N.R.A. . . . Not only has it proven impossible to secure compliance . . . on the part of individual producers, but it has proven impossible to secure compliance on the part of the code authorities themselves.[107]

What the NRA lacked, operators testified, was enforcement. "I liked the code," said one Fairmont operator. "If it had ways of enforcement, I would like it better."[108] Several supporters of the Guffey bill praised its allocation provisions, arguing that, without production controls, the incentives to cut prices would remain overpowering.

If it were possible for a code violator to be summarily put in jail, or summarily sent to Siberia, or summarily guillotined, we would want nothing more [than price control], because we would submit to what came out under the code. We would have no option then but to submit, but we have no such sanction, and will not have such sanctions by simply price control.[109]

[105]Waldo E. Fisher and Charles M. James, *Minimum Price Fixing in the Bituminous Coal Industry* (Princeton: Princeton University Press, 1955), pp. 29–33.
[106]U.S. Congress, Senate, Committee on Interstate Commerce, *Stabilization*, p. 159.
[107]Ibid., p. 160.
[108]Ibid., p. 120.
[109]Ibid., p. 59.

What is most notable about the testimony opposing the Guffey bill was what it did not include. Thus there was a relative absence of opposition to the bill's labor provisions, which amounted to the same "compulsory unionization" that operators found so objectionable in the Davis–Kelly bill. The southern operators who opposed the Guffey bill were now unionized and, with some exceptions, they praised the contribution of the United Mine Workers toward the stabilization of wages and described themselves as being satisfied with their present relationship with their workers. One operator, whose experience in the industry reached back to the turn of the century, testified that

I was in the strike of 1902 when the anthracite field was organized. Mr. Mitchell won that strike in the anthracite field and lost it in New River Field. I thought the anthracite people had lost and the New River people had won. I do not know whether I was right or not.[110]

Also absent from the testimony of opponents to the Guffey bill were the vitriolic attacks on government regulation that were such a major element of the political views of operators in the early 1920s. These operators were not proposing a return to the "free market" of the 1920s. They were unanimous in their advocacy of an extention of the NIRA. Nor were they necessarily opposed to state enforcement of price-fixing agreements. H. R. Hawthorne, speaking for the Smokeless Coal Association, a West Virginia operator association that was spearheading the opposition to the Guffey bill, testified that he favored government enforcement of prices fixed by the operators at the district level, and another Pocahontas operator signified that he would favor greater enforcement capability in a renewed NRA.[111] Another representative from the Smokeless Coal Association stated, in opposition to the Guffey bill, that the code was a success, and that with greater enforcement, it could become a "complete success."[112] James Francis, President of the Island Creek Coal Co., in West Virginia, and a leading figure in Appalachian Coals, Inc., favored an extension of the NRA that would prohibit sales below cost and would permit district-level output-allocation agreements.[113]

It was not state enforcement of cooperation per se that bothered southern operators, but state enforcement of a form of cooperation that would

[110]Ibid., p. 276.
[111]Ibid., pp. 218, 362.
[112]Ibid., p. 290.
[113]Ibid., p. 375.

be defined in conjunction with operators from other districts. Thus, while operators from Alabama and the Southwest opposed the Guffey bill because they feared that it would hamper their ability to compete with other fuels, the opposition of Appalachian operators centered almost entirely on the alleged unfairness of the allocation and price-fixing provisions. According to the bill, allocation on both the interdistrict and intradistrict levels would be carried out by boards of operators, which would base their decisions on the production record since 1919. The southern West Virginia operators, whose most notable gains in output had occurred in 1924–1926, under the regime of the Jacksonville scale, saw this scheme for what it probably was – an effort to afford some protection to the older, northern producing districts, in the words of one West Virginia operator, to grant "an old age pension to a coal mine."[114] One West Virginia newspaper editorial introduced into the record placed the Guffey bill squarely in the tradition of earlier efforts to constrain the expansion of southern markets.

The Pennsylvania industry has fought for a generation to put the southern Appalachian coal fields, embracing the highly productive territory in West Virginia, out of business. The fight began with the earliest development of these fields to the south. For two decades it has been waged largely around petitions for discriminatory freight rates before the Interstate Commerce Commission. . . . Now the destruction of the southern coal industry is aimed with one fell blow in the Guffey bill.[115]

"Nothing good for Kentucky coal ever came out of the state of Pennsylvania," testified a Hazard County operator.[116] The problem was not only the particular allotment formula contained in the bill, but the general principle that the market shares of West Virginia and Kentucky operators should be all subject to the influence of operators from Ohio and Pennsylvania. Thus, the Hazard County operator quoted above feared that "with the power to change allotments," the board of operators "might some day become a political weapon that we fear might beat whatever brains there are out of the state of Kentucky."[117]

Southern operators were also concerned about the price-fixing mechanism of the initial Guffey bill, which empowered a National Bituminous Coal Commission to set minimum prices for each district at the level of its average cost of production. The commission would also be able to

[114]Ibid., p. 196.
[115]Ibid., p. 141.
[116]Ibid., p. 338.
[117]Ibid., p. 333.

coordinate the price levels of competing districts. Here again, their fear was that the commission, with its "vague," "undefinable," and "dictatorial" powers, would manipulate the coal-price structure in such a way as to limit their capacity to compete.[118] "We do not believe that it is good public policy to subject the economic future of our state to the control of a politically appointed commission."[119] They repeatedly expressed fears that the criteria used by a national commission would be insufficiently "flexible" to take into account all of the commercially important pricing variables. Thus, a representative of the operators from Williamson County, West Virginia, worried that if prices were set inflexibly by average costs, West Virginia coal might be barred from the lake market.[120]

The months between the Senate hearings on the Guffey bill in February and March and the House hearings in June saw a couple of major developments. First, the NIRA was invalidated by the Supreme Court. In terms of legislative remedies to the disorganization of the coal industry, this left the Guffey bill as the only game in town. As *Coal Age* editorialized,

Few bituminous operators swept into the flight to chaos in 1925–33 will join the jubilee chorus with which so many industrialists and politicians have greeted the Schechter . . . decision. . . . Despite rising criticism of code operation and enforcement, operators as a whole frankly and freely acknowledge the outstanding, if temporary stabilization NIRA brought to the industry. Although proposals for permanent regulation . . . divided operators into two camps, what should have been a united front was breached only by disagreement as to the form and extent which supplementary legislation should take. In wiping out the code system, the court decision gives an answer which should close that breach and once again give the industry a common platform. . . . Legislation is admittedly necessary. . . . If the Guffey–Snyder bill can be amended . . . so as to allow reasonable experimentation while the industry is determining from experience what is and what is not desirable as fixed practice, it now offers the most convenient framework upon which the industry can build for future protection and public service.[121]

The second major development was the failure of the UMWA and the operators to come to an agreement on the terms on which the Appalachian contract was to be renewed. During the spring, when the UMWA granted several extensions of the strike deadline, the passage of the

---

[118]Ibid., p. 269.
[119]Ibid., p. 435.
[120]Ibid., pp. 416–17.
[121]*Coal Age* 40 (June, 1935): 233–4.

Guffey bill become a stake in the wage negotiations, as Guffey-bill supporters – both operators and the UMWA – implied that the price of a
new contract was its passage.[122] Charles O'Neill, the central Pennsylvania operator spokesman, told the House subcommittee that "I can say
here today that I have absolutely no hope of concluding a wage agreement on the present level of wages unless there is something done to
stabilize prices in the industry."[123]

Between the invalidation of the NIRA and the House hearings on the
Guffey bill in early June, the operators supporting state intervention met
with the UMWA in Washington to rewrite the bill, eliminating the allocation provisions, and placing the initiative in minimum-price setting
with the operators, rather than with the national commission, which
would now approve prices established by the district boards of operators. Minimum prices would be based on production costs in "minimum-
price areas," each of which encompassed several districts. Also, different
minimum prices could be set for different grades and sizes of coal.[124]
These changes made the bill more palatable to operators; yet many
southern operators continued to express their opposition to it. Tams,
himself a southern West Virginia operator, wrote that most southern
operators opposed the bill because "they reasoned that they could cut
prices, put their competitors out of business, and themselves survive
the battle."[125] With the NIRA option closed to them, opponents of the
bill now argued for district sales agencies, modeled after Appalachian
Coals, Inc., as the best alternative to a form of state intervention that
would limit their freedom of action. They favored "standard guides and
methods of cooperation," but, with respect to their price decisions, they
wanted the "elasticity and free play necessary and common in commercial transactions."[126]

We feel that any form of price regulation should be made as flexible and as
simple as possible and should be so constituted as to extend to the producers,
under reasonable limitations and restrictions, the right to conduct their business
as nearly as possible along normal lines.[127]

As was the case before the bill was revised, they did not believe that
the coordination of minimum prices could be carried out without some

[122]Johnson, *Politics*, p. 222; Parker, *Coal Industry*, p. 137.
[123]U.S. Congress, Senate, Committee on Interstate Commerce, *Stabilization*, p. 161.
[124]Fisher and James, *Minimum Price*, pp. 21–38.
[125]Tams, *Smokeless*, p. 71.
[126]U.S. Congress, Senate, Committee on Interstate Commerce, *Stabilization*, pp. 236–7.
[127]Ibid., p. 459.

districts being prejudiced. Thus, a northern Illinois operator opposed to the bill feared that his district would be deprived of the advantage of its proximity to Chicago.

We ask that no price be effective as to any producing field unless it shall be with the approval of a representative of the producing field on the board. We do not want our price fixed by a board composed of producers from the southern half of the state.[128]

The bill, with some slight revisions, was passed somewhat reluctantly by a Congress that was concerned about its constitutionality.[129] These fears turned out to be well grounded. The federal courts were deluged with injunctions against the collection of the tax (15 percent in the final bill) and against the bill's collective bargaining provisions, which extended the terms of a union contract agreed to by two-thirds of a district's workers and by operators representing two-thirds of a district's output over the entire district. On May 18, 1936, the act, whose operation had been hampered by the lack of a Congressional appropriation, the refusal of almost one-third of the industry to participate, and correlation controversies reminiscent of those under the NRA code, was declared unconstitutional by the Supreme Court, which objected particularly to its labor provisions.[130] A revised bill – the Guffey–Vinson bill – was immediately introduced, and, after dying with the 1936 Congressional session, was made into law in 1937, over similar objections to those expressed in opposition to its predecessors.[131] The new act gave less price-fixing authority to the district boards of operators, which now were to propose prices which the commission would establish, rather than, as before, establishing prices which the commission approved.[132]

The National Bituminous Coal Commission and the Bituminous Coal Division within the Department of the Interior, which succeeded it, were not able to establish minimum prices for the bituminous coal industry before the shift in demand produced by World War II had largely eliminated the conditions that produced price cutting. The commission's first price list was promulgated on November 30, 1937, but was repealed two months later after scores of operators succeeded in obtaining court in-

[128]Ibid., p. 567.
[129]Johnson, *Politics*, pp. 223–34.
[130]Ralph Hillis Baker, *The National Bituminous Coal Commission* (New York: AMS Press, 1941), pp. 56–62.
[131]U.S. Congress, Senate, Committee on Interstate Commerce, *To Regulate Interstate Commerce in Bituminous Coal*, Hearings on S. 4688, 74th Congress, 2nd Session, 1936, p. 141.
[132]Fisher and James, *Minimum Price*, pp. 31–2.

junctions freeing them from the act's provisions.[133] In July, 1939, the Commission's responsibilities were taken over by the Department of the Interior, which established a Bituminous Coal Division. This agency continued the Commission's second effort to set prices, and on October 1, 1940, three and one-half years after the Guffey–Vinson bill was passed, a new price schedule went into effect. However, by this time, another wartime coal boom was under way. Coal prices increased by over 50 percent between 1939 and 1944, and by May, 1942, maximum, not minimum prices were occupying the division's attention.[134]

Conclusion

The decade of the 1930s saw major changes in the attitude of coal operators to both collective bargaining and state intervention. Having earned a reputation as very successful and vociferous opponents of any kind of state intervention in industry during the 1920s, coal operators were appealing for state-enforced price fixing and production quotas by 1935. Having broken the back of the UMWA in 1926 and 1927, coal operators ten years later were praising the contributions of collective bargaining toward market stability. I have argued in this chapter that these changes, as well as the remaining divisions among operators over market organization, had their origins in the competitive conditions that they faced. Unprotected from self-destructive wage and price cutting by the collective bargaining agreements that they had abrogated a few years earlier, operators responded rationally by seeking to transform their competitive game and to organize themselves. Their willingness to risk doing so depended on their need for the cooperation of their competitors and on their perception of the sacrifices on their own part that the achievement of such cooperation would require. Thus, midwestern operators led the struggle for a more organized form of competition, and southern firms continued to advocate less costly methods of achieving the same results. In both cases, behavior was rooted firmly in material relations of production and in the collective action problems that they produced.

[133]Baker, *National*, pp. 159–63; Johnson, *Politics*, p. 234.
[134]Fisher and James, *Minimum*, p. 449; Johnson, *Politics*, p. 236.

PART III

8. Capitalists, workers, and the state

Introduction

In this chapter I return to the principal propositions of Chapters 1 and 2 in order to reexamine them in the light of the empirical material presented in Part 2 and in order to explore briefly some of their theoretical implications.

Do capitalists compete?

The most basic claim presented in this study is that capitalist relations of production generate conflict among capitalists, conflict that takes the form of economic competition. This may appear to be an obvious point, but, in spite of the evidence of capitalist competition that all of us have at our fingertips, economic conflicts among capitalists are still not taken seriously by many social theorists. For instance, Nicos Poulantzas, in one of the most influential works of political theory to be published during the past twenty years, argues that competition among capitalists, as well as competition among workers, is merely an effect, albeit a "terrifyingly real" one, of the *ideological* structure on the field of social relations.[1] My study of the bituminous coal industry leaves no room for doubt that, in that industry, at least, competition among firms was not an illusion, but was an unpleasant, continually present, fact of life. Its source was not the ideological structure but the same economic relations of production that generate the opposition between workers and capitalists. Capitalists were entirely correct in believing that their interests were in conflict. This conflict among capitalists was every bit as real as the conflict between workers and capitalists. In the words of *Black Diamond*, "there are some fundamentals which the employer should know by this time but which many persistently forget. . . . The enemy of labor is capital; the enemy of capital is labor and other capital."[2]

This conclusion would be move convincing, of course, if it were based

---

[1] Nicos Poulantzas, *Political Power and Social Classes* (London: New Left Books, 1973).
[2] *Black Diamond* 45 (August 8, 1910): 21.

on a study of an industry that was generally assumed to be noncompetitive, during the era of "monopoly capitalism," rather than on a notoriously competitive industry during the earlier, "competitive capitalistic," period. Granted, the present study does not contain the data to demonstrate that competition among capitalist firms was taken as seriously in other industries during other time periods as it was by coal operators before World War II. However, it does suggest some questions and some possible answers to them that are worth pursuing further and which may lead us to rethink the orthodox contrast between the era of competitive capitalism and the era of monopoly capitalism. First, there is the question of whether capitalists compete under conditions of monopoly capitalism. If we mean by *compete* the presence of competitive relations, then the answer clearly must be yes, in every industry not dominated by a single firm *and* protected by formidable entry barriers. Monopoly capitalism is still capitalism, and, by definition, capitalism implies the presence of capitalist relations of production, which are competitive relations. This does not, of course, settle the empirical issue of whether price cutting or other manifestations of competitive behavior take place in every market, but again, the answer appears to be quite clear. There *are* markets in the contemporary capitalist economy in which firms have effectively controlled price and other forms of competition for relatively long periods of time. However, the fact that firms are not actively competing in a particular market during a particular time period does not mean that the concept of competition has been rendered irrelevant by the unfolding of the laws of development of the capitalist economy. Rather, it simply means that in those markets capitalists have succeeded in organizing themselves – *for the time being*. This study suggests that the organization of markets is not the outcome of irreversible tendencies toward concentration and centralization, but is a contingent outcome of struggles among capitalists about market organization. This means that the appearance of stable oligopolistic markets should not lead us to discard the concept of competition, but rather to pursue the empirical questions of how competition is organized and under what conditions it will stay organized.

None of this is meant to suggest that major changes have not occurred in the capitalist economy, or that these changes have not touched on the degree and form of competition among firms. It does suggest, however, that we now are in possession of a new and powerful tool to use in conceptualizing these changes. Rather than relying on the rather blunt distinction between competitive capitalism and monopoly capitalism, it may be more fruitful to view historical changes within the capitalist economy in terms of changes in the nature of the competitive games played by capitalists. This would imply more industry-level studies that would give close attention to the market-structure variables discussed in Chapter 1, the nature of interfirm differences, the form that competition takes, and changes in the type of mechanisms available to capitalists to organize themselves out of these games. This approach has the advantage of focusing on the level of the industry rather than on that of the economy as a whole, thus accommodating the fact that at any one point in time, the degree to which the economy's various constituent markets are organized and the form that this organization takes varies greatly across industries. Another advantage of this approach is that it is better able to capture the contingent and reversible character of market organization. As the history of the coal industry demonstrates, market organization is not inevitable and, when it is achieved, it remains vulnerable to such disruptive factors as shifts in demand, technological and marketing innovations, and new entry. Finally, this approach expands the list of variables that we can use to make sense of different market situations to include variables that relate to a group of firms' capacity to communicate and detect defection, to their incentive to cooperate or defect, to the exact content of the competitive decision facing them, and to the identity, costs, and capabilities of the various available organizational mechanisms.

Economic competition and collective action

The fact that capitalists compete with one another does not mean that they have no common interests. As Jon Elster has written, "intra-class interaction . . . may and does occur in forms ranging from warfare through competition to mutual support. A major task of class theory is to explain when one or another of these will take place."[3] This is a task that has not yet been systematically addressed with respect to capitalists. I do so in this study with a model that integrates collective action theory and the economic theory of industrial organization. By depicting various competitive situations as games, we can predict the strategy within these games that will be selected by rational capitalist firms, thereby predicting whether their interaction will take the form of competition, cooperation, or warfare.

[3]Elster, *Making Sense of Marx*, p. 345.

I demonstrated in Chapter 1 that, because the fate of each capitalist firm depends on the behavior of all firms, competition places capitalists in collective action situations in which mutual cooperation can make everyone better off, but in which no individual firm has an incentive to cooperate.

These capitalist collective action problems arising from market relations among capitalist firms have been passed over by other collective action theorists, who tend to focus instead on the problem of interest group formation.[4] Thus, while Mancur Olson begins his book by depicting economic competition as a collective action problem in which rational self-interested behavior prevents firms from achieving as high a profit level as they could achieve by acting in concert, he disposes of this problem in a few sentences before proceeding to the issue that really concerns him.

About the only thing that keeps prices from falling in accordance with the process just described in perfectly competitive markets is outside intervention. Government price supports, tariffs, cartel agreements, and the like may keep the firms in a competitive market from acting contrary to their interests. Such aid or intervention is quite common. It is then important to ask how it comes about. How does a competitive industry obtain government assistance in maintaining the price of its product. . . . To obtain any such assistance from the government, the producers in this industry will presumably have to organize a lobbying organization; . . . *Just as it is not rational for a particular producer to restrict his output in order that there might be a higher price for the product of his industry, so it would not be rational for him to sacrifice his time and money to support a lobbying organization to obtain government assistance for the industry.*[5]

Similarly, in his critique of Marx's class theory, Olson again seems to situate the collective action problem of the capitalist class outside of their competitive market relationships.

If a person is in the bourgeois class, he may want a government that represents his class. But it does not follow that it will be in his interest to work to see that such a government comes to power. If there is such a government he will benefit from its policies, whether or not he has supported it, for by Marx's own hypothesis it will work for his class interests. Moreover, in any event one individual bourgeois presumably will not be able to exercise a decisive influence on the

[4]See Adam Przeworski, "Marxism and Rational Choice," *Politics and Society* 14 (1985): 379–409.
[5]Mancur Olson, *The Logic of Collective Action* (Cambridge, MA: Harvard University Press, 1971), pp. 9–10.

choice of a government. So the *rational* thing to do is to ignore his *class* interests and to spend his energies on his *personal* interests.[6]

In this passage, it is clear that the cooperative strategy involves political action, probably participation in a group or party devoted to the achievement of bourgeois political interests. This same perspective is evident in Olson's concluding discussion of "special interest" and "by-product" theories of collective action, where business organization means trade associations and general purpose business groups such as the Chamber of Commerce and the National Association of Manufacturers.[7]

Claus Offe and Helmut Wiesenthal criticize Olson for neglecting some critical differences between the collective action problems faced by workers and those faced by capitalists, and proceed to identify two other forms of capitalist collective action besides the employer's association – the fusion of units of capital within the firm and informal cooperation in the market – but they too focus their attention exclusively on the first type – the interest group.[8]

Association formation does present capitalists with problems of collective action, but these should not be viewed as *the* problem of capitalist collective action. As I emphasized in Chapter 1, capitalists must secure their positions in the market as capitalists before they can turn their attention to the common interests of capitalists. The problem of association formation should be viewed as a second-order problem, which exists alongside the more pressing problems of collective action generated in the market. There can be no doubt that this was the view of bituminous coal operators. For them, collective action and cooperation meant cooperative behavior *within* the market, not associational and political activity outside of the market. A study of collective action within the coal industry that focused on the formation of the National Coal Association or any of the various regional employers' associations would have completely overlooked the problems of market organization that were the principal concern of operators. At least in the bituminous coal industry, *the* problem of collective action was to organize competition so as to ensure the economic survival of individual firms.

The analysis of coal competition presented in the case study demonstrates that it is possible to conceptualize concrete competitive situ-

[6]Ibid., p. 106.
[7]Ibid., pp. 141–8.
[8]Claus Offe and Helmut Wiesenthal, "Two Logics of Collective Action: Theoretical Notes on Social Class and Organizational Form," *Political Power and Social Theory* 1 (1980): 67–115.

ations in terms of the simple game-theoretic models of Chapter 1. Several of the games discussed in Chapter 1 were present in the bituminous coal industry. During periods when they were prevented from cutting wages, coal operators played a relatively straightforward version of the pricing Prisoner's Dilemma, in which their choice of strategies was between maintaining a relatively high, cooperative price level and reducing prices. During the World War I coal boom, operators faced a version of the intertemporal Prisoner's Dilemma described in Chapter 1, in which firms cooperated by keeping prices from soaring to a level high enough to elicit hostile state intervention and a possible reduction in long-term profits. The most interesting game played by operators was the price and wage game, in which the price-cutting strategy was accompanied by wage reductions. The case study also demonstrates that the depiction of economic competition as a series of collective action problems not only makes theoretical sense but actually captures the way in which competition was *experienced* by bituminous coal operators. They clearly understood the state of their industry to be the outcome of their own often reluctant decisions, not as the product of reified "market forces."

The real test of the model is in how effectively it predicts behavior. The analysis of the pricing Prisoner's Dilemma in Chapter 1 identified a number of variables that determine whether a group of firms will cooperate or compete. These include such factors as the number of sellers, the number of buyers, the relations between buyers and sellers, the degree of product differentiation, and the cost structure of firms. The market structure characteristics of the bituminous coal industry led me to predict that the relations among coal operators would generally be competitive rather than cooperative. The historical evidence indicates that this was, in fact, the case. Complaints of an absence of cooperation constitute a thread running through the entire period studied.

Of all of the variables that contributed to this result, the single most important one was probably the short time frame of coal operators. For most of the period studied, operators did not appear to view competition as a supergame in which the payoff from any single ordinary game was relatively unimportant in relation to the long-term supergame payoff. Instead, they saw each ordinary game as an important contest in itself. Defection was viewed not as an "offensive" measure designed to take advantage of the cooperation of competitors, but as a necessary "defensive" strategy in a world in which other operators would be doing the same thing. Because defection was seen as a defensive move, a concern with "retaliation" was generally not present, and those variables that impede cooperation by hindering communication and detection among operators – the number of sellers, the lack of standardization, etc., – were probably not as important in determining the choice of strategy as the factors that determined the incentive structure of the individual games and that focused the attention of operators on the short term. These were discussed at length in Chapter 3. They include the generally depressed condition of the coal industry during this period, the relative importance of a single contract to the fortunes of the firm, the bargaining power of buyers, and the supply factors that made universal defection so much more attractive than unilateral cooperation. In this respect, it is instructive to recall the history of the Bituminous Coal Code. Although cooperation under the code was always precarious, the fact that the code had a terminal date was clearly one reason for the breakdown of the code's price structure during its final months in existence. Here, the natural proclivity of operators to discount future cooperative payoffs was reinforced by a law that, effectively, warned them that cooperation was unlikely to exist after a certain date. As that date approached, the value of future cooperation declined in relation to that of short-term defection and operators scrambled to secure contracts at whatever price they could. In the words of the operator quoted in Chapter 7, the axe replaced the chisel for price cutters. The history of the coal industry thus confirms Michael Taylor's analysis of the iterated Prisoner's Dilemma: Contingent cooperation is the dominant strategy only when the future is discounted at a low rate and the game is perceived to be of indefinite length. It also shows that neither of these conditions necessarily will hold in real-world contexts. This is probably especially the case in capitalist collective action games because capitalists are one of the few groups whose common interest is based on an achieved rather than an ascribed characteristic. It is the fact that their continued existence as capitalists was so precarious that imposed such a short time frame on coal operators. Workers and environmentalists, to name two other groups with common interests, are much less likely to see their interactions as having an impending finite end, and, therefore, are less likely to discount the future at a high rate.

Aside from the greater likelihood that the players will have a short-term orientation, there are several other ways in which the market organization games discussed in this book differ from the interest group formation game that has been the focus of most other collective action theory. In the first place, the stakes in the market organization game are higher than those in the interest group game. In both games, a firm's least-preferred outcome is that produced by the combination of its own unilateral cooperation and the defection of all other firms. In the interest group game, however, the penalty for unilateral cooperation is relatively small in relation to the firm's total resources. It is unlikely that the loss of the amount of a firm's dues to a trade association will have a material effect on the firm's prosperity. This is clearly not the case in the market organization game, where the unilateral selection of the cooperative price strategy could mean the loss of important business. This is especially true in industries such as the coal industry, where single contracts were large enough to have a significant impact on the firm's profits and survival in the market. Similarly, the advantages of free-riding are quantitatively greater in the market game than they are in the interest group game. In the former context, just as unilateral cooperation can mean the loss of an important contract, so can defection mean winning one. Again, this is in contrast to the interest group game, where the free-rider gains only the amount of its dues payment. The higher stakes mean that cooperation is riskier and that universal cooperation will be more difficult to achieve in the market game. In their article, "Two Logics of Collective Action," Clause Offe and Helmut Wiesenthal argue that the capitalist interest group problem is easier to solve than the interest group problem faced by workers because, in the former case, "central life interests" are not at stake.[9] The above analysis suggests that the capitalist market organization problem is *more* difficult to solve than the capitalist interest group problem precisely *because* the "central life interests" of firms are at stake.

Another difference between the market organization problem and the interest group problem is that, in the former case, the collective good, a higher price level, for instance, is provided *internally* through the cooperation of the firms; whereas, in the interest group case, the collective good sought by the group members (e.g., a preferential tax rate) is usually provided *externally* by the state.[10] Groups seeking externally produced goods are advantaged on at least two counts. First, if the external provider is the government, which, in the case of interest groups, it often is, the collective good is likely to be cheaper for the group members than if they would have to provide it themselves.[11] When the government provides a collective good to a group, the entire society of which

[9]Offe and Wiesenthal, "Two Logics," pp. 84–5.
[10]Russell Hardin, *Collective Action* (Baltimore: Johns Hopkins University Press, 1982).
[11]Ibid., pp. 52–3.

that group is a subset is footing the bill. A more important advantage for our purposes appears when we shift from the case of collective goods to the case of collective bads. When the collective bad is externally generated there is the possibility that the group will be privileged in Olson's sense, that is, that it will contain one or a few group members who value the elimination of the bad so highly that they will be willing to pay for it themselves. The cooperation of all group members is not always necessary, then, in order for the group's common interest to be achieved.[12] This is not the case in situations resembling the market organization problem, where the collective bad – low prices – is internally generated. Unless the industry is a monopoly, a single firm cannot unilaterally establish a cooperative market price. On the other hand, the defection of only a few firms is all that is necessary to set the market price at the lower, defection level. Finally, it will be more costly to police the behavior of many actors within the group than a single actor outside of the group.[13] This further hampers the cooperative effort in the former case.

The most important difference between the problem of interest group formation and the market organization problem lies in the impact of intraindustry heterogeneity. As Russell Hardin writes, "the principal issue in the politics of collective action is that perverse asymmetry in which some benefit to the detriment of others."[14] This has been evident throughout our entire study of collective action in the market, where we have repeatedly seen that firms often attempt to organize markets *against* their competitors. Because business associations do not concern themselves with the "central life interests" of their members, they are able to limit their activity to those areas in which unambiguous common interests exist. Thus, the National Coal Association skirted the issue of labor organization and wage differentials which was the principal "life interest" of coal operators. This pattern of keeping conflicts of interest outside of business associations is common. When they do enter, they may have the effect of facilitating cooperation. Thus, asymmetries in the way in which collective goods are evaluated may lead some members to pay a disproportionate share of the cost, simply because they are more desirous of seeing the good provided.[15] A more interesting case, again discussed by Hardin, is when the collective good can be defined

[12]Ibid., p. 54. Olson discusses privileged groups in *The Logic*, pp. 48–50.
[13]Hardin, *Collective Action*, p. 54.
[14]Ibid., p. 83.
[15]Ibid., pp. 67–8.

by cooperators in such a way as to benefit some members more than others. This is the case with tax legislation, which Hardin argues is the main arena of business interest group activity. When the firms in the industry differ from one another in ways that can be written into legislation, active cooperators can be rewarded by being placed in a position to propose particular loopholes that will benefit all members of the industry, but their own firms more than others.[16] In the case of business interest groups, then, interfirm differences can *improve* the likelihood of cooperation by providing additional incentives to cooperate. We have seen that this is not the case in market organization games, where cost and other differences among firms create a situation in which some firms have a compelling incentive to cooperate – they cannot afford to free-ride – while others cannot afford to cooperate. It is a particular strength of the framework developed in this study that it focuses our attention on such intraindustry heterogeneity and on its implications for collective action. In some cases, the obstacles to cooperation produced by differences among firms can be overcome through a sidepayment mechanism which compensates firms for cooperating when otherwise they would not choose to do so. The most prominent example of this in the coal industry was the collective bargaining agreements which, in the Central Competitive Field, compensated disadvantaged firms by allowing them to pay their workers lower wages. The regional differential built into the Appalachian Agreements of the 1930s had a similar effect, buying the participation of southern firms by enabling them to maintain some of their labor cost advantages. In other cases, however, interfirm differences that impede cooperation cannot be overcome, and they not only make voluntary cooperation in pursuit of a common interest less likely, but also make the very *existence* of a common interest less likely.

Another type of asymmetry among group members is their size and the amount of resources that they possess. In the interest group case, according to Olson, many industries constitute "privileged groups," because one or a few large firms find it worthwhile to provide the collective good themselves, regardless of whether or not others contribute.[17] To the extent that smaller firms take advantage of this willingness and free-ride, one can speak of the "exploitation of the great by the small."[18] There is a market analogy to this situation, small firms "exploiting" the

[16]Ibid.
[17]Olson, *The Logic*, p. 143.
[18]Ibid., p. 35.

monopolistic price level set by a dominant firm. However there is another market situation that produces a different result. Consider the low-cost firm with large financial resources. We have seen in Chapter 2 that such firms may be willing to endure a state of disorganized competition, with its attendant low profits, in the expectation that their competitors will not survive it, and their mortality will leave the stronger firms in a long-term position of dominance from which they could more than make up for their short-term losses. Here, where larger firms refrain from the cooperative behavior that their competitors need, the great are preying on the small rather than being exploited by them. The supporters of state intervention in the bituminous coal industry in the 1930s blamed the opposition of the larger coal companies on just this type of calculation. Thus, John L. Lewis explained the opposition of the Island Creek Coal Co. to the Guffey–Snyder bill in the following way.

Of course, it is true that the Island Creek Coal Co. is one of the few favored companies in the country, operating under ideal conditions, well managed, well financed, with a degree of efficient salesmanship. The Island Creek Coal Co. has been one of the favored few. Undoubtedly, if we revert to the dog eat dog policy in the coal industry, that company can continue living if any others can.[19]

Competition and the organization of markets

While the capitalist collective action framework developed in this study generates predictions about how firms will behave within various market games, its principal concern is with the way in which capitalist firms respond to the outcomes that such behavior produces. In particular, will firms try to transform their games, and if so, in what direction? The present model does not provide complete answers to these questions, but it does advance our understanding of the process of market organization in several ways. First, it suggests that we need to expand our notion of how firms interact with one another. The traditional focus of economic theory is on the exchanges that take place *within* markets. In particular, it attempts to tell us what output, price, and investment decisions will yield the maximum return for individual firms. Firms relate to workers, consumers, creditors, and suppliers directly as buyers and sellers of factors of production or of final products. Competition, whether it is oligopolistic or "perfect," refers simply to the fact that the outcome of a firm's interactions with suppliers and customers will be

[19]U.S. Congress, Senate, Committee on Interstate Commerce, *Stabilization*, p. 565.

affected by other firms' behavior, which combines behind their backs to create exogenous constraints – that is, a demand, supply, and price level. The principal effect of competition is to force competing firms to take measures to reduce their costs. Firms react to the unpleasantness of competition by seeking to minimize the interdependencies of the competitive relationship through advertising and product differentiation. The present study has demonstrated that not only do firms compete within markets and try to remove themselves from markets, they also seek to transform and reorganize their markets. Much of this competitive activity is directed toward changing the conditions under which competition takes place. Besides playing competitive games with each other, capitalist firms also struggle with each other over the rules of the games that they play. And, like players in other contexts, they are not above responding to an unfavorable situation by changing the rules and transforming the game. As Adolph Eichner said of the members of the sugar industry, "although not revolutionaries, they were . . . prepared to overthrow the existing structure of markets when they could see no other alternative to their eventual destruction."[20] This is an insight that is missing in most game-theoretic models of competition. Besides attempting to reduce their costs of production, coal operators tried to change the parameters of their competitors' environment by raising their labor and transportation costs, and by seeking to expand their own strategic possibilities by redefining their relationship with their workers and winning the capacity to cut wages. In all of these cases, economic competition consisted of conflict *about* the organization of markets, as well as conflict *within* markets.[21]

In drawing our attention to the *re*organization of markets, this study poses an important question that has been almost completely overlooked by economists: How do markets become organized? As Almarin Phillips has written, markets "are not unorganized, unregulated meetings of buyers and sellers. They are organized to rather extreme detail."[22] While my focus has been on the organization of price competition, this is by no means the only aspect of market organization. Even when price competition is unregulated, a network of legal and extralegal conven-

[20]Adolph Eichner, *The Emergence of Oligopoly* (Baltimore: Johns Hopkins University Press, 1969), pp. 101–2.
[21]This expression plays on Adam Przeworski's argument that class struggle involves struggles about class as well as struggles among classes. See *Capitalism and Social Democracy* (Cambridge: Cambridge University Press, 1985), p. 79.
[22]Phillips, *Market Structure*, p. 175.

tions govern other aspects of competitive activity, many of which have come to be recognized as "unfair trade practices." Such market organization is the outcome of a social process, one that should not be taken for granted by social scientists. In the words of two other writers, "an industry does not automatically organize itself, there is no natural, immutable, indefeasible scheme of order. No industrial structure comes into existence as a result of the 'automatic working' of 'economic forces.' "[23] Like other sets of social relations, markets must continually be produced and reproduced. Moreover, market organization is not a once-and-done accomplishment. Organized markets are vulnerable to new technology, new products, new marketing techniques, new forms of business organization, and new competitive pressures.

How well does the model presented in Chapters 1 and 2 explain the dynamics of the process of market organization in the bituminous coal industry? The model suggests, first, that faced with suboptimal outcomes, capitalist firms will attempt to organize their competition. This proposition is certainly confirmed by the history of the coal industry. During the sixty years covered by this study, coal operators whose profits suffered by the failure of their competitors to cooperate consistently tried to elicit their cooperation. However, this does not mean that each firm will embrace every proposal to organize competition. In fact, much of the present study was devoted to explaining the conflicts among operators over the various proposals to organize their markets.

The most important factor differentiating firms with respect to this decision to organize is the relationship between their present payoff (P) and their prospective payoff in the reorganized market (R). If $P>R$, then the firm will have nothing to gain by market organization and can be expected to oppose it. This situation was present in one of the games described above: the Prisoner's Dilemma played by firms differentiated by unionization. In any Prisoner's Dilemma situation in which a significant portion of the players are organized – or forced to cooperate – the remaining privileged defectors will receive profits that are either greater than the profits generated by universal cooperation or are very close to those profits, and will have no incentive to support the extension of organization to cover their own behavior. This was why nonunion operators resisted any attempts to raise their production costs to the "cooperative" level; whether, as in the case of the uniform mine-safety law

[23] Walton H. Hamilton and Helen R. Wright, *A Way of Order for Bituminous Coal* (New York: Macmillan, 1928), p. 55.

movement, the early national association movement, the ICC rate controversies, and the NRA code proposals, they originated with operators; or, as in the case of the UMWA organization drives, with mine workers. From the point of view of these firms, further organization of competition would have resulted in their being organized out of an advantageous competitive position. Unionized operators found themselves in a similar position as union output declined during the 1920s and their payoffs fell below the level that would have been produced by universal defection. Just as the nonunion firms resisted being placed in a relatively disadvantaged position, so the unionized operators resisted being kept in a position that was disadvantageous not only in comparison with universal cooperation but also in comparison with universal defection. Having repeatedly failed in their efforts to raise the level of cooperation in the industry, they sought to escape from their semiorganized state by breaking with the union, preferring the suboptimal universal defection outcome to the "sub-suboptimal" unilateral cooperation outcome. On the other hand, there are costs associated with destroying a form of market organization, as well as creating one. Thus, the allegiance of Illinois operators to the Central Competitive Field agreement probably sprung as much from the certainty that the well-organized Illinois miners would not passively accept the abrogation of their contracts as from the relatively protected market position of Illinois coal.

Firms for which $P<R$ may still resist a proposed organization of competition because such attempts at market organization often impose costs on the firms in the market. It follows that, when costs of an organizational mechanism are low, firms in this $P<R$ category will favor it. This will occur, first of all, in the case of internal mechanisms, which impose few, if any, costs on any firms in the market. Thus, in the bituminous coal industry, internal mechanisms were continually being embraced by capitalists. They were opposed only out of a fear that they would be in violation of the antitrust statutes, never because they would have hindered the autonomy of operators or in any way threatened their market positions. Second, in the kind of semiorganized market characterized by the game in which not all firms are unionized and the nonunion firms have access to a defection strategy not available to their unionized competitors, the extension of cooperation does not impose much in the way of costs on those firms who are already forced to cooperate. We would expect these latter firms to support an organizational mechanism that would raise their profits by increasing the level of cooperation in the industry. And again, there can be no doubt that the Central Com-

petitive Field operators were strong supporters of any measure that would raise labor costs and/or transportation costs (and subsequently prices) in the southern Appalachian fields.

When the organization of the market does involve the imposition of costs, a firm's reaction to it is determined by the magnitude of these costs and the degree to which the firm "needs" the cooperation of its competitors. In the movement to organize competition, firms minimize costs before they maximize cooperation. Market organization proceeds in a sequential movement, beginning with less costly mechanisms and progressing to more costly ones only if the former mechanisms are ineffective and the need for organization remains great. Both sets of appeals for state intervention to organize the coal industry – those that originated in the Midwest before World War I and those that culminated in the passage of the Guffey Acts – were part of a sequence of efforts that began with mergers and internal organizational mechanisms, proceeded to private external mechanisms (in particular, the collective bargaining agreements enforced by the UMWA), and that continued to the state only when these other efforts had failed. It appears, then, that when a proposal to organize competition has been put forth, and a firm is facing a situation in which $R>P$, the first question that we should ask in determining its probable position to market organization is whether a less costly form of market organization has been attempted.

We have seen in Chapters 1 and 2 that the success of various organizational mechanisms in a particular market is linked to its market structure; to the nature of the product, and to the nature of the relationships between capitalists and workers, and between buyers, sellers, suppliers, and creditors. Our analysis of the coal industry led us to expect that less costly mechanisms would result in failure and that a persistent need for a reorganization of competition would eventually lead capitalists to the state. Indeed, this is what occurred. The unionization that took place in the 1890s and the 1930s certainly contributed to the organization of the market but it did not introduce the controls on output and entry that would have been necessary to "stabilize" the industry during periods of stagnating demand. As for the internal measures and the merger movements, they also enjoyed some limited success at the district level, but had no impact on the more important competition between districts. Our examination of the Guffey bill testimony has shown that, when operators turned to the state, it was reluctantly, and with the feeling that no other alternatives were left.

A firm's need for organization is determined by the magnitude of its short-term payoff, both with and without a reorganization of the market, and on its prospective payoff should the market be left in an unorganized state over the long term. There appears to be a qualitative difference between suboptimal profits below zero and suboptimal profits above zero. In other words, it is not only the suboptimality of profits that leads capitalists to seek to organize competition, but also their absolute level. While capitalists are almost always willing to increase cooperation through low-cost internal mechanisms, their willingness to suffer costs in order to organize competition depends upon the presence of the dangerously low profits that occur during periods of reduced demand or overproduction. It is the capitalists with the lowest profits who are most willing to pay the costs of market organization. Just as suboptimal profits, in themselves, are insufficient to push capitalists toward market organization, optimal profits are not necessarily sufficient incentives to pull them in that direction. We saw that in the 1880s and 1890s high-cost capitalists, who feared that they would not be able to compete at the competitive price, required side payments that ensured that their profits would be positive as well as optimal.

One issue concerning the relations among capitalists that has attracted a lot of scholarly attention has been the question of "Who controls the corporations?" This question is usually traced back to the Berle and Means classic, *The Modern Corporation and Private Property*.[24] The ensuing debate has focused principally on three interrelated issues: (1) Have the legal owners of corporations – the stockholders – relinquished effective control over the operation of these corporations to a professional group of managers whose interests diverge from those of owners? (2) Do corporations controlled by owners behave any differently in the market than corporations controlled by managers? and (3) To what extent are corporations themselves controlled by financial institutions, interlocking directorates, and interest group networks of the kind first identified by Sweezy?[25]

The answers to the first two of these questions now seem to be fairly clear: Ownership continues to constrain management behavior, and profit maximizing continues to be the rule of corporate market behav-

[24] Adolph A. Berle and Gardiner C. Means, *The Modern Corporation and Private Property* (New York: Macmillan, 1932).
[25] Paul Sweezy, "Interest Groups in the American Economy," in the National Resources Committee, ed., *The Structure of the American Economy* (Washington, DC, U.S. Government Printing Office, 1939).

ior.[26] However, the answer to the third question is less evident. On the one hand, it appears to be the case that direct intervention by financial institutions in the operation of corporations takes place only rarely. On the other hand, it remains a possibility that financial institutions use their strategic position in the flow of capital to impose control over corporations in the form of constraints which limit but do not eliminate corporate discretion.[27] The present study was not framed in terms of the debate over corporate control, but it can perhaps illuminate it in two ways. The focus of the corporate-control debate, as evidenced by the title of Mintz and Schwartz's important recent contribution, *The Power Structure of American Business*, is on top-down control – on power relations among corporations.[28] The collective action framework adopted here demonstrates that there is also a "bottom-up" logic to capitalist class organization. The history of the bituminous coal industry demonstrates that, quite apart from the interests of a hegemonic fraction of capital that exercises control over the flow of investment funds, an independent logic of class organization originates from the competition experienced by firms in the various markets that constitute the economy. I have demonstrated above that the interests of financial institutions and those of firms in individual industries are not always congruent; and, even when they are, financial institutions are not always placed to enforce those interests. In fact, on the basis of these two dimensions – congruence or lack of congruence between financial and industrial interests, and the presence or absence of a financial capacity to enforce its interests on manufacturers – four situations are possible. Things become even more complicated when we recognize that the logic of class organization from below also generates conflict within industries, creating the possibility of alliances between financial institutions and one set of industrial firms against another set of competing firms.

The second point is methodological. A major strength of the corporate-control research tradition has been its strong empirical focus. The painstaking reconstruction of corporate interlocks has revealed much about the structure of corporate America. What is lacking, however, is convincing evidence of the impact of this structure on corporate behavior. Why was this structure created? What problems does it resolve? Whose

---

[26]Edward Herman, *Corporate Control, Corporate Power* (New York: Cambridge University Press, 1981).
[27]Beth Mintz and Michael Schwartz, *The Power Structure of American Business* (Chicago: University of Chicago Press, 1985).
[28]Ibid.

interests are advanced by it?[29] Such questions cannot be answered by a positional analysis alone. Again, it appears likely that this approach could be enriched by the collective action framework embodied in the present study, the strength of which lies precisely in its capacity to link interest and behavior, demonstrating why firms may seek to create an intercorporate network, and providing the critical link between strategy and structure.

Capitalists and workers

Among those political analysts who do acknowledge the existence of economic competition among capitalists, most tend to discount its relevance in structuring political conflict. Typical is the following sentence by Michael Useem about those in the "highest circles of corporate leadership": "What divides them is modest compared to what separates them from those who would presume to exercise power over economic decisions from bases other than corporate power."[30] This study suggests not only that capitalist competition is important in the economic arena, but that it has important political consequences as well, combining with (and sometimes superseding) the conflictual relations between workers and capitalists to structure political conflict. This book confirms the traditional Marxist thesis that relations of production structure political conflict among workers and capitalists, yet it does so in a somewhat untraditional way that injects this old thesis with new meaning.

In the conventional interpretation, the phrase "relations of production" refers exclusively to relations *between* workers and capitalists. Capitalist relations of production define the positions of workers and capitalists in such a way that their interests are mutually contradictory. The interests of capitalists in profits and capital accumulation push them to reduce labor costs, in opposition to the interests of workers in high wages and satisfying working conditions. This structurally determined opposition of interests is expected to issue in economic and political conflict between the two principal classes.

In some respects, we have seen, this conventional view of interclass relations has been confirmed by my study of the bituminous coal industry. The importance of wage cutting in the above analysis leaves no

[29]Mintz and Schwartz's study is notable in attempting to connect structure and behavior.
[30]Useem, *The Hidden Circle*, p. 6.

room for doubt that the interests of operators regarding the distribution of the product between wages and profits and the organization of the workplace conflicted with that of workers and that conflict resulted. This much is undeniable; no study of the coal industry, or of any other capitalist industry, for that matter, can fail to find some very real basis for labor–capital conflict. My point is not that worker versus capitalist conflict did not take place, but that it was itself structured by the competitive relations among capitalists.

Whatever the structure of the underlying interests, it is clear that class struggle in the bituminous coal industry took the form of capital and labor alliances, as well as labor and capital conflict. There are two ways in which this empirical data can fit the traditional labor versus capital model. First, one might argue that, in allying with capitalists, workers were not pursuing their true interests, but were acting out of a false consciousness that their interests coincided with those of capitalists. Although this argument may be valid in other contexts, it cannot be sustained in the case before us. The interests pursued by the UMWA were higher wages, better working conditions, and job security. The union's early leadership should be credited with seeing that, between the interest of workers in a high wage and the interest of operators in a stable wage, there was common ground. The initiative behind the original Central Competitive Field agreements lay with the workers. The following excerpt from a statement made by the District President of the UMWA in West Virginia is interesting because it captures the degree to which the collective action of capitalists was viewed by workers as a problem for *workers*, in fact a worker problem too important to be left in the hands of capitalists.

There are certain operators . . . asking their employees to accept a reduction in wages, saying that if the mine workers would accept this reduction, it would enable the operators to get in the market, and furnish the miners steady work. Operators of the type just mentioned are to the fair operators who want to maintain the present prices what a non-union miner is to the union miner. . . . *The miners want the cooperation of the operators to stabilize the coal industry.* . . . We feel that the operators who are attempting to unstabilize the coal industry should not be given any consideration at the hands of the United Mine Workers of America, and that they will not receive any consideration so far as I am concerned.[31]

[31]*Coal Age* 15 (February 13, 1919): 327, emphasis added.

The fact that workers and capitalists have some conflicting interests does not mean that all of their interests are in conflict. For workers, a stable organized coal market means regularity in employment, a stable, high wage level, and improved working conditions. Workers even share the interest of capitalists in high profits, as long as those profits are used to finance future wage increases and productive investment.[32] And in the coal industry, where market organization implied unionization, the organization of capitalist competition directly enhanced the capacity of workers to pursue those interests that contradicted those of capitalists.

A second way in which the simple labor versus capital model could be accommodated to fit the history of the bituminous coal industry is through the possibility that those operators who were advocates of collective bargaining and regulation were enlightened capitalists, motivated by their long-term class interests. Therefore, their alliance with workers was a tactical, one step backward, two steps forward, kind of maneuver, a brief phase in the interclass struggle. Several historians have found such groups of class-conscious capitalists espousing a corporate liberal ideology of conciliation and interclass cooperation behind many pre–World War II reforms.[33] However, there are several problems with applying this argument to the coal industry, in particular, and to problems of market organization, in general. First, there is the possibility, discussed in Chapter 1, that the interests of any individual firm or group of firms does not necessarily coincide with the long-term interests of the capitalist class. Thus, even if enlightened capitalists existed, we have no reason to believe that their material position would enable them to behave in accord with the long-term interests of their class. It is probably true that the closer the issue is to the economic position of the individual firm, the less disposed will it be to act in any way other than in pursuit of its *individual* interests. Michael Useem argues convincingly that some corporate officials have an understanding of their class interests, but the arenas in which this class interest is activated – corporate philanthropy, campaign contributions, "aditorials," and "social responsibility" – are, as Useem acknowledges, distinguished precisely in that they do *not* touch on the immediate life-and-death concerns of individual firms.[34] The coal operators' problem was not that they were ignorant or greedy,

[32]Adam Przeworski and Michael Wallerstein, "The Structure of Class Conflict in Democratic Capitalist Societies," *American Political Science Review* 76 (1982): 215–38.
[33]See, for instance, James Weinstein, *The Corporate Ideal and the Liberal State* (Boston: Beacon Press, 1968).
[34]Useem, *The Hidden Circle*, pp. 195, 117.

but that the structure of their competitive relations did not always allow them to act in the market on the basis of their personal characteristics. As Phil Murray, Vice President of the UMWA, testified, "the bituminous coal operators, individually, are splendid gentlemen, but collectively they are a frantic mob, wholly incapable of regulating or standardizing their own businesses."[35]

Because of this disjunction between individual and class interests, it is not always easy, without the benefit of hindsight, to see where the long-term interests of capitalists really lie. In the coal industry, it is arguable that the true bearers of the long-term interests of the capitalist class were those operators who could produce the best coal at the lowest price – precisely those operators who *opposed* the form of interclass conciliation represented by the Central Competitive Field collective bargaining framework.

This study suggests that the interclass struggle between workers and capitalists and the intraclass struggle among capitalists exert a mutual influence on each other, and that one cannot understand the connection between relations of production and political and economic conflict unless one takes into account *both* these aspects of production relations. Competitive relations among capitalist firms structure interclass conflict in two ways. First, it is competitive pressure which "activates" the conflict of interest between workers and capitalists within the firm. Competition from other firms forces capitalists to try to reduce costs by seizing control of the labor process and reducing wages. One reason that workers in the more oligopolized sectors of the economy, where price competition has been effectively organized, enjoy more rights and higher wages is simply because the relative relaxation of competitive pressures enables firms to afford them. Our capitalist collective action framework suggests another way in which competition among capitalists affects worker–capitalist conflict. Capitalist firms sometimes face competitive games that generate suboptimal outcomes that they wish to escape. When they are unable to organize themselves through voluntary cooperative activity, workers may be able to force them to cooperate by restricting output or by preventing certain forms of cost cutting. To the extent that they are successful, workers organize capitalists. Because the Prisoner's Dilemma structure of these games always provides a temptation for firms to free-ride, if they can get away with it, such worker–capital alliances for the purpose of organizing capitalist competition will

[35]U.S. Congress, Senate, Committee on Interstate Commerce, *Stabilization*, p. 148.

always to some extent be alliances against other, free-riding, capitalists. This will especially be the case, however, when the organization of competition has a differential impact within the industry, perhaps, as in the coal industry, because of intraindustry cost differences, or perhaps, as in the mid-nineteenth-century English textile industry studied by Marvel, because of differences in the type of technology employed.[36] In either case, the labor–capital alliance will be face to face not with individual free-riders, but with groups of firms for whom free-riding may be the only viable strategy, and who cannot afford to cooperate. Most important, the structure of capitalist competition does not remain constant. As the history of the coal industry vividly demonstrates, the competitive games played by operators change, and these changes alter the pattern of both intra- and interclass conflict.

This pattern of class conflict – a labor–capital alliance against other capitalists – was also present in the pre–World War II garment industry, and for the same reason that it existed in the bituminous coal industry – capitalist firms relied on workers to organize competition among capitalists.[37] Like the coal industry, the garment industry contained a large number of firms whose principal competitive weapon was wage cutting. And as was the case with coal operators, clothing manufacturers accepted collective bargaining in part in the hope that a worker-enforced standardization of wages and working conditions would effect the organization of competition that capitalists could not achieve on their own. In the words of the president of the manufacturers' association, they hoped that the union would "protect the legitimate manufacturers from the small fry who are cutting into their trade." The International Ladies Garment Workers Union sought to achieve this goal through "authorized strikes" conducted against nonunion shops "with the mutual consent and cooperation" of the unionized employers. Garment manufacturers responded to the recessionary conditions of the 1920s in the same manner as did coal operators, reducing wages and reluctantly weakening the union, although unlike coal operators they did not seek to eliminate the union as a force in the industry. On the contrary, in 1929, manufacturers met with the union at their joint conference and, in the words

---

[36]Marvel, "Factory Regulation."

[37]The following account of the garment industry is based on Stanley Vittoz, *New Deal Labor Policy and the American Industrial Economy* (Chapel Hill: University of North Carolina Press, 1987), pp. 35–47. This book, which also contains case studies of the coal and cotton textile industries, employs a framework that in several respects parallels that which is developed in the present volume.

of a spokesman for manufacturers, "vouchsafed our support to the strengthening of the demoralized union." By 1933, garment manufacturers, even more than coal operators, felt the need for "a publicly sanctioned institutional framework for the negotiation and administration of industry wide employment standards."

In the coal and garment industries, then, capitalist relations among capitalists structured the conflict between workers and capitalists, generating a capitalist–worker alliance seeking to force other capitalists to cooperate. However, in both cases, this outcome was possible only because workers had successfully organized themselves in prior struggles against capitalists.[38] While workers organized capitalists, capitalists did not organize workers. This was an achievement of workers in their struggle against capitalists.

In general, then, the capitalist relations of production that structure political and economic conflict are not simply relations that oppose workers to capitalists; they also oppose capitalists to each other: "The enemy of labor is capital; the enemy of capital is labor and other capital." These two aspects of capitalist production relations interact in complex ways. At the level of the individual firm, capitalists seek to lower labor costs at the expense of workers in order to maximize their own profits. However, as this study has demonstrated, the outcomes produced by such behavior can be undesirable for capitalists as well as for workers, creating the basis for a collaborative effort to organize competition. But the form that this effort takes and the pattern of intraindustry conflict that it generates will depend both on the strength of workers vis-à-vis capitalists *and* on the economic basis of divisions among capitalists.

Capitalists and the state

A major theme in Marxist writing on the state, and one which has persisted from the work of Marx and Engels through current controversies, is the inability of capitalists to provide the conditions required for the reproduction of their own class domination and the consequent need for the state to intervene to organize the interests of capitalists. The principal concern of most work in this area has been on the related questions of why the democratic state acts to pursue the interests of the capitalist class, and to what extent the state is autonomous with respect

[38]Ibid., p. 119.

to those interests.[39] Because this study has concentrated on capitalist firms rather than state actors, it does not provide us with the means to address these particular questions, which focus on the state side of the state–capital relationship. However, by approaching the state–capital relationship from the other side – as we have been led to it by capitalists trying to pursue their interests – we have gained some insight into the following related problems, which are also important: (a) Why do capitalists seek to organize themselves? (b) Why are they unable to organize themselves? and (c) Why do capitalists oppose state intervention to organize themselves?

In considering the needs of capitalists that are met by the state, most writers focus on two categories of collective action problems. The first concerns their desire to provide themselves with an optimal amount of the various public goods required for the production and marketing of commodities. These include an adequately developed transportation and communication system as well as an educated and motivated workforce. The second concerns their political interest in maintaining their domination and in preempting or repressing any challenges to their societal position from below.[40] The present study suggests that besides wishing to provide themselves with standard public goods and to protect themselves against threats from *other* groups, capitalists also wish to protect themselves from each other. As I argued in Chapter 1, the most basic interest of every firm is to stay in the market, and the most basic threat to that interest comes from other firms. Capitalist competition places capitalists in a situation in which their pursuit of their individual survival generates competitive behavior that, collectively, is self-destructive. Their response is to try to organize themselves out of those situations, sometimes turning to the state to help them do so. Thus, independent of their conflict with workers, capitalists may require state intervention to protect themselves from each other.

We should not forget, however, that the interests of any set of firms, even if it comprises the majority of an important industry, does not necessarily coincide with the interest of the capitalist class, which is an interest in long-term growth. Thus, the attack on government regulation

[39]Two recent surveys of Marxist writing on the state are Martin Carnoy, *The State in Political Theory* (Princeton: Princeton University Press, 1984) and Bob Jessop, *The Capitalist State* (New York: New York University Press, 1982).
[40]This distinction corresponds roughly to James O'Connor's distinction between "accumulation" and "legitimation." See *The Fiscal Crisis of the State* (New York: St. Martin's Press, 1973).

has been led by neoclassical economists who argue that, in providing cartel profits or protecting competitors from entry, it interferes with the free market's production of an optimal long-term outcome.[41] Similarly, in Jon Elster's interpretation of *The German Ideology*, competition is seen by Marx as being in the interest of capitalists.[42] On the one hand, capitalists seek determinedly to escape free competition; yet, on the other hand, competition appears to be in the long-term interests of the capitalist class. This apparent contradiction can be resolved if we remember that all free markets are, in fact, organized to some degree against self-destructive competitive behavior. *Some* degree of market organization is necessary for "free" competition to take place and is therefore in the interest of the capitalist class.

This is true both for the economic reasons discussed above and for political reasons – unrestrained competition produces adverse political consequences. However, not every attempt by capitalists to organize themselves is in the interest of their class, and neither is every state-enforced organization of competition. This statement carries with it two important implications, both of which are confirmed by our coal-industry study. First, capitalists seek to organize their competition, sometimes with state assistance, in pursuit of their short-term interest in profits and survival in the market. This is what motivated the operators who sought state intervention in the form of the Guffey Acts after the demise of the NIRA, not their interest in the long-term interests of capital. Second, other considerations move public officials besides the long-term interests of the capitalist class, and while they have to be concerned about the general profitability and prosperity of the capitalist economy, their concern with the profitability of particular industries and their willingness to organize them is the outcome of indeterminate political factors.

There were two dimensions to the state's interest in coal. First, because of coal's importance to the national economy, public officials had a very real interest in a steady, uninterrupted coal supply. Second, simply because of their numbers, their militancy, and their organization, the state had to be interested in the welfare of miners. Extremely oppressive conditions in the coal fields were likely to have political repercussions. The state was interested in the profits of the bituminous coal industry

---

[41]The neoclassical "economic theory of regulation" was first articulated by George Stigler. See *The Citizen and the State* (Chicago: University of Chicago Press, 1975).
[42]Elster, *Making Sense of Marx*, p. 410.

only so far as they affected the coal supply and conditions in the mine fields. Since the state had the capacity to assume control of coal production and distribution during an emergency, its interest in profitability *per se* was minimal. State intervention in the bituminous coal industry during World War I was directed toward the maintenance of a continuous supply of coal at a "reasonable" price. When coal profits suffered as a result of initial low prices, the Fuel Administration raised prices – not to give operators profits but to provide them with an incentive to increase output. In the 1920s high coal prices and threatened shortages moved legislators from the consuming states to push fact-finding legislation. Interestingly, the state's interest in uninterrupted coal production probably led it to refrain from intervening to enforce collective bargaining agreements during the latter half of the 1920s. Nonunion coal production was seen as a safety-valve in the event of a coal strike. The presence of a substantial "unorganized" segment of the industry left the economy less vulnerable to a UMWA strike and therefore decreased the dependence of the state on the union.[43] As for the 1930s, state intervention in the coal industry to organize coal competition was probably more than anything else a reflection of the strength of the United Mine Workers. This was certainly true of the early NIRA period, when the UMWA pressured the president to pressure operators to agree to a wage contract. And although there was substantial operator support for the Guffey legislation, it was the threat of a coal strike that led Roosevelt to force it through a less than enthusiastic Congress. Moreover, according to Fisher and James, what congressional support there was for these bills was motivated less by a desire to preserve the capital of owners than by a desire to establish a cost floor that would support better wages.[44]

When capitalist firms seek state intervention to organize their competition, it is often in direct contradiction of the interests of other competing firms in the same industry, sometimes in contradiction of the long-term interests of the capitalist class, and almost always in opposition to the interests of firms in other industries. Thus, the state, whenever it intervenes to organize capitalists necessarily does so *against* some capitalists. This provides one way of interpreting Marx's statement that the bourgeois state is "nothing more than the mutual insurance of the bourgeois class against its individual members, as well as against the

[43]Dubofsky and Van Tine, *John L. Lewis*, p. 119.
[44]Fisher and James, *Minimum Price*, p. 310.

exploited class," and Engels's similar remark that the state is "the organization that bourgeois society takes on in order to support the general external conditions of the capitalist mode of production against the encroachments as well of the workers as of individual capitalists."[45]

This study demonstrates that a principal obstacle preventing capitalists from organizing themselves is the structure of their competitive relations. Competition generated gaming situations in which the noncooperative strategy was consistently dominant. The political awareness of capitalists – their ability to perceive common interests and the necessity of acting on them – played no role in the politics of market organization in the coal industry. There were operators – Phil Penna, Charles O'Neill, Charles Hosford, J. D. A. Morrow – whose names regularly appeared in accounts of meetings of operators and who could be characterized as "industrial statesmen." However, the inability of operators to organize themselves did not result from a dearth of such men, but from the material relations which structured the behavior of all operators, including the industrial statesmen. Competing in a depressed industry in which the risks of unilateral cooperation were extremely high, operators were unable to cooperate, even when they desired to do so. Most importantly, operators were prevented from cooperating by the fact that they did not share a common interest in market organization. As we have seen, the efforts of coal operators to reorganize the national market were primarily efforts by northern firms to organize their southern competitors *out* of the market.

In the coal industry, state intervention was always the organizational mechanism of last resort. An initial inability to organize themselves did not immediately generate demands by operators for state intervention. The reason for this, I have argued, is that state intervention is costly to capitalists. First, enforced cooperation deprives individual firms of their dominant defection strategy. Universal cooperation in the Prisoner's Dilemma is always the *second* preference; each firm would prefer that it be allowed to defect while its competitors cooperate. Second, more than any other organizational mechanism, state intervention creates the possibility that hostile actors will gain influence over a firm's policy. In part, this refers to workers and consumers; fear of the legislative consequences of a public distrustful of coal operators was a major determinant of coal

---

[45]The Marx quote is from a review of Girardin's *Le Socialisme et l' Impot* cited by Elster, *Making Sense of Marx*, p. 409. The Engels quote is from Friedrich Engels, *Anti Duhring* (Moscow: Foreign Languages Press, 1962).

politics during the early 1920s, when operators vehemently opposed
even the mildest form of fact-finding legislation. However, besides the
fear of actors whose interests were in opposition to industry as a whole
or even to the coal industry as a whole, operators were worried that
state intervention would place *competitors* in positions of power. Just as
this study demonstrates that even in a world with a passive working
class, capitalists still face important organization problems, it also demonstrates that, in such a world, they still have good reason to fear the
state.

The record of the debate over state intervention in the 1930s shows
clearly that the main source of opposition on the part of capitalists was
not that the members of anticapitalist social groups would gain control
over coal operators, but that other capitalists would gain such control.
Thus, a spokesman for Consolidation Coal Company told the Senate
that:

we believe that the determination of prices upon which we are to sell our coal,
if left in the hands of our competitors, as it must be in these district boards,
finally set up by a coal commission in Washington, of people who know nothing
of our business, know nothing of our coals, our competitive relationships, and
who know nothing about us – we believe that we will find it impossible to
maintain our business.[46]

Another operator told the Senate that the:

district board [which set prices under the Guffey–Vinson bill] is made up of an
even number of producers in the district, with one additional member. Now,
these men are producers of coal; they are in competition with their neighbors.
. . . They must fix their neighbors' prices as they "deem necessary and proper."
If they deem it necessary to have the prices thus and so, they may make a profit,
and the other man will not.[47]

Conflicts over state intervention, like other struggles over market organization, are often struggles among groups of capitalists, each seeking
to enforce a set of rules that will place it in an advantageous position
with respect to competitors. Some capitalists oppose state intervention
for the same reason that others support it: It is often a weapon in the
competitive struggle among capitalists.

[46]U.S. Congress, Senate, Committee on Interstate Commerce, *To Regulate*, p. 128.
[47]Ibid., p. 136.

Bibliography

Aurand, Harold W. *From the Molly Maguires to the United Mine Workers: The Social Ecology of an Industrial Union, 1867–1897*. Philadelphia: Temple University Press, 1971.

Bain, Joe. *Barriers to New Competition*. Cambridge, MA: Harvard University Press, 1965.

Baker, Ralph Hillis. *The National Bituminous Coal Commission*. Baltimore: Johns Hopkins University Press, 1941.

Baratz, Morton. *The Union and the Coal Industry*. Port Washington, NY: Kennikat, 1973.

Berle, Adolph A., and Means, Gardiner C. *The Modern Corporation and Private Property*. New York: Macmillan, 1932.

Berquist, F. E., et al. *Economic Survey of the Bituminous Coal Industry Under Free Competition and Code Regulation*. Washington, DC: U.S. National Recovery Administration, Work Materials, No. 69, 1936 (Mimeographed).

Black Diamond (1885–1926).

Bonbright, James C., and Means, Gardiner C. *The Holding Company*. New York: Augustus M. Kelley, 1969.

Bowman, John R. "Economic Competition and Collective Action: The Politics of Market Organization in the Bituminous Coal Industry, 1880–1940." Unpublished Ph.D. dissertation, University of Chicago, 1984.

Bunting, David, and Barbour, Jeffrey. "Interlocking Directorates in Large American Corporations." *Business History Review* 45 (Autumn, 1971): 317–36.

Burns, Arthur R. *The Decline of Competition*. New York: McGraw-Hill, 1936.

Carnoy, Martin. *The State in Political Theory* (Princeton: Princeton University Press, 1984).

Caves, R., and Porter, M. "From Entry Barriers to Mobility Barriers: Conjectural Decisions and Contrived Deterrence to New Competition." *Quarterly Journal of Economics* 91 (1977): 241–61.

Chamberlin, Edward H. *The Theory of Monopolistic Competition*. Cambridge, MA: Harvard University Press, 1962.

Coal Age (1911–1940).

Corbin, David Alan. *Life, Work, and Rebellion in the Coal Fields: The Southern West Virginia Miners, 1880–1922*. Urbana: University of Illinois Press, 1981.

Davis, G. Cullen. "The Transformation of the Federal Trade Commission, 1914–1929." *Mississippi Valley Historical Review* 49 (December, 1962): 437–55.

Devine, Edward T. *Coal: Economic Problems of the Mining, Marketing, and Consumption of Anthracite and Soft Coal in the United States*. Bloomington: American Review Service Press, 1925.

Dewey, Donald. *Monopoly in Economics and Law*. Chicago: Rand McNally, 1959.

Dooley, Peter C. "The Interlocking Directorate." *American Economic Review* 59 (June, 1969): 314–23.

Dubofsky, Melvyn, and Van Tine, Warren. *John L. Lewis: A Biography*. New York: Quadrangle, 1977.

Edwards, Corwin D. *Control of Cartels and Monopolies: An International Comparison*. Dobbs-Ferry, NY: Oceana Publications, 1967.

Eichner, Adolph, *The Emergence of Oligopoly*. Baltimore: Johns Hopkins University Press, 1969.

Eis, Carl. "The 1919–1930 Merger Movement in American Industry." *Journal of Law and Economics* 12 (October, 1969): 267–96.

Elster, Jon. *Logic and Society*. London: Wiley, 1978.

    Making Sense of Marx. Cambridge: Cambridge University Press, 1985.

    "Marxism, Functionalism, and Game Theory." *Theory and Society* 11 (1982): 453–82.

Encaoua, David, Geroski, Paul, and Jacquemin, Alexis. "Strategic Competition and the Persistence of Dominant Firms: A Survey." In *New Developments in the Analysis of Market Structure*. Edited by Joseph E. Stiglitz and G. Frank Mathewson. Cambridge, MA: MIT Press, 1986, pp. 55–86.

Engels, Friederich. "The Abdication of the Bourgeoisie." In *Articles on Britain*, by Karl Marx and Friederich Engels. Moscow: Progress Publishers, 1975, pp. 393–8.

    Anti-Duhring. Moscow: Foreign Languages Press, 1962.

Farr, Grant. "The Origins of Recent Labor Policy." *University of Colorado Studies, Series in Economics*, No. 3, 1959.

Fellner, William. *Competition among the Few*. New York: Alfred A. Knopf, 1949.

Fisher, Waldo E., and Bezanson, Anne. *Wage Rates and Working Time in the Bituminous Coal Industry*. Philadelphia: Temple University Press, 1932.

Fisher, Waldo E., and James, Charles M. *Minimum Price Fixing in the Bituminous Coal Industry*. Princeton: Princeton University Press, 1955.

Fritz, Wilbert G., and Veenstra, Theodore A. *Regional Shifts in the Bituminous Coal Industry with Special Reference to Pennsylvania*. Pittsburgh: Bureau of Business Research, University of Pittsburgh, 1935.

Gilbert, Richard. "Preemptive Competition." In *New Developments in the Analysis of Market Structure*. Edited by Joseph E. Stiglitz and G. Frank Mathewson. Cambridge, MA: MIT Press, 1986, pp. 90–123.

Goldsmith, Raymond, and Parmelee, Rexford C. *The Distribution of Ownership in the 200 Largest Nonfinancial Corporations*. U.S. Temporary National Economic Committee Investigation of the Concentration of Economic Power, Monograph No. 29. Washington, DC: Government Printing Office, 1941.

Graebner, William. *Coal Mining Safety in the Progressive Period: The Political Economy of Reform*. Lexington: University Press of Kentucky, 1976.

    "Great Expectations: The Search for Order in Bituminous Coal, 1890–1917." *Business History Review* 48 (Spring, 1974): 49–73.

Hamilton, Walton H., and Wright, Helen. *The Case of Bituminous Coal*. New York: Macmillan, 1928.

    A Way of Order for Bituminous Coal. New York: Macmillan, 1926.

Haney, Lewis, H. *Business Organization and Combination*. New York: Macmillan, 1921.

Hannah, Leslie. "Mergers." In *Encyclopedia of Economic History*. Edited by Glenn Porter. New York: Scribners, 1980, pp. 639–51.

Hardin, Russell. *Collective Action*. Baltimore: Johns Hopkins University Press, 1982.

Hawley, Ellis W. *The New Deal and the Problem of Monopoly*. Princeton: Princeton University Press, 1966.

Hay, G., and Kelley, D. "An Empirical Survey of Price Fixing Conspiracies." *Journal of Law and Economics* 17 (April, 1974): 13–38.

Herman, Edward. *Corporate Power, Corporate Control*. New York: Cambridge University Press, 1982.

Heermance, Edgar. *Can Business Govern Itself?* New York: Harper and Bro., 1932.

Hendry, James B. "The Bituminous Coal Industry." In *The Structure of American Industry*. Edited by Walter Adams. New York: Macmillan, 1961, pp. 74–112.

Hevener, John W. *Which Side Are You On: The Harlan County Miners, 1931–1939*. Urbana: University of Illinois Press, 1978.

Hilferding, Rudolf. *Finance Capital: A Study of the Latest Phase of Capitalist Development*. London: Routledge, and Kegan Paul, 1981.

Himmelberg, Robert F. *The Origins of the National Recovery Administration*. New York: Fordham University Press, 1976.

Hirschman, Albert O. *Exit, Voice, and Loyalty*. New Haven: Yale University Press, 1970.

Hollander, S. G. "The United States." In *Resale Price Maintenance*. Edited by B. S. Yamey. Chicago: Aldine, 1966, pp. 65–100.

Howard, J. E. "Collusive Behavior." *Journal of Business* 27 (July, 1954): 196–204.

Hunt, Edward E., Tryon, F. G., and Willits, Joseph. *What the Coal Commission Found*. Baltimore: Williams and Wilkins, 1925.

Jacquemin, Alexis. *The New Industrial Organization: Market Forces and Strategic Behavior*. Cambridge, MA: MIT Press, 1987.

Jessop, Bob. *The Capitalist State*. New York: New York University Press, 1982.

Johnsen, Julia, ed. *Selected Articles on Government Ownership of Coal Mines*. New York: H.W. Wilson, 1923.

Johnson, James P. *A "New Deal" for Soft Coal*. New York: Arno, 1979.
   The Politics of Soft Coal. Urbana: University of Illinois Press, 1979.

Jones, Eliot. *The Trust Problem in the United States*. New York: Macmillan, 1922.

Jordan, William A. *Airline Regulation in America: Effects and Imperfections*. Baltimore: Johns Hopkins University Press, 1970.

Keynes, John Maynard. *The General Theory of Employment, Interest, and Money*. New York: Harcourt, Brace and World, 1936.

Kolko, Gabriel. *Railroads and Regulation*. Princeton: Princeton University Press, 1965.
   The Triumph of Conservatism. New York: The Free Press of Glencoe, 1963.

Kotz, David. *Bank Control of Large Corporations in the United States*. Berkeley: University of California Press, 1978.

Lambie, Joseph T. *From Mine to Market: The History of Coal Transportation on the Norfolk and Western Railway*. New York: New York University Press, 1954.

Lamoreaux, Naomi. *The Great Merger Movement in American Business, 1895–1904.* Cambridge: Cambridge University Press, 1985.

Leonard, N.H. "The Bituminous Coal Industry." In *The Structure of American Industry.* Edited by Walter Adams. New York: Macmillan, 1950, pp. 29–62.

Lindblom, Charles. *Politics and Markets.* New York: Basic Books, 1977.

Lubin, Isador. *Miners' Wages and the Cost of Coal.* New York: Macmillan, 1924.

Luce, R. D., and Raiffa, H. *Games and Decisions.* New York: Wiley, 1957.

MacAvoy, Paul W. *The Economic Effects of Regulation.* Cambridge, MA: MIT Press, 1965.

  Federal Milk Marketing Orders and Price Supports. Washington, DC: American Enterprise Institute, 1977.

McDonald, David J., and Lynch, Edward A. *Coal and Unionism: A History of the American Coal Miners' Unions.* Silver Springs, MD: Lynald Books, 1939.

McNulty, Paul. "Economic Theory and the Meaning of Competition." *Quarterly Journal of Economics* 82 (November, 1968): 639–56.

Macrosty, Henry W. *The Trust Movement in British Industry.* New York: Agathon Press, 1968.

Maloney, Michael, McCormick, Robert E., and Tollison, Ralph D. "Achieving Cartel Profits through Unionization." *Southern Economic Journal* 46 (October, 1979): 628–34.

Mansfield, Harvey C. *The Lake Cargo Coal Rate Controversy.* New York: Columbia University Press, 1932.

Marvel, H. "Factory Legislation: An Interpretation of the Early English Experience." *Journal of Law and Economics* 20 (1977): 379–402.

Marx, Karl. *Capital,* Volume 1. New York: Modern Library, 1936.

  Capital, Volume 3. New York: International Publishers, 1975.

  The Eighteenth Brumaire of Louis Bonaparte. New York: International Publishers, 1963.

  Grundrisse: Foundations of the Critique of Political Economy. New York: Vintage, 1973.

  The Poverty of Philosophy. New York: International Publishers, 1963.

Miller, J. P. *Unfair Competition.* Cambridge, MA: Harvard University Press, 1941.

Mineral Industry, Its Statistics, Technology, Trade (1893–1941).

Mintz, Beth, and Schwartz, Michael. *The Power Struggle of American Industry.* Chicago: University of Chicago Press, 1985.

Moody, John. *The Truth about the Trusts.* New York: Greenwood, 1968.

National Industrial Conference Board. *The Competitive Position of Coal in the United States.* New York: National Industrial Conference Board, 1931.

Neale, Alan D., and Goyder, D. G. *The Antitrust Laws of the United States of America.* New York: Cambridge University Press, 1980.

Nelson, James C. "The Motor Carrier Act of 1935." *Journal of Political Economy* 44 (August, 1936): 464–504.

Nelson, Ralph. *Merger Movements in American Industry.* Princeton: Princeton University Press, 1959.

O'Connor, James. *The Fiscal Crisis of the State.* New York: St. Martin's Press, 1973.

Offe, Claus, and Ronge, Volker. "Theses on the Theory of the State." *New German Critique* 9 (Fall, 1975): 137–47.

Offe, Claus, and Wiesenthal, Helmut. "Two Logics of Collective Action: Theoretical Notes on Social Class and Organization Form." *Political Power and Social Theory* 1 (1980): 67–115.

Olson, Mancur. *The Logic of Collective Action.* Cambridge, MA: Harvard University Press, 1971.

  The Rise and Decline of Nations. New Haven: Yale University Press, 1982.

Palamountain, Joseph C., Jr. *The Politics of Distribution.* Cambridge, MA: Harvard University Press, 1955.

Papandreou, A. G., and Wheeler, J. T. *Competition and Its Regulation.* New York: Prentice-Hall, 1954.

Parker, Glen L. *The Coal Industry: A Study in Social Control.* Washington: American Council on Public Affairs, 1940.

Pearce, Charles A. *Trade Association Survey.* U.S. Temporary National Economic Committee Investigation of the Concentration of Economic Power, Monograph No. 18. Washington, DC: Government Printing Office, 1941.

Pennings, Johannes M. *Interlocking Directorates.* San Francisco: Jossey-Bass, 1980.

Pfeffer, Jeffrey, and Salancik, Gerald R. *The External Control of Organizations: A Resource Dependence Approach.* New York: Harper and Row, 1978.

Phillips, Almarin. *Market Structure, Organization, and Performance.* Cambridge, MA: Harvard University Press, 1962.

Pibran, Karl. *Cartel Problems.* Washington, DC: Brookings Institution, 1935.

Posner, Richard A. *Antitrust Law: An Economic Perspective.* Chicago: University of Chicago Press, 1976.

  The Robinson–Patman Act. Washington, DC: American Enterprise Institute, 1976.

  "Theories of Economic Regulation." *Bell Journal of Economics and Management Science* 5 (Autumn, 1974): 335–56.

Poulantzas, Nicos. *Political Power and Social Classes.* London: New Left Books, 1973.

Przeworski, Adam. *Capitalism and Social Democracy.* Cambridge: Cambridge University Press, 1985.

  "Marxism and Rational Choice." *Politics and Society* 14 (1985): 379–409.

  "Toward a Theory of Capitalist Democracy." Unpublished Paper, University of Chicago, 1980.

Przeworski, Adam, and Wallerstein, Michael. "The Structure of Class Conflict in Advanced Capitalist Societies." *American Political Science Review* 76 (1982): 215–38.

Rappoport, Anatol. "Prisoner's Dilemma – Recollections and Observations." In *Rational Man and Irrational Society?* Edited by Brian Barry and Russell Hardin. Beverly Hills: Sage, 1982.

Rasmussen, Wayne D., Baker, Gladys, L., and Ward, James. *A Short History of Agricultural Adjustment.* U.S. Department of Agriculture Information Bulletin No. 391. Washington, DC: Government Printing Office, 1976.

Reynolds, Lloyd. "Cutthroat Competition," *American Economic Review* 30 (December, 1940), pp. 736–47.

Risser, Hubert E. *The Economics of the Coal Industry.* Lawrence, KS: Bureau of Business Research, School of Business, University of Kansas, 1958.

Schattschneider, E. E. *Politics, Pressure, and the Tariff.* New York: Prentice-Hall, 1935.

Schelling, Thomas C. "Hockey Helmets, Concealed Weapons, and Daylight Savings: A Study of Binary Choices with Externalities." *Journal of Conflict Resolution* 17 (September, 1973): 381–428.

The Strategy of Conflict. Oxford: Oxford University Press, 1960.

Scherer, F. M. *Industrial Market Structure and Economic Performance.* Chicago: Rand McNally, 1980.

Schmookler, Jacob. "The Bituminous Coal Industry." *The Structure of American Industry.* Edited by Walter Adams. New York: Macmillan, 1954, pp. 76–113.

Schotter, Andrew. *An Economic Theory of Institutions.* New York: Cambridge University Press, 1981.

Schurr, Sam H., and Netshert, Bruce C. *Energy in the American Economy.* Baltimore: Johns Hopkins University Press, 1960.

Shubik, Martin. *Strategy and Market Structure.* New York: Wiley, 1959.

Smith, R. A. "The Incredible Electrical Conspiracy," Parts One and Two. *Fortune* (April and May, 1961).

Snidal, Duncan. "Coordination versus Prisoner's Dilemma: Implications for International Cooperation and Regimes." *American Political Science Review* 79 (1985): 923–42.

Stevens, William S. "A Classification of Pools and Associations Based on the American Experience." *American Economic Review* 3 (September, 1913): 545–75.

Stigler, George. *The Citizen and the State.* Chicago: University of Chicago Press, 1975.

"A Theory of Oligopoly." *Journal of Political Economy* 72 (February, 1964): 44–61.

The Organization of Industry. Homewood, IL: Richard D. Irwin, 1968.

Suffern, Arthur E. *Conciliation and Arbitration in the Coal Industry of America.* Boston: Houghton-Mifflin, 1915.

The Coal Miners' Struggle for Industrial Status. New York: Macmillan, 1926.

Sweezy, Paul. "Interest Groups in the American Economy." In *The Structure of the American Economy.* U.S. National Resources Committee. Washington, DC: Government Printing Office, 1939, pp. 307–17.

Tams, W. P. *The Smokeless Coal Fields of West Virginia: A Brief History.* Morgantown, WV: West Virginia University Library, 1963.

Taylor, Michael. *Anarchy and Cooperation.* London: Wiley, 1976.

Thompson, Alexander M. *Technology, Labor, and Industrial Structure of the U.S. Coal Industry: A Historical Perspective.* New York: Garland Publishing Co., 1979.

Thorelli, Hans B. *The Federal Antitrust Policy.* Baltimore: Johns Hopkins University Press, 1955.

Tryon, F. G. "Effect of Competition Conditions on Labor Relations." *Annals of the American Academy* 111 (June, 1924): 83–95.

U.S. Bureau of Mines. *Minerals Yearbook.* Washington, DC: Government Printing Office, 1932–1941.

U.S. Congress, House of Representatives, Committee on the Judiciary, Antitrust Subcommittee. *Interlocks in Corporate Management.* Washington, DC: Government Printing Office, 1965.

U.S. Congress, House of Representatives, Committee on Ways and Means. *Stabilization of the Bituminous Coal Industry.* Hearings on H.R. 8479, 74th Congress, 1st Session, 1935.

U.S. Congress, Senate, Committee on Interstate Commerce. *To Regulate Interstate Commerce in Bituminous Coal.* Hearings on S. 4668, 74th Congress, 2nd Session, 1936.

 Stabilization of the Bituminous Coal-Mining Industry. Hearings on S. 1417, 74th Congress, 1st Session, 1935.

U.S. Congress, Senate, Committee on Mines and Mining. *To Create a Bituminous Coal Commission.* Hearings on S. 2935, 72nd Congress, 1st Session, 1932.

U.S. Geological Survey. *Mineral Resources of the United States.* Washington, DC: Government Printing Office.

U.S. Interstate Commerce Commission. *Association of Bituminous Coal Operators of Central Pennsylvania v. Pennsylvania Railroad Company.* 23 ICC 385, 1912.

 Eastern Bituminous Coal Investigation. 140 ICC 3, 1928.

 Investigation and Suspension Docket Nos. 26, 26-A, 26-B, and 26C. In the Matter of the Investigation and Suspension of Advances in Rates for the Transportation of Coal by the Chesapeake & Ohio Railway Company, Baltimore & Ohio Railway Company, Norfolk and Western Railway Company, the Kanawha & Michigan Railway Company, and their Connections. 22 ICC 604, 1912.

 Investigation and Suspension Docket No. 774. Bituminous Coal to Central Freight Association Territory. 46 ICC 66, 1917.

 John W. Boileau et al. v. Pittsburgh & Lake Erie Railroad Company et al. 22 ICC 640, 1912.

 John W. Boileau et al. v. Pittsburgh & Lake Erie Railroad Company et al. 24 ICC 129, 1912.

 Lake Cargo Cases 1930. 181 ICC 37, 1932.

 Lake Cargo Coal Rates. 46 ICC 159, 1917.

 Lake Cargo Rates, 1925. 101 ICC 513, 1925.

 Rates, Charges, Regulations, and Practices Governing Transportation of Anthracite Coal. 101 ICC 363, 1925.

Useem, Michael. *The Hidden Circle.* New York: Oxford University Press, 1984.

Vittoz, Stanley. *New Deal Labor Policy.* Chapel Hill, NC: University of North Carolina Press, 1987.

Watkins, Myron. *Public Regulation of Competitive Practices in Business Enterprise.* New York: National Industrial Conference Board, 1940.

Weinstein, James. *The Corporate Ideal and the Liberal State.* Boston: Beacon Press, 1968.

Whitney, Simon. *Antitrust Policies: American Experience in Twenty Industries,* 2 vols. New York: Twentieth Century Fund, 1958.

Wieck, Edward A. *The American Miners' Association.* New York: Russell Sage, 1940.

Wilcox, Clair. *Public Policies toward Business.* Homewood, IL: Richard D. Irwin, 1971.

  The Structure of Industry. U.S. Temporary National Economic Committee Investigation of the Concentration of Economic Power, Monograph No. 27. Washington, DC: Government Printing Office, 1941.

Williamson, Oliver E. "Wage Rates as a Barrier to Entry: The Pennington Case in Perspective." *Quarterly Journal of Economics* 82 (1968): 85–115.

Zeitlin, Maurice. "Corporate Ownership and Control: The Large Corporation and the Capitalist Class." *American Journal of Sociology* 79 (March, 1974): 1,073–119.

  "On Class Theory of the Large Corporation: Response to Allen." *American Journal of Sociology* 81 (January, 1976): 894–903.

Name index

Subject index

agricultural policy, 67
Amalgamated Association of Miners of the United States, 105
American Miners' Association, 104–5
antitrust law: as a contraint on collective action by coal operators, 127–9, 182–3, 189–90; prohibitions on consolidation, 35–6; prohibitions on contracts in restraint of trade, 62–3; prohibitions on internal mechanisms, 53–4
Appalachian Coals, Inc., 183, 192, 208
Assurance Game, 14–15

banks, as organizers of competition, *see* creditors
basing points, *see* delivered prices; coal industry
Battle of the Sexes, game of, 30
Bituminous Coal Code, 173; creation of, 191–6; operation of, 196–202
bituminous coal industry, *see* coal industry
buyers: number and bargaining power of as affecting cooperation in pricing Prisoner's Dilemma, 18–19; as organizers of competition, 56–7; *see also* coal industry

capitalism: and economic competition, 3–5, 210–12; and interests of capitalists, 4, 13, 230–1, 234–5; *also see* capitalist relations of production
capitalist collective action: conditions facilitating, 17–23, 216–17; contingent nature of, 212–13; through external mechanisms, 54–62; through internal mechanisms, 45–54; through public mechanisms, 62–8; *see also* coal industry; railroads; United Mine Workers of America
capitalist collective action problems: and collective action theory, 213–21; derived from accumulation and legitimation requirements, 234; derived from the conflict with workers, 2–3; derived from the investment decision, 29; derived from the length-of-work-

ing-day decision, 27–8; derived from the pricing decision, 5–16, 23–7; derived from the product differentiation decision, 29; derived from the standardization decision, 29–30; derived from the wage decision, 28; elimination of, 33–9; intertemporal, 28–9; and the problem of market organization, 221–8; solutions to, 39–68; when firms differ according to their capacity to defect, 26–7; 87–8; when firms differ according to their costs, 24–6, 41, 86–7; *see also* coal industry
capitalist relations of production, 2–5, 131–2, 149, 211–12, 228–33, 237
capitalists, competition among, *see* competition
capitalists, interests of, *see* class consciousness; competition
cartels, 13; state-enforced, 66–7
Central Competitive Field, 107; *see also* coal industry; coal operators
Chicken, game of, 29
Civil Aeronautics Board, 66
class conflict between workers and capitalists, 2–4, 228–33; *see also* coal industry; coal operators; competition; United Mine Workers of America
class consciousness, 14–15, 229–31, 237
class organization, *see* capitalist collective action; capitalist collective action problems
coal: differences in quality of, 78–80; physical properties of, 77–8
Coal Distribution Act, 160
coal industry: as a "boom/bust" industry, 74, 140; bargaining power of consumers in 71–3; basing-point pricing in, 199–200; collective bargaining in, 105–10, 115–16, 153–8, 160–1, 168–70, 194–6, 207–8; consolidation in, 89–90, 124–5, 176–8; days worked in, 98–9; demand in, 73–4, 83, 94–6, 134–5, 139–40, 149–50, 158, 164; 178–9; district sales agencies in, 182–4, 208; East–West competition in, 94–101, 105–7; efforts to moderate price increases in, 136, 142–3; entry condi-

tions in, 76; excess capacity in, 115; exit conditions in, 76; external organizational mechanisms in, 91–2 (*see also* railroads; United Mine Workers of America); fair trade codes in, 181–2; freight rate controversies in, 122–3; high fixed costs in 74–5; increased entry in during World War I, 150; interfirm differences in, 78–82, 87–8; internal organization organizational mechanisms in, 103, 106, 125–7, 131, 136, 162, 174–6, 181–4, 199–200; intertemporal pricing Prisoner's Dilemma in, 134–6; labor costs in, 81–2; labor unions in, 104–5, 107–10 (*see also* United Mine Workers of America); lack of concentration in, 71–2; lack of standardization in, 77–8; major markets in, 83–5; major producing districts in, 79–80; mechanization in, 80–1; nationalization of, 140–1; North–South competition in, 110–11, 116–24, 170–1; obstacles to consolidation in, 89–90, 181; obstacles to cooperation in, 70–8, 216–17; organization of competition by railroads in, 111–14, 131; organization of competition by workers in, 88, 91–2, 107–10 (*see also* United Mine Workers of America); output in, 96–7; post World War I boom in, 139–40; price and wage cutting in, 102–7, 124, 151, 179; price cutting in, 197–203; price games in, 88–9, 117, 124, 130, 134–6, 174, 196–7, 203; price increases in, 134–5, 139–40, 158, 210; prices in, 100–1; 114; price–wage games in, 86–8, 96–7, 117–19, 130, 151–3, 173, 179–80, 223–5; standardization problems in, 77–8; state intervention in, 136–9, 141, 235–8; strikes in, 103–4, 106–7, 153–8, 160–1, 169–70, 202; transaction characteristics in, 71–3; transportation conditions in, 76–7; transportation costs in, 81–2; wage cutting game in, *see* coal industry, price–wage games in; wage cutting in, 82–3, 86, 116, 151, 164–8 (*see also* coal industry, price and wage cutting in); wage differentials in 108–10, 116, 151, 165, 194–5, 208, 220; wage game in, *see* coal industry, price–wage games in; wage–price game in, *see* coal industry, price–wage games in; wage–price games in, *see* coal industry, price–wage games in; wages in, 82–3, 108–10, 198; *see also* United Mine Workers of America; coal operators

coal mine safety laws, 121–2
coal operators: attitude toward NIRA, 190; and debate over Davis–Kelly bill, 187–9; efforts to moderate price increases, 136, 142–3, 159; efforts to stabilize wages, 162; high discount rate of, 216–17; opposition to collective bargaining in late 1920s, 167–8; opposition to interstate collective bargaining in 1922, 153–8; opposition to state intervention, 140–7, 158–61, 188–90, 205–7, 237–8; organizational need of, 87–8, 99–100, 139, 147, 152, 179–80, 184, 191, 196; public hostility toward, 140–1; resistance to unionization in South, 120–1; support for state intervention, 127–9, 189–90, 203–10; support of collective bargaining, 105–8, 119–20, 155–6, 162, 185–6, 193–4; *see also* Bituminous Coal Code; coal industry
collective action, *see* capitalist collective action
collective action problems, *see* capitalist collective action problems
collective bargaining, *see* coal industry; coal operators; United Mine Workers of America
combination, *see* consolidation
competition: as a collective action problem, 5–13, 213–28, 237; and conflicts about market organization, 222, 237–8; as a constitutive element of capitalism, 3, 210–13; in a depressed market, 13; economic theory of, 5–8, 221–2; importance in structuring interclass struggle, 131–2, 149, 170–1, 231–3; and interests of capitalists, 3–5, 23–7, 29, 230–5; *see also* coal industry
competitive equality, 108–10
consolidation, as a means to eliminate competition, 33–9; *see also* coal industry
consumers, *see* buyers
coordination problems, 29–30
corporation: debate over control of, 227–8; as device to eliminate competition, 36–7.
cost differences, and cooperation in pricing Prisoner's Dilemma, 24–7; *see also* coal industry
cost structure, and cooperation in pricing Prisoner's Dilemma, 20; *see also* coal industry
costs of market organization, *see* market organization, costs of
credible threats, and cooperation in pricing Prisoner's Dilemma, 21–2